*access to history*

# The Experience of Warfare in Britain: Crimea, Boer and the First World War 1854–1929

*Alan Farmer*

**HODDER**
EDUCATION
AN HACHETTE UK COMPANY

Study Guide author Angela Leonard

The Publishers would like to thank the following for permission to reproduce copyright material:

**Photo credits: p.3** Getty Images; **p.32** *tl, tr* Michael Nicholson/CORBIS, *br* Illustrated London News/Mary Evans, *bl* Bettmann/CORBIS; **pp.38, 39** SSPL via Getty Images; **pp.52, 61** Getty Images; **p.63** Time & Life Pictures/Getty Images, **p.78** Hulton-Deutsch Collection/CORBIS; **p.79** Getty Images; **p.86** Popperfoto/Getty Images; **p.88** CORBIS; **p.92** Getty Images; **p.108** Bettmann/CORBIS **p.100** Getty Images, **p.115** Hulton-Deutsch Collection/CORBIS; **p.130** Mary Evans Picture Library; **p.158** S. Forster/Alamy; **p.199** Hulton Deutsch Collection/CORBIS; **pp.172, 190, 191, 207** Getty Images.

**Acknowledgements:** Abacus for an extract from *The Rise and Fall of the British Empire* by Lawrence James, 1995. Alan Sutton for an extract from *Women's Factory Work in World War 1* by Gareth Griffiths, 1991. Arnold for an extract from *Britain and the Great War 1914–1918* by J.M. Bourne, 1989. Blackwell for an extract from *The Making of Modern British Politics, 1867–1939* by M. Pugh, 1982. Cambridge University Press for an extract from *Lloyd George: Rise and Fall* by A.J.P. Taylor, 1961. Faber & Faber for an extract from *The Downfall of the Liberal Party, 1914–1935* by Trevor Wilson, 1966. HarperCollins for an extract from *Age of Lloyd George: Liberal Party and British Politics, 1890–1929* by K.O. Morgan, 1978. Headline Review for an extract from *Forgotten Victory: The First World War – Myths and Realties* by Gary Sheffield, 2002. *History Review* for an extract from 'Florence Nightingale: Icon and Iconoclast R. E. Foster Sifts Myth from Reality in the Life of the "Lady with the Lamp", Who Died 100 Years Ago' by R.E. Foster, 2010. Hodder Education for an extract from *Access to History: The British Empire, 1815–1914* by Frank McDonough, 1994. Longman for extracts from *Blighty: British Society in the Era of The Great War* by G. DeGroot, 1996 and *Women and the First World War* by Susan Grayzel, 2002. Macmillan for an extract from *The Evolution of the British Welfare State: A History of Social Policy since the Industrial Revolution* by Derek Fraser, 1973. Macmillan for an extract from *The Making of Modern Britain* by Andrew Marr, 2009. Oxford University Press for extracts from *English History 1914–1945* by A.J.P. Taylor, 1965 and *Mrs Duberly's War: Journal and Letters from the Crimea, 1854–6* by Christine Kelly, 2007. Pimlico for an extract from *The First World War* by John Keegan, 1999. Sidgwick & Jackson for an extract from *The Imperial War Museum Book of the First World War* by Malcolm Brown, 1991. Viking for an extract from *The Destruction of Lord Raglan: A Tragedy of the Crimean War, 1854–55* by Christopher Hibbert, 1984.

Every effort has been made to trace all copyright holders, but if any have been inadvertently overlooked the Publishers will be pleased to make the necessary arrangements at the first opportunity.

Hachette UK's policy is to use papers that are natural, renewable and recyclable products and made from wood grown in sustainable forests. The logging and manufacturing processes are expected to conform to the environmental regulations of the country of origin.

Orders: please contact Bookpoint Ltd, 130 Milton Park, Abingdon, Oxon OX14 4SB. Telephone: (44) 01235 827720. Fax: (44) 01235 400454. Lines are open 9.00–5.00, Monday to Saturday, with a 24-hour message answering service. Visit our website at www.hoddereducation.co.uk

© Alan Farmer
First published in 2011 by
Hodder Education,
An Hachette UK Company
338 Euston Road
London NW1 3BH

Impression number     5  4  3  2
Year                               2015  2014  2013  2012

Cover image: *For King and Country* (1917), by E.F. Skinner, © Imperial War Museum (IWM_ART_006513)
Typeset in 10/12pt Baskerville and produced by Gray Publishing, Tunbridge Wells
Printed in Great Britain by MPG Books Group

A catalogue record for this title is available from the British Library.

ISBN: 978 1444 110104

# Contents

# Dedication

## Keith Randell (1943–2002)

The *Access to History* series was conceived and developed by Keith, who created a series to 'cater for students as they are, not as we might wish them to be'. He leaves a living legacy of a series that for over 20 years has provided a trusted, stimulating and well-loved accompaniment to post-16 study. Our aim with these new editions is to continue to offer students the best possible support for their studies.

# 1

# Introduction: The Experience of War 1854–1929

**POINTS TO CONSIDER**

Between 1854 and 1918 Britain fought three major wars: the Crimean War, the Boer War and the First World War. Without doubt, the First World War – the Great War as contemporaries called it – had the greatest effect, impacting on the lives of virtually all Britons, servicemen and civilians alike. But all three wars had repercussions, militarily, politically, socially and economically. This introductory chapter aims to provide you with a framework for understanding the context of the wars. It will do this by examining the following issues:

- Britain's position in the world 1854–1929
- The impact of war 1854–1918

**Key dates**

| | |
|---|---|
| 1854–6 | Crimean War |
| 1857–8 | Indian Mutiny |
| 1899–1902 | Boer War |
| 1914–18 | First World War |

## 1 | Britain's Position in the World 1854–1929

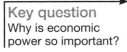

**Key question**
Why was Britain a great world power?

Throughout the period 1854–1929, Britain was a great world power. Its power rested on its economic strength, the Empire, the Royal Navy, the British army, and political and social stability.

### Economic strength

**Key question**
Why is economic power so important?

By 1850, Britain had become the home of the world's first urban industrialised economy. By 1850, Britain accounted for 50 per cent of the world's trade in coal, cotton and iron and its **gross national product** (GNP) was higher than that of China and Russia combined. The steady expansion of the British economy was achieved with only two per cent of the world's population. (Britain's population grew from nine million in 1801 to 18 million in 1851 and 36 million by 1901.) Large cities mushroomed. A whole new banking and finance system based in London spread its influence around the world. By 1870, Britain was both the workshop of the world and the world's banking house.

**Key term**

**Gross national product**
The total value of all goods and services produced within a country plus the income from investments abroad.

## Economic decline?

By 1900, Britain's economic position was no longer so strong. Germany and the USA had become serious industrial rivals and Britain seemed to be falling behind in a number of new areas (for example, motor car production and electrical goods). Some thought this was due to inadequate investment in pure and applied science.

However, the British economy was stronger than many pessimists feared. Although by the late nineteenth century Britain ran a trade deficit in 'visible' exports, this deficit was more than bridged by 'invisibles'; that is, money generated by insurance, banking and shipping. By 1914, Britain's merchant fleet carried one half of all the world's sea-borne traffic. Britain's trade balance was kept in the black by returns on its overseas investments. London remained the world's financial centre, **sterling** the world's main currency.

Even in technology, between 1876 and 1900 some 15 per cent of all the world's significant inventions were of British origin. British facilities for imparting scientific and technological instruction improved significantly in the 50 years after 1870 as the government (and big business) began to fund university research and university expansion. The government also funnelled large sums of money into scientific projects designed to improve the armed services: the **Admiralty**, for example, subsidised the development of wireless technology.

## The Royal Navy

Throughout the eighteenth and nineteenth centuries the Royal Navy ruled the waves. As well as ensuring Britain's security, the navy maintained trade routes with the Empire and with other commercial partners. It was an important factor in European politics and proved invaluable in a host of colonial campaigns, providing safe passage for the troops, coastal bombardment and protection for bridgeheads ashore.

## Naval decline?

During the late nineteenth century, naval vessels changed from sail and wood to steam and steel. New developments forced Britain to keep modernising its navy – a costly business. After centuries of very slow change, warships could now be obsolete on completion. With the ever-changing technology and the constant threat of new weapons appearing, there were occasional doubts about whether the Royal Navy could defend Britain adequately. Naval expenditure between 1889 and 1897 increased by 65 per cent. Nevertheless, the Royal Navy's relative advantage continued to erode. In 1883, Britain had 38 **capital ships** compared to the 40 belonging to the combined fleets of France, Russia, the USA, Japan, Germany and Italy. By 1897, the ratio had slipped to 62:97. After 1900, Britain no longer ruled all the waves.

More fears were generated in the first decade of the twentieth century when Germany began to build a large fleet. Britain's response was a huge shipbuilding programme, ensuring that the Royal Navy maintained its supremacy.

While it did not always capture the headlines, the navy's strength underpinned Britain's performance in the Crimean War, the Boer War and the First World War, ensuring that troops could be sent to where they were needed

## The army

**Key question**
How efficient was the British army?

For most of the period 1854–1929 the army was relatively small (rarely more than 130,000 strong in peacetime, excluding the troops stationed in India) compared with the armies of the major continental powers. The army's function was essentially two-fold: home defence and maintenance of the Empire. Military leaders had to meet steadily expanding commitments within the constraints of tight budgetary limits and voluntary enlistment (until 1916).

### The composition of the army

Harsh discipline, poor conditions and low wages meant that the army constantly had manpower problems. While a few men may have dreamed of foreign adventure, the vast majority of the rank and file were unskilled, casual labourers who joined the army through economic necessity.

As the nineteenth century wore on, there were changes in the national and social composition of the army. In 1851, Irishmen had constituted 37 per cent of all non-commissioned personnel.

Tough-looking and often bearded, Highlanders of the 42nd Regiment posing before the camera in 1856.

By 1913, the Irish element was only nine per cent. **Demographic** changes meant that the army drew increasingly on recruits from urban areas rather than from the countryside. Most officers preferred men from agricultural backgrounds, assuming that those brought up in the open air were better fitted than town dwellers to be soldiers. The reality may have been different. The experience of soldiers in the American Civil War (1861–5) suggests that those born in towns lived longer than those born in rural areas, probably because they had more resistance to germs. Disease was a far greater killer of soldiers in the nineteenth century than battle.

**Demographic**
To do with population size and distribution.

Key term

## The officer class
Most army officers came from the landed classes or from high-ranking military families. Many public schools specialised in preparing boys for the army. In some regiments, especially the cavalry and guards, most officers were from aristocratic families. Only a few officers managed to advance their careers without money or patronage.

## British colonial success
Virtually every year between 1854 and 1914, the army saw active service overseas in:

- campaigns of conquest
- actions to suppress insurrections
- expeditions to avenge perceived wrongs or to overthrow a dangerous enemy.

The army generally performed well. **Garnet Wolseley**, Britain's most successful late nineteenth-century soldier, claimed that officers and men benefited from 'the varied experience and frequent practice in war'.

In most colonial wars, the army was successful because it was far better armed than its opponents. Despite this huge advantage, some campaigns were first-rate achievements, requiring considerable improvisation, given the immense diversity of the foes, terrain, weapons and tactics encountered. The skills of the Royal Engineers were essential in building roads, bridges and forts and providing telegraphic communications and sometimes rail transportation. In general, the army depended on personal qualities of courage and resolution, a highly disciplined organisation and innovative leadership.

**Garnet Wolseley**
Wolseley fought in the Crimean War, in India, Canada and Africa. He later became Commander-in-Chief of the British army.

Key figure

## Colonial troops
Given the difficulty of recruiting at home, Britain made use of colonial troops, especially in India. Using local troops was cheap. Moreover, in tropical colonies, indigenous soldiers had far lower rates of mortality and sickness than Europeans. But some Britons mistrusted colonial troops, doubting their commitment and efficiency. Overreliance on Indian troops almost led to catastrophe in 1857 when a large part of the Indian army in Bengal mutinied. The Indian Mutiny (see page 66) was suppressed only after 14 months of hard fighting. Britain lost 11,000 men, 9000

of whom died from sickness or sunstroke.) Given the need for internal control and possible external threat, 75,000 British troops were permanently stationed in India from 1858 to 1914 in addition to over 150,000 Indian troops.

## Positives and negatives

Despite the army's success in most colonial campaigns, in all three major wars there were problems:

- In the Crimean War, there were administrative and supply issues.
- In the Boer War, problems initially stemmed from poor leadership.
- In the First World War, the army learned the lessons of fighting a continental war the hard way. This resulted in the deaths of hundreds of thousands of men.

However, in each case, army leaders learned from the mistakes:

- While the Crimean army suffered over the winter of 1854–5, it did not suffer unduly the following winter.
- The army defeated the main Boer armies and then waged a difficult, but ultimately successful war, against opponents who used **guerrilla tactics**.
- In 1918, the British army played a crucial role in winning the First World War.

## The Empire

Economic and naval supremacy enabled Britain to acquire an extensive Empire. By 1919, it amounted to a quarter of the world's land surface and population. While the Empire is now regarded with a mixture of embarrassment and indifference, in the period covered by this book it was a source of considerable pride to most Britons. It was perceived as:

- conferring great-power status on Britain
- providing Britain with reliable sources of food and raw materials and a captive market for British exports
- providing the Royal Navy with important naval bases from which it was able to dominate the world's sea lanes.

## Imperial expansion

The acquisition of Empire was not the result of a co-ordinated policy of conquest. It was rather the case that colonies were picked up almost in a fit of absence of mind. New territories came under British rule largely because of a number of local circumstances. In many cases they were acquired for defensive or strategic reasons or to safeguard trading interests that were under threat. Some colonies were acquired because enterprising individuals like Cecil Rhodes in southern Africa (see page 80) decided to act as independent buccaneers.

Pre-1880, Britain's main imperial rivals were France and Russia. After 1880, other powers – principally Germany, Italy and Japan – also sought Empire. In the 'scramble for Africa' between 1880 and 1900, 90 per cent of the continent was appropriated by European

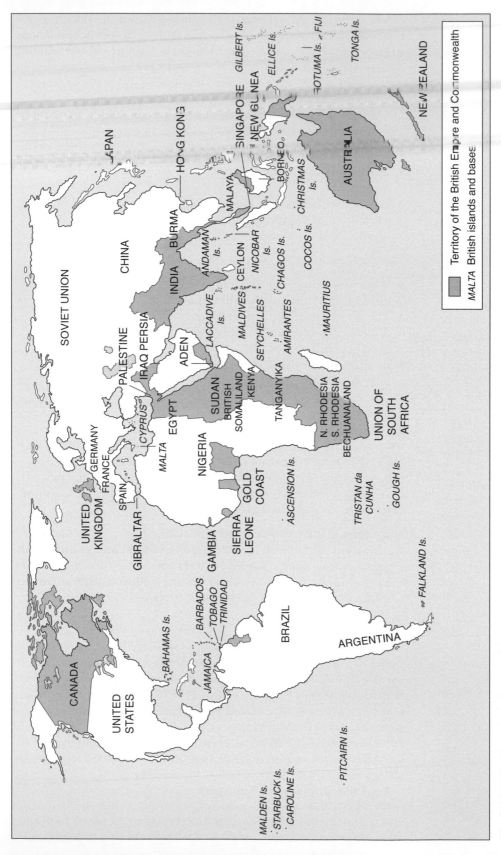

Territory of the British Empire and Commonwealth

*MALTA* British islands and bases

The British Empire at its height in 1920.

powers. Britain acquired nearly five million square miles, France 3.5 million while Germany, Belgium and Italy shared 2.5 million square miles between them. European involvement in Africa was a complex matter. Economic interest was certainly a factor. Britain was concerned that it might find itself barred from markets and sources of raw materials if other countries grabbed huge chunks of land. However, successive British governments took little notice of business lobbies. Britain's overarching economic and strategic interests were their main concern. They were prepared to defend those interests whenever they were threatened by European rivals or local nationalist movements.

## The importance of India

India – the **jewel in the crown** – was the most important part of the Empire. The largest single element of British army spending was devoted to the Indian army. While the Royal Navy's first task was to defend Britain, its second was to protect the trade route to India. Lord Curzon, perhaps the most famous Viceroy of India, claimed that 'as long as we rule India, we are the greatest power in the world. If we lose it, we shall drop straightaway to a third rate power'. After the Indian Mutiny, the whole civil and military system of British India was reorganised: the involvement of the **East India Company** in the operation of British rule was ended. The British government adopted full responsibility for most of the sub-continent, an area larger than all of Europe (excluding Russia) with a population of 300 million people by 1900.

## Political divisions

For much of the nineteenth century, imperial affairs were not an especially important or divisive subject of discussion in British politics. However, in 1872, Conservative leader Benjamin Disraeli injected the issue of Empire into domestic politics by criticising the Liberal government's policy towards India. As prime minister (1874–80) he put the consolidation of British power in India at the heart of his imperial crusade. His main aim was probably simply to associate the Conservative Party with patriotism in order to make a new appeal to the electorate.

William Gladstone was the dominant British politician of the nineteenth century. A high-minded Liberal, he won four general elections between 1868 and 1892. Alarmed at Disraeli's **jingoism**, he emerged from retirement in 1880 and, campaigning to win the Scottish constituency of Midlothian, attacked Disraeli's 'imperialist ambitions', accusing him of inflaming the British public to display 'unworthy emotions' such as 'lust for glory, aggressiveness and chauvinism'. The Midlothian campaign helped Gladstone to triumph in the 1880 election. Somewhat ironically, given the fact that the Liberals were less imperialist than the Conservatives, the Empire expanded more rapidly under Gladstone than under Disraeli.

## Imperial support

The greatest imperial enthusiasts came from the public schools, from army and naval officers and from colonial administrators and businessmen. But many middle- and working-class Britons also supported imperialism. The extent of working-class support has generated controversy. While some historians doubt whether the working class was ever particularly supportive of the Empire, others think large numbers of workers were won over to – or manipulated into supporting – imperialism. There is no doubt that in the period 1880–1920 there was considerable imperial propaganda. This was reflected in newspapers, school textbooks and popular literature. The fact that so many Britons emigrated – some 1.5 million in the five years before 1914 – also strengthened imperial consciousness, superimposing on Britons the concept of Empire citizenship.

## Imperial hotch-potch

The Empire was never a uniform association. There was no single constitution, religion, language or system of law. The colonies had very little in common with each other except their link with Britain. Essentially, they were divided into two broad categories:

**Key question**
Why was the Empire perceived to be of such importance to Britain?

- the colonies of settlement
- the dependent or crown colonies.

The colonies of settlement – Canada, Cape Colony, Australia and New Zealand – were founded by people of British or European origin. By the second half of the nineteenth century, Australia, Canada and New Zealand had moved to almost full independence. After 1907, the self-governing colonies were referred to as dominions. The idea that the introduction of self-government implied the imminent break-up of the Empire was not the case. The dominions probably became more dependent on British investment and British defence after they had been granted self-government than before.

The hotch-potch of dependent colonies had few white settlers and were ruled by small groups of British officials. After 1858, power in India was shared between a viceroy, the India Office, a secretary of state and a Council for India. India apart, the British government generally left day-to-day management of the Empire to officials in the Colonial Office. They, in turn, entrusted responsibility to administrators in the colonies themselves. Frederick Lugard, appointed High Commissioner of Northern Nigeria in 1900, found himself ruling a vast area with a civilian staff totalling 104 and a military force of 2000–3000 Africans under 200 British officers and non-commissioned officers (NCOs). Arguably the Empire was something of a bluff, held together less by force than by a mixture of cajolery and guile, and by local collaboration, especially in India.

## The cost of Empire

Despite strong imperialist sentiment, British governments – Conservative and Liberal alike – were far from fully committed to the business of running the Empire. They hoped to maintain it on the cheap. In 1914, fewer than 6000 people, mainly from affluent middle-class backgrounds, were employed to administer the whole Empire.

However, the major cost of Empire for Britain was defence, not administration. Britain's hope that the colonies would contribute to their own defence costs was barely realised. British taxpayers footed most of the Empire's defence bill.

### Did the Empire benefit Britain?

While some companies undoubtedly made large profits from the Empire, most of Britain's trade was with countries outside the Empire: with Europe, the USA, the Far East and Latin America, Britain's share of total trade with the Empire declined from 49 per cent in 1860 to 36 per cent in 1929. Nevertheless, the Empire provided a good market for British products well into the twentieth century.

The Empire countries varied greatly in the economic benefits that they conferred on Britain. India dwarfed all the others, accounting for nearly 40 per cent of Britain's colonial exports. Australia, Canada, South Africa and New Zealand (in that order of importance) were Britain's next most important imperial trading partners, taking over 40 per cent of its colonial exports. The rest of the dependent colonies had relatively little economic significance.

Arguably many of the things which supposedly made the Empire worthwhile – emigration, high returns on capital investment, increased trade – were not in the end sufficiently powerful to transform the vast defence expenditure into an overall balance of financial gain. But most Britons continued cheerfully and proudly to shoulder the tax costs of the Empire.

## Political stability

**Key question**
To what extent was Britain politically stable?

Most Britons were proud of their system of government which they perceived as being democratic.

### British democracy?

For most of the period 1854–1929, Britain was far from being a genuine democracy. Less than a third of (essentially rich) men had the vote in 1854. Only 60 per cent of men had the vote by 1914. Not until 1918 were women (over the age of 30) able to vote in general elections. Not until 1928 did women get the vote on the same terms as men. Men ruled. More specifically, rich men ruled. The landed gentry dominated the House of Lords, controlled the House of Commons and were a majority in virtually all cabinets pre-1905.

### Political divisions

The Conservatives and Liberals dominated the political scene until 1918. The Conservatives tended to defend the *status quo*: the Liberals tended to be more supportive of reform. Interest in politics was high throughout the period. Political meetings often attracted vast audiences and most men had strong partisan convictions.

### Laissez-faire government

For most of the period, parliament did not impinge much on people's lives. Britain's lack of extensive government machinery was seen as a 'good thing' by most – lightly taxed – Britons who espoused *laissez-faire* principles. They contrasted their position

**Key term**

*Laissez-faire*
The principle that governments should not interfere in people's lives or in economic matters.

**Table 1.1:** British governments 1854–1929

| Party | Prime Minister | In office |
|---|---|---|
| Whig/Peelite coalition | Lord Aberdeen | 1852–5 |
| Liberal | Lord Palmerston | 1855–8 |
| Conservative | Lord Derby | 1858–9 |
| Liberal | Lord Palmerston | 1860–65 |
| Liberal | Lord John Russell | 1865–6 |
| Conservative | Lord Derby | 1866–8 |
| Conservative | Benjamin Disraeli | Feb.–Dec. 1868 |
| Liberal | William Ewart Gladstone | 1868–74 |
| Conservative | Benjamin Disraeli | 1874–80 |
| Liberal | William Ewart Gladstone | 1880–5 |
| Conservative | Marquess of Salisbury | 1885–6 |
| Liberal | William Ewart Gladstone | 1886 |
| Conservative | Marquess of Salisbury | 1886–92 |
| Liberal | William Ewart Gladstone | 1892–4 |
| Liberal | Earl of Rosebery | 1894–5 |
| Conservative | Marquess of Salisbury | 1895–1902 |
| Conservative | Arthur Balfour | 1902–5 |
| Liberal | Sir Henry Campbell-Bannerman | 1905–8 |
| Liberal | Herbert Asquith | 1908–15 |
| Coalition | Herbert Asquith | 1915–16 |
| Coalition | Lloyd George | 1916–22 |
| Conservative | Andrew Bonar Law | 1922–3 |
| Conservative | Stanley Baldwin | 1923–4 |
| Labour | Ramsay MacDonald | 1924 |
| Conservative | Stanley Baldwin | 1924–9 |

favourably with that of most Europeans who (they believed) were harassed by armies of petty officials and subjected to all-pervasive systems of control. Until the start of the twentieth century, Britons were affected more by local than central government.

## The monarchy

Britain's monarchy probably helped to maintain political calm. Queen Victoria's longevity – she ruled from 1837 to 1901 – led to her becoming a symbol of stability. Her golden and diamond jubilees (in 1887 and 1897) were occasions of national celebration. Edward VII (1901–10) and George V (1910–35) were also popular. The monarchs were essentially figureheads, their political power strictly limited. But in practice, particularly at times of crisis, they could exert some influence.

## Haves versus have-nots

**Key question**
Was Britain socially stable?

The real 'haves' were the landed classes who wielded huge political, economic and social power. At the other end of the social spectrum were paupers for whom the workhouse was the last welfare resort. By the late nineteenth century most Britons lived and laboured in the mushrooming industrial towns. Many worked long hours for poor wages and often lived in squalor.

Nevertheless, there was little overt social unrest. This may have had something to do with the fact that there was not one, but many, working classes: skilled, semi-skilled and unskilled workers were far from united. It was probably more to do with the fact that real living standards were rising. This was reflected in the rise in life expectancy: under 40 in the early Victorian period: 53 by 1911 and over 60 by the 1920s.

### Religious divisions

In some respects religion continued to divide Britons more than class. While late Victorian Britain was overwhelmingly Christian, Christianity was a source of social and ideological discord. The deepest divide was between Protestants (the vast majority of Britons) and Catholics (most of whom were of Irish stock). But the division between Church and Chapel was also important. Church-goers tended to vote Conservative, Chapel-goers Liberal. Chapel-going **nonconformists** were themselves a diverse group. The Wesleyan Methodists were the largest sect but there were also Presbyterians, Baptists, Congregationalists, Quakers and Unitarians. Religious discord helped to push into the background latent resentment between skilled and unskilled workers, between manual and white-collar workers and between rich and poor.

**Key term**

**Nonconformists** Protestants who rejected the authority (and some of the practices) of the Church of England.

### National divisions

By 1913, over 75 per cent of Britons were English. Most Scots, Welsh and Northern Irish were also proud to call themselves British. The same could not be said of southern Irish Catholics. Ireland was the least integrated part of the British state and political life for much of the period was dominated by Irish nationalists' demands for recognition of Ireland's separate identity.

### The gender divide

Women, who on average lived longer than men, were a majority of the population. Emigration (largely by men) tilted the balance still further towards females. Most Britons, whatever their political persuasion, wealth or gender, believed woman's place was the home, where indeed most nineteenth-century women spent a great deal of their time, thanks to frequent childbirth. In the early twentieth century some women – Suffragettes – fought for votes for women. But they did not fight for equal rights as such. The prevailing view was that men and women had different but complementary social roles.

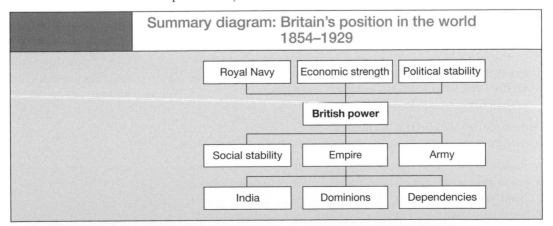

Summary diagram: Britain's position in the world 1854–1929

## 2 | The Impact of War 1854–1918

Key dates

Crimean War: 1854–6

Boer War: 1899–1902

First World War: 1914–18

Between 1854 and 1918, as well as fighting three major wars, Britain fought numerous colonial wars. These included the Indian Mutiny (1857–8), the Abyssinian War (1868), the Ashanti War (1873–4), the Zulu War (1879), the Afghan War (1879–80), the Egyptian War (1882) and the Sudan campaign (1880).

### The nature of the major wars

Key question
Why are the three major wars so difficult to compare?

The Crimean War, waged against Russia, involved substantial mobilisation of men and resources. However, the war was relatively limited in terms of both scale and time. Moreover, Britain's French and Turkish allies played crucial roles, French forces greatly exceeding British forces by 1855. Although the British army fought well in 1854, supply and medical problems over the winter of 1854–5 decimated the army. The bulk of Britain's 20,000 fatalities died from disease, not battlefield action.

The Boer War, a colonial rather than a great power conflict, involved some 450,000 British troops and dragged on for two and a half years. Some 5774 British soldiers were killed in action, 22,529 were wounded and 16,000 died from disease.

The First World War was on an altogether different scale. By 1918, 5.2 million men had served in the army. In addition, over 640,000 had served in the Royal Navy and 291,000 in the Royal Flying Corps/RAF. Over 723,000 Britons died in the war and a further 1.7 million were wounded. The war was a total war in which the state utilised all its resources in order to achieve victory.

### Patriotism and the media

Key question
Why were the British people so patriotic?

All three wars were supported by the mass of the population. The British public was strongly patriotic. Men **rushed to the colours** in the Boer War but particularly in the First World War. Patriotism may well have been generated by the popular press. But it is just as likely that jingoistic newspapers like the *Daily Mail* reflected the public's views. Papers that were seen as unpatriotic were unlikely to sell. Only in the First World War, did the government make a deliberate attempt to limit freedom of information and to issue propaganda material in an effort to maintain morale and commitment.

**Rushed to the colours**
Volunteered to enlist in the army.

Key term

Newspapers did not just toe the government line:

- In the Crimean War, war correspondents like Russell of *The Times* revealed the army's failings.
- In the Boer War, the Liberal press campaigned against the dreadful conditions in the South African concentration camps.
- In the First World War, newspapers were critical of government and military leaders.

Although the bulk of the population supported the wars, there were opponents, mainly from the left of the political spectrum.

- Radicals (like Richard Cobden) opposed the Crimean War.
- Radical Liberals (like David Lloyd George) opposed the Boer War.
- Socialists (like Keir Hardie) opposed the First World War.

## The political impact

All three wars had important political consequences. Perceived government failure led to Palmerston replacing Aberdeen as prime minister in 1855 and Lloyd George replacing Asquith in 1916. The First World War helped to bring about major parliamentary reform, the decline of the Liberal Party and the rise of Labour. It also saw a massive expansion of government control and intervention, far beyond anything previously experienced or envisaged.

## The imperial impact

All three wars were connected with Empire:

- Britain fought the Crimean War in part because it feared that Russia posed a threat to India.
- The Boer War was fought to preserve Britain's position in southern Africa.
- Britain's relations with Germany in the early twentieth century were soured by Germany's *Weltpolitik* ambitions.

If the wars were fought in defence of Empire, the Empire came to Britain's defence in the Boer War and the First World War. Some 200,000 dominion and colonial troops died fighting on the Allied side between 1914 and 1918. The consciousness of shared sacrifice probably strengthened the imperial bond. However, the war may also have helped to weaken British imperial rule.

- In 1917, Indian Secretary Edwin Montagu promised that after the war, India would be given greater powers of self-government.
- The war helped bring about southern Ireland's independence.
- After 1918, ideas of equality, mass democracy and national self-determination placed strains on the idea of imperialism.

## The financial and economic impact

The wars had to be paid for. This was done by raising taxes and by government borrowing, resulting in an increase in the **national debt**. The Crimean War and the Boer War had only a limited effect on Britain's finances and economic development. The First World War had a far greater impact. Arguably, it led to the loss of overseas markets and left Britain in hock to the USA. However, it is equally arguable that the war had a limited impact on general economic trends and that Britain was able to pay for it with relative ease. It is certainly the case that Britain's great wealth and manufacturing capacity enabled it to fight and win all three wars.

## The social impact

The Crimean War and Boer War had only a limited impact on society. The same could not be said of the First World War. Some historians think that the Great War had huge consequences for Britain's social evolution, especially with regard to state involvement in all aspects of life, general welfare development, the redistribution of wealth, and for women's roles. However, other historians claim that the continuities between pre- and post-First World War were more significant than the changes. Arguably:

**Key question**
Did the First World War strengthen or weaken imperial bonds?

**Key terms**

*Weltpolitik*
A German word meaning 'world policy'; that is, Germany's imperialist ambitions.

**National debt**
The money borrowed by a government and not yet paid back.

- The social measures that were introduced were a continuation of the expansion in state welfare in late Victorian and Edwardian Britain.
- Most of the war's effects were of short-term significance.
- Social change would have occurred if there had been no war.

## Conclusion

Britain waged a series of successful wars between 1854 and 1918, wars which enabled the country to establish and maintain the greatest empire in the world's history. Despite its military success pre-1918, preserving peace seemed to be the greatest of Britain's national interests post-1918. The cost of the First World War in human and financial terms made politicians and public recoil from the prospect of a new war. The country, it seemed, had everything to lose and little to gain from another major war. That war – the Second World War – came in 1939. It proved that Britain did indeed have everything to lose and little to gain from involvement in a major conflict.

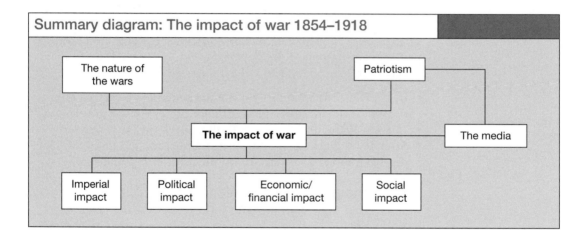

Summary diagram: The impact of war 1854–1918

# The Crimean War 1854–6

## POINTS TO CONSIDER

It is possible to argue that the 'Crimean War' is wrongly named. The war did not begin or end in the Crimea and the conflict there was only part of a much wider struggle. However, given that most of Britain's fighting occurred in the Crimea, the name is apt. In Britain the war has become a byword for military incompetence. It is best remembered for the Charge of the Light Brigade, for Florence Nightingale and for popularising the cardigan and the balaclava. In some respects this trivialises a major war, the only conflict between 1815 and 1914 involving more than two of Europe's great powers and a war in which over 500,000 men died. This chapter will consider the following issues:

- The causes of the war
- The British army
- Fighting in the Crimea in 1854
- The winter of 1854–5
- The war 1855–6
- The wider war
- Peace

## Key dates

| | | |
|---|---|---|
| 1815 | | Treaty of Vienna: end of Napoleonic Wars |
| 1850–2 | | Holy places dispute |
| 1853 | February–May | Menshikov mission |
| | October | War between Russia and Turkey |
| 1854 | March | Britain and France declared war on Russia |
| | September | Battle of Alma |
| | October | Battle of Balaclava |
| | November | Battle of Inkerman |
| 1855 | | Fall of Sevastopol |
| 1856 | | Treaty of Paris |

# 1 | The Causes of the War

After the Treaty of Vienna in 1815, Europe's great powers – Austria, Russia, Britain, Prussia and France – enjoyed nearly four decades of international peace. But the weakness of the ramshackle Ottoman (or Turkish) Empire was a major problem dividing the five great powers. The Turkish government at Constantinople (modern Istanbul) claimed authority over territories that included much of the Balkans, Asia Minor, the Middle East and the coast of North Africa. If the Ottoman Empire fell apart, its collapse could easily endanger European peace.

## Holy Places dispute

In 1848, Louis Napoleon, a nephew of Napoleon Bonaparte, was elected French President. In 1852, he became Emperor Napoleon III. Determined to pursue an active foreign policy, he supported **liberal** causes and hoped to destroy the 1815 peace settlement which endeavoured to contain France. He was thus keen to challenge Russia, the country most associated with **autocracy** and with ensuring that France did not again dominate Europe.

The situation in the **Near East** gave Napoleon III an opportunity to oppose Russia. In 1740, French Catholic monks had been granted the right to look after the holy places in Palestine. However, Greek Orthodox monks, backed by Russia, had gradually taken over control of them. In 1850, the Ottoman Sultan was presented with a French demand for the reinstatement of the full rights of Catholic monks. The dispute over the guardianship of the holy places was basically a test of whose influence prevailed at Constantinople. In December 1852, after a two-year diplomatic struggle, the Sultan handed over the keys to the holy places to Catholic priests. Tsar Nicholas I, outraged by this French triumph, determined to take firm action.

## British policy

In December 1852, Lord Aberdeen became head of a coalition government in Britain. Lord Palmerston (see pages 52–3) was appointed Home Secretary while Lord John Russell became Foreign Secretary. (He was soon replaced by the Earl of Clarendon.) Nicholas had established good relations with Aberdeen in the 1840s and hoped to revive the good rapport. In January 1853, the Tsar held a series of conversations with Sir Hamilton Seymour, British ambassador to Russia, in which he suggested a 'gentleman's agreement' between Russia and Britain for dealing with the supposedly imminent collapse of the Ottoman Empire. Russell's polite response to the Seymour conversations was misunderstood by Nicholas, who thought he had Britain's sympathy. In fact, Aberdeen's cabinet was divided. Some, like Aberdeen, hoped to maintain good relations with Russia. But others, like Palmerston, were suspicious of Nicholas's intentions, suspicions that increased in January 1853 when Russian troops concentrated on the borders of Moldavia and Wallachia – a clear threat to Turkey.

**Key question**
Was the Crimean War an accident waiting to happen?

**Key dates**

Treaty of Vienna: end of Napoleonic Wars: 1815

Holy places dispute: 1850–2

**Key terms**

**Liberal**
In the mid-nineteenth century, liberals supported democracy and greater freedom generally (e.g. freedom of speech and religion).

**Autocracy**
A form of government where one (unelected) ruler has total power.

**Near East**
The area which today comprises Turkey and many of the countries of the Middle East.

**Key question**
What were Tsar
Nicholas's aims in
1853?

**Key date**
Menshikov mission:
February–May 1853

## The Menshikov mission

In February 1853 the Tsar sent a high-powered mission, headed
by Prince Menshikov, to Constantinople. Menshikov demanded
that:

- the keys to the holy places be given back to the Orthodox monks
- the Tsar should be recognised as the protector of all Christians
  living in the Turkish Empire. (Since Orthodox Christians
  amounted to over one third of the Sultan's subjects, such a right,
  if conceded, would reduce Turkey to the status of a Russian
  protectorate.)

Menshikov's demands aroused anger and nationalist fervour
in Constantinople and Lord Stratford de Redcliffe, the British
ambassador, encouraged the Sultan to stand firm. In May, Russia
announced that unless it received the satisfaction it required,
its troops would occupy Moldavia and Wallachia. Although
theoretically autonomous, the two Danubian provinces were still
formally under Ottoman control.

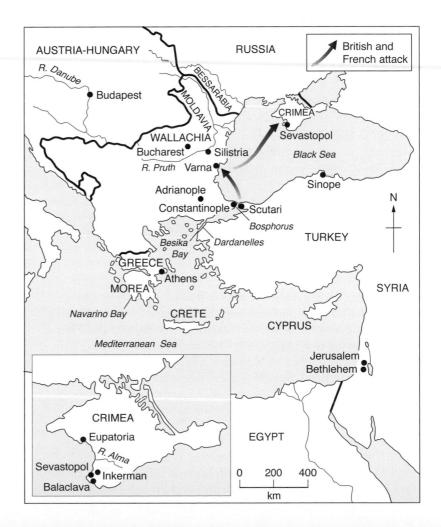

The start of the
Crimean War.

## British and French intervention

De Redcliffe urged Britain to take a strong line. He had the support of Palmerston, who argued that Russia would back down if firmly opposed. Aberdeen remained cautious. While not convinced that Russia was plotting Turkey's destruction, he was concerned that it might try to win control over Constantinople, with the dire prospect of Russian warships sailing through the **Straits** as they pleased. Aberdeen's efforts to find a peaceful solution were hampered by the divisions within his cabinet and by a surge of **Russophobia** among the British public. Liberals and **Radicals** became excited at the prospect of challenging the Russian autocracy.

In June, British ships were sent to Besika Bay just outside the Dardanelles as a gesture of support for the Turks. They were soon joined by a French fleet. By opposing Russia, Britain could not escape co-operation with France, even though Aberdeen did not trust Napoleon III. The possibility of a French attack on Britain had been taken seriously in the years 1851–3. It was somewhat ironic that the Royal Navy, recently strengthened to protect Britain from French attack, was now allied with the power it was primarily designed to fight.

In July, Nicholas ordered his troops into Moldavia and Wallachia. He stated that Russian forces would withdraw when the Turks accepted Menshikov's earlier demands. Turkey, confident of British and French support, was not prepared to give way.

## The Vienna Note

In an attempt to defuse the crisis, Austria organised a conference in Vienna hoping to find a formula that would satisfy the Tsar's honour while safeguarding Turkey's integrity. The diplomats proposed that the Sultan should make a few concessions to the Tsar and should consult both Russia and France about his policy towards Ottoman Christians. In return, Russia should leave the **Principalities**. In August, Russia accepted the Vienna Note. But the Sultan, with the backing of de Redcliffe, insisted on some amendments. These were rejected by the Tsar.

## War

In October, Turkey declared war on Russia. Turkish troops crossed the Danube and attacked the Russians in Wallachia in a series of indecisive clashes. In November, the British and French fleets, violating the 1841 Straits Convention, sailed through the Dardenelles to the Sea of Marmara. On 30 November, a squadron of the Russian Black Sea Fleet annihilated a Turkish squadron at Sinope. The so-called 'massacre' of Sinope, depicted – wrongly – by the British press as an illegitimate action by Russia, cranked Russophobia in Britain to new heights. This helped those like Palmerston who wanted to resist Russia. In January 1854, the British and French fleets sailed into the Black Sea.

In February, Russia broke off diplomatic relations with Britain and France. On 27 February, a British and French joint note was sent to the Tsar demanding a withdrawal of Russian troops from Moldavia and Wallachia. The note was ignored. On 27 March, France declared war on Russia. Britain did so the following day.

## Responsibility for war

**Key question**
Which country was most to blame for the Crimean War?

### Russian responsibility?

Tsar Nicholas was responsible for a series of miscalculations which led to confrontation with Turkey. His exaggerated sense of honour led him to reject several diplomatic attempts to resolve the crisis in 1853–4.

### British responsibility?

British policy was criticised by a few contemporaries and has been criticised since, most recently by historian Orlando Figes. Radical MPs Richard Cobden and John Bright believed that Russia's demands were reasonable. They were on stronger ground when they claimed that the issues were not vital enough for Britain to go to war. Figes argues that the Crimean War was the first in history launched to appease British public sentiment – media-inspired paranoia about Russia – rather than in pursuit of any coherent national purpose. He is not totally correct. Britain went to war with a purpose: that of thwarting – assumed – Russian plans to dismantle the Ottoman Empire and seize Constantinople, actions which would have threatened British naval supremacy in the eastern Mediterranean.

Other critics have focused blame on the divided councils of Aberdeen's government in which the prime minister was pacific and anti-Turkish while Palmerston was bellicose and anti-Russian. Arguably, if Britain had taken a more consistent line – hard or soft – war would have been averted. Certainly Aberdeen regretted until his death his failure to push more strongly for peace. But Palmerston, hugely experienced in foreign affairs, insisted that Britain must stand firm against the Russian invasion of Moldavia and Wallachia. He promoted anti-Russian feeling with all the means at his command, undermining Aberdeen's government's attempts to find a diplomatic solution. Palmerston was very much in alignment with British opinion, which regarded Russia as a dangerous reactionary force whose expansionist designs had to be resisted. Vigorous action by Britain in 1853 might have persuaded Russia to reduce its demands before it was too late. Once that stage passed, it is difficult to see what Aberdeen's government could have done to avoid war unless it was prepared to permit the Turks to be crushed by Russia and to see Britain's honour trampled.

### French responsibility?

France's culpability lay mainly in initiating the crisis by raising the issue of the holy places. Napoleon III can be accused of playing to the gallery at home, regardless of the likely repercussions.

## Turkish responsibility?

Although the Turks may appear to be the hapless victims of great power politics, they were by no means innocent of warlike intentions. Western support presented them with an opportunity to stand firm against Russia.

## Diplomatic efforts to make peace in 1854

Britain and France declared war on Russia in order to protect the integrity of the Ottoman Empire. However, their war aims were not identical. Essentially, Napoleon III wanted a quick victory to raise his prestige both at home and abroad. Palmerston, by contrast, wanted the widest possible campaign to reduce Russian power. In a memorandum, which Palmerston drew up for the cabinet in March 1854, he proposed carving up Russia:

- Finland would be returned to Sweden.
- The Baltic provinces would be given to Prussia.
- Poland would become independent.
- Austria would gain Wallachia and Moldavia.
- The Ottoman Empire would regain the Crimea and Georgia.

Aberdeen dismissed this as totally unrealistic, a view shared by most of the cabinet at the time and by most historians since. Aberdeen's main concern was to bring Austria into the war on the Anglo-French side. Opposing Russia's occupation of the Principalities, Austria's foreign minister, Buol, was keen to support Britain and France. But Emperor Francis Joseph had no wish to go to war with Russia. In June 1854, Austria, with Prussian backing, demanded Russian evacuation of the Principalities. In July, Russia withdrew and the area, with Turkish agreement, was occupied by Austrian troops. The Balkan issue had thus been effectively solved. Austria now took the lead in promoting diplomatic moves to end the war. The Four Points, accepted by Britain and France in August, became the basis of peace proposals for the rest of the conflict:

- Russian guarantees of the Principalities were to be replaced by a European guarantee.
- The Danube was to be a free river.
- The 1841 Straits Convention, banning warships from sailing through the Straits, was to be revised 'in the interests of the balance of power'.
- The Sultan's Christian subjects were to be placed under European protection.

The Tsar's rejection of the Four Points in September left Britain and France with little option but to fight.

## The choice of the Crimea

For Britain and France, the war was initially something of an anti-climax. Given that Constantinople was in no danger, allied forces, which had initially landed at Gallipoli, were moved to Varna (in present-day Bulgaria), intending to raise the siege of Silistria. But the Russians were already in the process of retreating, abandoning Moldavia and Wallachia before the allied troops had fired a shot

in anger. Britain and France could now have declared victory. But
having sent their troops so far, British and French governments and
publics wanted to strike a blow against Russia.

In late July cholera struck the military camp at Varna. British
military hospitals were unable to cope with the situation and
hundreds of men died. As troop morale crumbled, the Duke of
Newcastle, the Secretary of State for War, urged Lord Raglan, the
head of the British expeditionary force, to attack the Crimean port
of Sevastopol. Its capture would destroy Russian naval power in the
Black Sea. Raglan, who knew little about the state of Sevastopol's
fortifications or the strength of its garrison, had some misgivings.
But anxious to do something, he agreed to the invasion of
the Crimea.

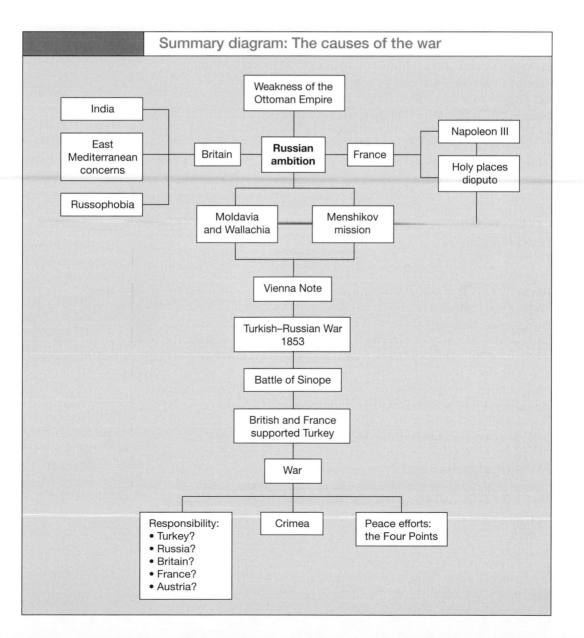

## Summary diagram: The causes of the war

# 2 | The British Army

The 26,000 strong British army that sailed for the Crimea in September 1854, composed of five infantry divisions and one cavalry division, was described by *The Times* as 'the finest army that has ever left these shores'. But its dashing appearance only served to camouflage problems in command and organisation. In many respects the army had been neglected since 1815, not altogether surprisingly given four decades of European peace. Moreover, little attention had been paid to the likelihood that it would have to fight a continental war.

**Key question**
What were the British army's main weaknesses in 1854?

## The influence of Wellington

Given parliamentary preoccupation with **retrenchment** and public indifference, the army to a large extent after 1815 was run by the military high command without interference. The fact that the army had triumphed over France in the **Peninsula War** and at **Waterloo** and also performed well in campaigns against non-European forces, especially in India, strengthened the forces of conservatism and complacency, both within the army and politically. The Duke of Wellington was Commander-in-Chief in 1827–8 and again from 1842 to 1852. Even when not in that position he exercised massive authority over military affairs. Although not entirely opposed to new ideas, he took the view that what had served the army well in the past was the surest guarantee of continuing success. He also believed that calls for reform were really no more than calls for further economies.

## Lord Raglan

In 1854, Lord Raglan was appointed to command the British expeditionary force. He had served on Wellington's staff in the Peninsula War and at Waterloo and had subsequently been Wellington's military secretary. No one doubted Raglan's bravery. At Waterloo, his right elbow had been shattered by a musket-ball and he had let the surgeon amputate his damaged arm without a murmur. Nor was his administrative ability in question. He also had many personal qualities: diplomacy, patience, loyalty to subordinates and devotion to duty. 'Raglan', said Wellington, 'is the sort of man who would die rather than tell a lie'. Unfortunately, he was 65 years old in 1854, had seen no active service since 1815, and had never commanded a force in his life.

## Divisional command

The quality of British military command was a cause of some concern. Only one of Raglan's five infantry **divisional** commanders was under 60, and he, the Duke of Cambridge, was the queen's 37-year-old cousin who had not seen action before. The chief engineer Sir John Burgoyne was 72. An army commanded by such men was unlikely to be innovatively led. Moreover, only two of the infantry divisional commanders had led anything larger than a **battalion** into action.

**Key terms**

**Retrenchment**
The cutting of government spending.

**Peninsula War**
The war in Portugal and Spain between British and French forces (1808–14). The Duke of Wellington commanded British troops for most of the war.

**Waterloo**
The Battle of Waterloo was fought in 1815. British forces (led by Wellington) and Prussian forces (led by Blucher) defeated Napoleon Bonaparte.

**Division(al)**
A division was a formation of two or more brigades. It usually comprised some 4000–5000 men.

**Battalion**
Another name for a regiment, comprising in theory but rarely in practice 1000 men.

## British officers

There were signs of growing professionalism among sections of the officer corps. But the actual experience of command was necessarily confined to colonial wars and many officers had seen no active service at all. The system of buying commissions ensured that wealth often triumphed over ability. Officers were drawn principally from the landed aristocracy and gentry, and from families with a military tradition. Very few rank-and-file soldiers sought or received commissions. Such restricted recruitment enabled officers to perpetuate the values of the officer gentlemen with accepted standards of behaviour and a heightened sense of honour and duty. While these were positive attributes, too many officers joined the army because it provided them with a fashionable and not too strenuous existence.

## Military administration

Military administration in 1854 was a shambles. So many ministers and officials were involved that even contemporary experts became lost in the maze:

- The Secretary of State for War and the Colonies was theoretically responsible for military policy and for political oversight of all troops outside Britain.
- The Secretary-at-War looked after military financial and legal matters.
- The Commander-in-Chief saw to discipline, appointments, promotions and the army's general state of readiness.
- The Adjutant-General dealt with recruiting, discipline, pay, arms and clothing.
- The Quartermaster-General was responsible for movement, quartering, barracks, camps and transport (though no transport corps existed).
- The Board of General Officers advised the Adjutant-General on clothing and equipment.
- The Home Secretary administered the **yeomanry** and the **militia** and the distribution of regular troops in Britain.
- The Ordnance Office controlled the engineers and the artillery as well as the army's ammunition needs.
- The Commissariat, a department of the Treasury, was responsible for food, fuel and transport.

Such a cumbersome structure inevitably produced rivalries, procrastination and inertia. Periodically, ministers had discussed plans for reform. But successive cabinets were too timid to override the hostility of Wellington and other senior officers to any change that would diminish the authority and independence of the Commander-in-Chief or subject the army to greater political control.

**Key terms**

**Yeomanry**
Volunteer cavalry who served in Britain.

**Militia**
A home defence force raised from volunteers or by ballot in an emergency.

## The problem of military commitments

The army's main commitments were home and imperial defence. Given that Britain was shielded by the Royal Navy and that foreign invasion seemed a remote possibility, the demands of domestic security generally took second place to those of imperial defence. Most soldiers served overseas, often for long periods.

## The problem of expenditure

A passion for economy raged in parliament after 1815, affecting all areas of government spending. The army budget declined from £43 million in 1815 to £9.5 million in the 1840s.

## The problem of manpower

The army rarely had more than 115,000 men. Soldiers served 21 years in the infantry and 24 years in the cavalry. Long service overseas exacted a heavy toll in human life and health, particularly in tropical stations like India. (Between 1839 and 1853 there were 58,139 deaths.) The army's manpower problems were compounded by its failure to attract sufficient recruits.

## The problem of poor conditions

Soldiering was not a popular occupation among the labouring classes. This was largely because of poor conditions of service:

- Most barracks, whether in Britain or abroad, were overcrowded and insanitary.
- Army food was monotonous. The standard diet was a daily ration of one pound of bread (450 g) and three-quarters of a pound (340 g) of meat.
- A soldier's basic pay was poor, 1s. a day for infantry. A deduction of 6d. a day was made for food.
- Army authorities discouraged marriage among the rank and file. The families of married soldiers were expected to live in the same barrack rooms as the rest of the men.
- The army disciplinary code was severe. Soldiers could be flogged for a variety of crimes and misdemeanours. (In 1846 the maximum number of lashes was reduced to 50.)
- Army routine was monotonous: **drill**, drill and more drill.

Given these conditions, the army was something of a refuge for the dregs of society: misfits, drunkards and criminals.

**Key terms**

**1s. (one shilling)** Twelve old pence (12d.) – or 5 pence in modern money.

**Drill** Basic training including marching and learning to handle weapons.

## Efforts at reform pre-1854

The 1830s and 1840s were decades of reform in civilian society. The army was not wholly immune to calls for change:

- Military reformers tried to generate demands for remedial action in specialist journals like the *United Service Magazine.*
- Many officers displayed a paternalistic concern for their men.
- Lord Howick, Secretary-at-War (1835–9) and Colonial Secretary (1846–52), attempted to bring about military change. Hoping to make army life more attractive, he introduced a more wholesome diet and sought to improve barrack accommodation.

But efforts to ameliorate the lot of the ordinary soldier were often frustrated:

- The administrative system made it difficult to achieve wide-ranging reform.
- Parliament, anxious to save money, showed a conspicuous neglect of the soldier.

## The situation by 1854

Since 1815 no one had seriously considered what seemed the remote contingency of troops being called on to fight a major war in Europe. Thus little thought had been given to concerted action by brigades or divisions, let alone **staff work** and large-scale administrative co-ordination. Yet in 1854, the army, resented if not openly despised by many civilians, was expected to achieve a quick and comprehensive victory over the Russians. In the circumstances, it is a tribute to the professionalism and bravery of many of its officers and men that the army, only one battalion of which had seen recent active service, fought as well as it did. The fact that the infantry were armed with the **Minié rifle** (soon to be replaced by the lighter **Enfield rifle**) gave British troops an undoubted advantage over Russians still armed with smoothbore muskets.

## The French army

The French expeditionary force initially consisted of 40,000 infantry, plus artillery and cavalry. This number was soon to grow to about 120,000. French divisional commanders were notably younger than their British equivalents. Most French officers had acquired recent campaign experience in Algeria. Promotion from the ranks was commonplace and the officer class was more professional than its British equivalent. The most striking area of French superiority was in organisation and supply. Properly trained French staff ensured that pay, rations, medical services and supply arrangements were as lavish as possible and efficiently administered.

## The Russian army

In 1854, the Russian army was over one million strong. Its conscripted rank and file (many of whom were convicted prisoners) suffered worse conditions of service than their British counterparts. Most Russian officers were from the landowning class and many took their professional military duties lightly.

## The Turkish army

On paper, the Turkish army was 700,000 strong. In reality, it was probably only half that strength. Turkish forces were poorly led, poorly equipped, poorly trained and poorly supplied.

## The Royal Navy

While the Royal Navy had been greatly reduced in size after 1815, it had kept up with new developments, not least the coming of steam and iron ships. But given the limitation of engines, steam power

**Key terms**

**Staff work**
Preparatory planning and administrative work undertaken by the commanding officer's personal team.

**Minié rifle**
This fired the minié ball, an inch-long lead ball that expanded into the groove of the rifle-musket's barrel. It was far more accurate than the smoothbore musket. The latter had an effective range of less than 100 yards; the minié rifle was accurate at over 400 yards.

**Enfield rifle**
An improved version of the minié rifle-musket.

was still an auxiliary to sail in the 1850s. In 1854, the navy had difficulty finding enough men to fit out expeditions to both the Baltic (see pages 42–4) and Black Seas.

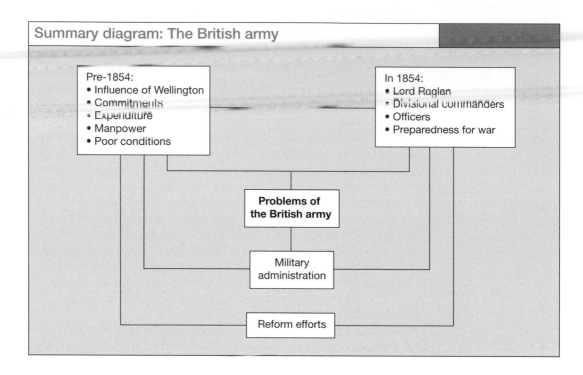

**Summary diagram: The British army**

Pre-1854:
- Influence of Wellington
- Commitments
- Expenditure
- Manpower
- Poor conditions

In 1854:
- Lord Raglan
- Divisional commanders
- Officers
- Preparedness for war

**Problems of the British army**

Military administration

Reform efforts

## 3 | Fighting in the Crimea in 1854

On 14 September 1854, allied troops began landing at Kalamita Bay, north of Sevastopol. British soldiers went ashore in full dress uniform, carrying:

- four and a half pounds (2 kg) of salt beef
- the same weight of biscuits
- a greatcoat and blanket
- a knapsack
- a spare pair of boots and a spare shirt
- a water canteen
- cooking apparatus
- rifle and bayonet
- 50 rounds of ammunition.

### The Battle of Alma

St Arnaud, the French commander, wanted to march immediately on Sevastopol. But Raglan insisted on rounding up wagons, baggage animals and supplies from the surrounding countryside. On 19 September, the allied army – 63,000 strong – finally moved south, making contact with the enemy in the early afternoon. The Russian Commander-in-Chief, Prince Menshikov, had only 33,000 men. After a fitful exchange of artillery fire, the Russians withdrew to a strong position behind the River Alma.

**Key question**
What were Raglan's main mistakes in 1854?

**Battle of Alma: September 1854**

Key date

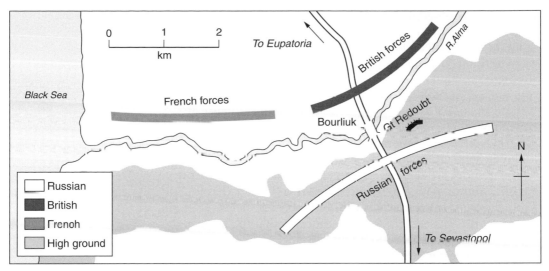

Map of the Battle of Alma.

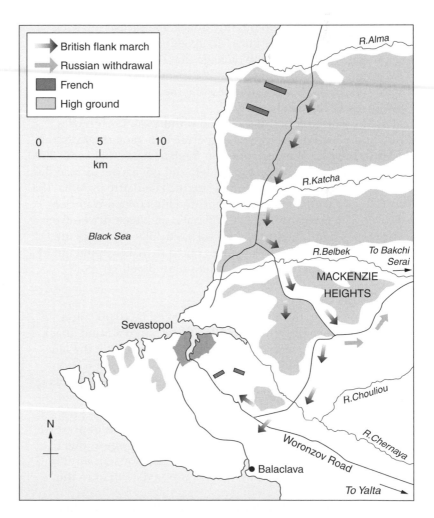

The march to
Sevastopol from
Alma.

St Arnaud proposed that the French forces attack on the right next to the sea. Protected by the guns of the fleet, they would scale the West Cliff and roll up the Russian left flank while British troops advanced against the Russian centre and right flank. Raglan listened with his customary politeness to St Arnaud's impassioned arguments. Privately he considered the French commander had underestimated Russian strength but not wishing to cause an unseemly altercation, he assured St Arnaud that he could rely on the 'vigorous co-operation' of the British army.

On 20 September, at 1.00p.m., the British advance began. Coming under artillery fire, the troops halted and lay patiently for 90 minutes, waiting to see how the French attack developed. French troops scaled the West Cliff but lacked sufficient strength to roll up the Russian left. Raglan, informed that the French needed support, ordered his men to advance again. Across a two-mile front, the British lines marched down to the Alma. The 2nd Division, struggling round the village of Burliuk, came under heavy fire from Russian guns. Troops of the Light Division, further left, made quicker progress. Once across the Alma, they headed uphill, bayonets fixed, and captured the Great Redoubt. Exposed to enemy artillery fire and infantry attack, the British fell back. Two British nine-pounder guns, dragged into position by Colonel Dickinson, inflicted so much damage that the enemy retreated. This cleared the way for a general British advance. The Grenadier Guards seized the Great Redoubt while the Highland Brigade drove back 12 Russian battalions.

The Russians now began a general withdrawal. Lord Lucan, who led the British cavalry, was desperate to pursue the Russians and turn the retreat into a rout. But Raglan, aware that some 3000 Russian cavalry were lurking to his left, did not agree. Instead, he ordered his men to bivouac for the night. The Battle of Alma, the first full-scale battle between European nations since Waterloo, was over. The Russians had lost 5700 men and been driven from a strong position. The British had suffered 1500 casualties, the French under 1000. While the allies failed to make capital out of the Russian retreat, the campaign had started well.

## The Siege of Sevastopol

On 23 September, the allied army, reinforced by 10,000 men, began its advance on Sevastopol. Raglan favoured a rapid attack from the north and many Russians later attested that if the allies had done as he wished there would have been nothing to stop them marching into the town. However, Raglan's chief engineer, Sir John Burgoyne, believed the Russian defences posed a serious obstacle. St Arnaud, who was fatally ill, agreed. He advocated attacking Sevastopol from the south. Raglan, anxious to preserve allied accord, deferred to the French. This decision was one of the most crucial of the war. Meanwhile Menshikov sent most of his army towards the north-east where it posed a threat to the allied flank.

On 26 September, British forces entered Balaclava, a fishing port too small to serve as a supply base for both armies. Raglan, poorly advised by Admiral Lyons, chose to remain at Balaclava. Consequently, the French, now led by General Canrobert, went to bays further west. Raglan's decision to stay at Balaclava was to place an enormous strain on his army: it was committed to defending the allied flank from attack at the same time as laying siege to Sevastopol.

Raglan, not anticipating a protracted siege, pressed for an assault on Sevastopol. But Canrobert insisted that the city's defences must first be reduced by artillery bombardment. Given allied inaction, the Russians had time to improve Sevastopol's defences. Admiral Kornilov, who had **scuttled** part of his fleet at the mouth of the harbour, blocking allied ships' access, inspired the defenders while Colonel Totleben strengthened the town's fortifications. The Russian army was also steadily reinforced. The allies had thus frittered away their victory at the Alma.

By 17 October the allies had dragged 126 siege guns into position and the cannonade finally began. Facing them on the landward side of Sevastopol were 341 Russian guns: double the number of a few weeks earlier. An allied naval bombardment, coinciding with the land cannonade, led to damage to several warships and 500 casualties. The allied land bombardment was more effective, so much so that had the allies attacked they would probably have captured Sevastopol. But Canrobert was not prepared to do so and the Russians were able to patch up their defences. This pattern was repeated over several days: a successful bombardment, a failure to attack and Russian repairs carried out under cover of darkness.

## The Battle of Balaclava

On 25 October, a Russian army of 25,000 foot soldiers, 34 squadrons of cavalry and 78 guns advanced towards Balaclava, aiming to:

- cut the Worontsov road connecting Balaclava to Sevastopol
- threaten Balaclava itself.

After overrunning Turkish outposts along the Causeway Heights, several thousand Russian cavalry charged the 93rd Highland Regiment, 550-men strong. Sir Colin Campbell told his men to stand or die. They stood in two lines (standard practice was to arrange infantry facing cavalry attack in squares) and managed to turn aside the enemy cavalry. But the 93rd could not check the Russian assault single-handed. This task fell to the British cavalry. The Heavy Brigade, comprising 800 men, led by General Scarlett, faced at least twice that number of Russian cavalry pouring over the Causeway Heights. Scarlett led the counter-charge. After a few minutes of desperate fighting, the Russians fled. The Heavy Brigade, charging uphill, had won an amazing victory, losing only 10 dead.

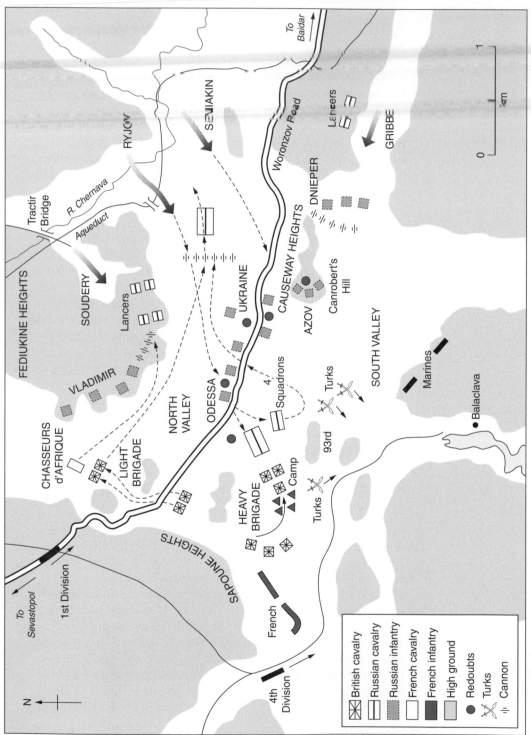

Map of the Battle of Balaclava.

Key question
Who was most to
blame for the Charge
of the Light Brigade?

## The Charge of the Light Brigade

Major General the Earl of Cardigan, head of the 664-strong Light
Brigade, watched the triumph of the Heavy Brigade with some
envy. An arrogant snob, Cardigan was Lucan's brother-in-law. But
the two men, neither of whom had previously seen any active
service, hated each other. Their long enmity had only intensified
in the Crimea. Cardigan's officers wanted to launch themselves
against the fleeing enemy. But Cardigan, having no orders from
Lucan, refused to attack. (Lucan later claimed that he had told
Cardigan to take advantage of any reasonable opportunity.)

### Raglan's order

Raglan, on the Sapoune Heights, had little immediate control
over operations. Annoyed by the loss of initiative, he sent a
verbal message to Lucan requesting him to occupy the ground
the Russians were vacating. Without infantry to assist him, Lucan
declined to regard the message as an order. Taking advantage of
the respite, the Russians set about removing the guns from the
Turkish redoubts on the Causeway Heights that they had earlier
overrun. The exasperated Raglan now composed a new order for
Lucan. 'Lord Raglan wishes the cavalry to advance rapidly to the
front, follow the enemy and try to prevent the enemy carrying away
the guns. Troop Horse Artillery may accompany. French cavalry is
on your left. Immediate.'

### Nolan's role

Captain Louis Nolan was the staff officer chosen to deliver the
message. He was selected probably because he was an excellent
horseman and could ride rapidly down the steep descent into
the valley below. But excitable, conceited and openly scornful of
both Lucan and Cardigan, he was far from the ideal messenger.
Nolan handed Lucan the order. Lucan read its contents with some
consternation. He then announced that such an attack would be
'useless'. Nolan replied that Raglan's orders were that the cavalry
should attack immediately.

'Attack, sir!' said Lucan. 'Attack what? What guns, sir? Where
and what to do?'

Nolan waved his arm in a contemptuous gesture down the valley.
'There, my Lord. There is the enemy! There are your guns!'

### Lucan's role

Lucan, who lacked Raglan's high vantage point, could not see the
guns on the far side of the Causeway Heights. Nolan's angry wave
gave Lucan the impression that he had been ordered to attack the
mass of Russian guns at the far end of the valley some 2000 metres
away. Lucan, realising that such an attack would be suicidal,
rode over to Cardigan and ordered him to advance towards the
main Russian army. Even Cardigan, who was spoiling for a fight,
hesitated.

'Certainly, sir', Cardigan replied. 'But allow me to point out to
you that the Russians have a battery in the valley in our front, and
batteries and riflemen on each flank.'

'I know it', said Lucan. 'But Lord Raglan will have it. We have no choice but to obey.'

Cardigan turned away murmuring, 'Well, here goes the last of the Brudenells!' (Brudenell was Cardigan's family name.)

## Cardigan's role

Cardigan gave the order to advance. The 13th Light Dragoons and the 17th Lancers led the brigade, followed by the 4th and 11th Hussars, with the 8th Hussars in the third line. Ahead were 20 battalions of Russian infantry, supported by over 50 guns. These forces were deployed on both sides of and at the opposite end of the valley. It would take the Light Brigade some seven minutes to cover the distance.

As the horsemen trotted down the valley, Nolan suddenly dashed before Cardigan who led the charge, waving his sword and shrieking at him. Nolan probably realised that the cavalry were heading in the wrong direction and was trying to avert disaster. But at this very moment a splinter from an exploding Russian shell tore into his chest and killed him. The Light Brigade thus continued its charge 'into the mouth of hell' as Alfred, Lord Tennyson later graphically described it (see page 34).

Artillery and musket fire soon poured into its ranks from three sides, causing the leading men to break into a charge before they were ordered to do so. Reaching the Russian guns, the cavalry hacked at the gunners. Then, seeing Russian cavalry drawn up

Who was most to blame? (clockwise from top left) Lucan? Cardigan? Nolan? Raglan?

behind the guns, Cardigan turned and trotted back down the valley. His men followed, running the same gauntlet of fire as they retreated. The whole incident lasted barely 20 minutes. Of the 664 men who charged, 110 were killed, 130 wounded and 58 taken prisoner. Some 500 horses died. Cardigan made no effort to rally or find out what had happened to his men. Enraged by what he considered Nolan's insolence, he left the battlefield, went on board his private yacht and drank champagne.

### The aftermath of the Charge

The futility of the Light Brigade's action and its reckless bravery prompted French General Bosquet to state: 'C'est magnifique, mais ce n'est pas la guerre.' ('It is magnificent but it is not war.') He continued, in a rarely quoted phrase: 'C'est de la folie.' ('It is madness').

Raglan's dispatches on the incident were published in an edition of the *London Gazette* on 12 November. Raglan blamed Lucan for the Charge. While accepting that he might have misunderstood the order, Raglan believed that Lucan should have exercised his discretion. Furious at being made a scapegoat, Lucan responded by claiming that throughout the campaign Raglan had allowed him no independence at all and required that his orders be followed to the letter. Lucan's criticism of his superior was not tolerated and in March 1855 he was recalled to Britain, where he continued to defend himself, blaming Raglan and Nolan. Although he never again saw active duty, he was made a member of the Order of the Bath in July 1855. Cardigan who had merely – indeed bravely – obeyed orders, blamed Lucan for giving him those orders. Leaving the Crimea at his own request, he returned home a hero and was promoted to Inspector General of the Cavalry.

The Charge has been a subject of controversy ever since. It is usually seen as a classic example of military ineptitude. In reality, it was an accident, types of which happen in most wars. It was also a relatively small-scale affair. Moreover, it also had some success, the Light Brigade inflicting more casualties on the Russians than it suffered. But the notion of a tragic blunder, redeemed by heroic sacrifice, was set in stone by Alfred, Lord Tennyson, the **Poet Laureate**.

### Tennyson's Poem

Tennyson's reading of Russell's account of the Charge in the *The Times* (which glorified British valour) inspired him to dash off a poem in a few minutes. After agonising over whether to retain the phrase 'Someone had blundered', he sent the poem for publication in the *Examiner* on 9 December. The poem was well received by civilians and soldiers alike and secured a permanent place in the collective memory of the public. Several generations of schoolchildren, required to learn poetry by heart, found that the stirring poem, with its sing-song rhythm, was ideally suited to memorisation.

### 1

Half a league, half a league,
  Half a league onward,
All in the valley of Death
  Rode the six hundred.
'Forward, the Light Brigade!
'Charge for the guns!' he said.
Into the valley of Death
  Rode the six hundred.

### 2

'Forward, the Light Brigade!'
Was there a man dismay'd?
Not tho' the soldier knew
  Someone had blunder'd:
Theirs not to make reply,
Theirs not to reason why,
Theirs but to do and die:
Into the valley of Death
  Rode the six hundred.

### 3

Cannon to right of them,
Cannon to left of them,
Cannon in front of them
  Volley'd and thunder'd;
Storm'd at with shot and shell,
Boldly they rode and well,
Into the jaws of Death,
Into the mouth of Hell
  Rode the six hundred.

### 4

Flash'd all their sabres bare,
Flash'd as they turn'd in air,
Sabring the gunners there,
Charging an army, while
  All the world wonder'd:
Plunged in the battery-smoke
Right thro' the line they broke;
Cossack and Russian
Reel'd from the sabre stroke
  Shatter'd and sunder'd.
Then they rode back, but not
  Not the six hundred.

### 5

Cannon to right of them,
Cannon to left of them,
Cannon behind them
  Volley'd and thunder'd;
Storm'd at with shot and shell,
While horse and hero fell,
They that had fought so well
Came thro' the jaws of Death,
Back from the mouth of Hell,
All that was left of them,
  Left of six hundred.

### 6

When can their glory fade?
O the wild charge they made!
  All the world wonder'd.
Honour the charge they made,
Honour the Light Brigade,
  Noble six hundred.

*The Charge of the Light Brigade*, Alfred Lord Tennyson, 1870.

## The results of the Battle of Balaclava

The Battle of Balaclava, coupled with the driving back of a Russian attack on the Inkerman Heights on 26 October ensured that the Russian advance on Balaclava was halted. The siege of Sevastopol thus continued. However, the Russians confined the British to a narrow area between Balaclava and Sevastopol and also commanded the important Worontsov road. British positions guarding the approaches to Balaclava were vulnerable. Menshikov now commanded 120,000 men. Raglan had 25,000 troops and the French some 40,000.

## The Battle of Inkerman

Early on 5 November the Russians launched an attack on Inkerman Ridge. Their moves were hidden, first by rain and then by fog. The fighting quickly broke up into a series of isolated encounters which were impossible to direct or co-ordinate. All over the battlefield,

Battle of Inkerman: November 1854

Key date

small units of British infantry took on much larger numbers of Russian troops. Around 9.00a.m., as the mist began to clear, it seemed that the Russians were certain to drive back the British forces. However, French soldiers now came to the rescue, helping to turn the tide of battle. Soon after noon, the Russians retreated, leaving the allies in possession of Inkerman Ridge.

The Russians lost 11,000 casualties, the British 597 killed and 1860 wounded, the French 130 killed and 750 wounded. While the allies had won a great victory, Clarendon, the Foreign Secretary, wrote that the British army might be unable to sustain another such 'triumph'.

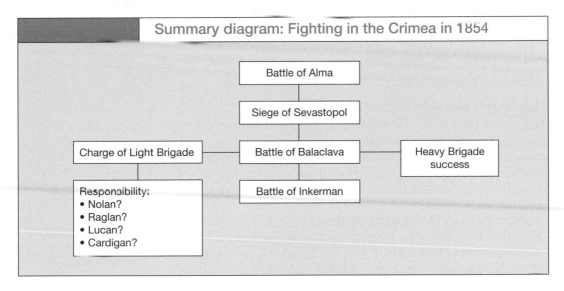

## Summary diagram: Fighting in the Crimea in 1854

- Battle of Alma
- Siege of Sevastopol
- Charge of Light Brigade — Battle of Balaclava — Heavy Brigade success
- Responsibility:
  - Nolan?
  - Raglan?
  - Lucan?
  - Cardigan?
- Battle of Inkerman

## 4 | The Winter of 1854–5

**Key question**
Who was responsible for the British army's suffering in 1854–5?

Although the allied armies had fought well, they were still no nearer capturing Sevastopol. Raglan, aware of the army's administrative shortcomings, warned the Duke of Newcastle of the dangers of wintering in the Crimea. In reply, Newcastle declared that the Crimean winter was one of the mildest in the world.

### The problem of supply

On 13 November, James Filder, the Commissary-General, wrote to the Treasury that:

> I am full of apprehension as to our power of keeping this army supplied during the coming winter … In this crowded little harbour [Balaclava] only a proportion of our vessels can be admitted at a time … With all the siege and other stores which are being disembarked, we can do little more than land sufficient supplies to keep pace with the daily consumption of the troops; and to add to our difficulties, the road from the harbour to the camp, not being a made one, is impassable after heavy rains; our obstacles in these respects will increase as the winter comes. We shall have many more stores to convey than we have hitherto had – fuel, for instance.

On 14 November, the situation became worse. A terrible storm resulted in the loss of more than a score of ships, carrying much-needed stores. (The *Prince*, for example, carried a huge amount of warm clothing while the *Progress* carried enough hay to feed all the horses in the British army for three weeks.) On land, scores of tents were blown to shreds. The storm was in part to blame for what now occurred. However, as Fildor recognised, the situation had been grim before the storm. In Balaclava there was no lack of stores. The problem lay in efficiently organising the supplies and moving them up to the soldiers on the heights above Balaclava.

As the rank and file suffered, the careless luxury displayed by certain officers did not help matters:

- Cardigan dined and slept aboard his private yacht.
- Colonel Griffiths came to the Crimea with a French chef.
- Lord Rokeby brought a patent water closet to the Crimea (which French troops soon stole for boiling soup).

## The harsh winter

The winter 1854–5 was one of the worst Crimean winters in living memory, sometimes so cold that icicles formed on the moustaches of men at night. While such cold spells were rarely prolonged, the weather was also wet. Given the shortage of tents and the lack of firewood, men were unable to cook or stay dry and warm.

## Congestion in Balaclava harbour

Over the winter, Balaclava became a place of nightmarish chaos. Much of the blame rested with Admiral Boxer, who was in charge of transport arrangements. His inefficiency led to ships arriving at Balaclava without notice and with nobody sure what supplies they carried. In Balaclava there were insufficient landing stages. On the port's crowded quayside, there was total confusion. Everything was piled together, consumables often rotting in the open air.

## The problem of transport

Transporting supplies from Britain to Balaclava (4000 miles; 6500 km) was easy. It was the transport from Balaclava to the siege lines (just six miles; 9.5 km) that was the problem. Russian control of the Worontsov road initially deprived the army of the only metalled road up the Sapoune Ridge. However, the Russians abandoned their position on 6 December, before the worst of the winter set in, so the Commissariat could not use this as an excuse. The freezing or muddy tracks were less of a problem than the lack of forage to feed the pack animals, which in turn prevented more transport animals being brought in to improve the situation. The Commissariat thus found it impossible to provide the troops above Balaclava with basic necessities: food, fuel, tents and clothing. Eventually, in January 1855 a railway contractor, Samuel Peto, was brought in to lay a track from Balaclava to the heights above the port.

**Key terms**

**Cholera**
An infection of the intestine caused by bacteria transmitted in contaminated water. The disease causes severe vomiting and diarrhoea which leads to dehydration that can be fatal.

**Scurvy**
A disease caused by deficiency of vitamin C. The symptoms are weakness and aching joints and muscles, progressing to bleeding of the gums and other organs.

**Gangrene**
This usually results from infected wounds or frostbite. Body tissue decays as a result of failure in the blood supply, usually to an arm or a leg. Amputation of the affected limb was the only cure in the 1850s.

## Administrative incompetence

Army administrators found themselves entangled in a bureaucratic mesh. Departmental jealousies cut across the path to efficiency. No one, it seemed, was able to act. Even when the appalling state of the army was common knowledge, the Treasury lived in a world apart. The government finally sent out Colonel MacMurdo with independent purchasing powers to form a much-needed transport corps. It was a costly undertaking and when he sent in his requisitions, Sir Charles Trevelyan, Secretary to the Treasury, replied saying, 'Colonel MacMurdo must limit his expenditure', to which MacMurdo replied, 'When Sir Charles Trevelyan limits the war I will limit my expenditure'.

## The medical situation

As more and more men went down with **cholera**, **scurvy**, **gangrene**, **typhus**, **typhoid**, **frostbite** and **dysentery**, the medical situation became dire. Early in the campaign, it was evident that hospital conditions for both the wounded and those who were ill were appallingly inadequate. Hospital tents, food and medicines were scarce. Medical orderlies had no transports to move the sick. The filthy, verminous and overcrowded hospital at Balaclava provided little comfort for sick and wounded men. Those who were shipped off to the hospital at Scutari fared no better.

Soon letters reached horrified relatives in Britain of the dreadful conditions, conditions confirmed and denounced by *The Times* and other newspapers. It was at Scutari that Florence Nightingale battled to improve matters. She found men piled up in corridors, lying on unscrubbed floors and crawling with vermin. In her early days at Scutari more than 1000 patients were suffering from acute diarrhoea and there were only 20 chamber pots to go round. Privies were blocked up and an inch of liquid filth floated over the floor. Men died in dreadful numbers.

Dr Blake, surgeon of the 55th, kept a medical history of his regiment, whose average strength in 1854–5 was 818. He treated:

- 640 men for fever, including typhus: 57 died.
- 368 cases of respiratory diseases, including pneumonia and tuberculosis: 17 died.
- 1256 cases of infections of the bowels and stomach, including dysentery: 76 died.
- 96 cases of cholera: 47 died.

Six men died from frostbite, three from scurvy, four from diseases of the brain and 21 from 'unknown causes'. Blake also treated:

- nine men for heart disease
- 98 for diseases of the eyes
- 290 for boils and ulcers
- 90 for **venereal diseases**
- 41 for wounds caused by flogging.

---

**Key terms**

**Typhus**
A dangerous fever transmitted by lice, fleas, mites or ticks. There are many different forms but they share the symptoms of fever, headache, pains in muscles and joints, and delirium.

**Typhoid**
An infectious disease, usually contracted by drinking infected water. The symptoms include fever, headache, loss of appetite and constipation.

**Frostbite**
Damage to part of the body, usually a hand or foot, resulting from exposure to extreme cold. This may lead to gangrene.

**Dysentery**
An infection of the bowel causing painful diarrhoea. This results in dehydration which can be fatal. Dysentery occurs wherever there is poor sanitation.

**Venereal diseases**
Diseases transmitted predominantly by sexual intercourse.

In total, he treated a total of 3025 cases of sickness, compared with 564 men treated for wounds. Blake had few medical supplies. 'The hospital accommodation through the greater part of the winter', he wrote, 'was so limited that it was necessary to fill the few tents literally as full as they could hold'.

Raglan was well aware of the deficiencies in the army's medical care. In December 1854, he issued a General Order that was highly critical of the treatment of the sick and wounded. Unfortunately, little money had been spent in planning for something which no one expected to happen. Moreover, the mid-Victorian army medical services often attracted the least competent and most callous members of (what could be in the nineteenth century) a callous profession.

---

## Profile: Roger Fenton 1819–69

| 1819 | – Born in Heywood, Lancashire, son of a banker |
| 1840 | – Graduated from University College, London |
| 1840–4 | – Studied art in London and Paris |
| 1847 | – Qualified as a solicitor |
| 1851 | – Began to take an active interest in photography |
| 1852 | – Visited Russia: his photographs from Russia helped to establish his fame |
| 1853 | – Founder of the Photographic Society |
| 1855 | – Went to the Crimea to photograph the troops |
| 1861–2 | – Abandoned photography, selling his equipment |
| 1869 | – Died |

Fenton went to the Crimea in February 1855 as the first official war photographer at the insistence of Prince Albert. It was hoped his photographs might counteract the anti-war reporting of *The Times*. Location photography in 1855 was no easy matter. Fenton carried his bulky equipment in a converted wine-wagon. Given the primitive photographic technology, he was unable to take action shots. Thus, most of his 350 photographs were either carefully posed pictures of men or images of the landscape. Many of his photographs were of the officers. 'If I refuse to take them', he said. 'I get no facilities for conveying my van from one locality to another.' His pictures tend to portray war as a gorgeous pageant and he avoided making pictures of dead or injured soldiers. On returning from the Crimea, his prints were displayed in a London gallery and also published in bound volumes.

Fenton was not the only photographer in the Crimea. James Robertson and the Frenchman Jean-Charles Langlois also took photographs. Newspapers in the 1850s lacked the technology to print photographs. However, the *Illustrated London News* sent several artists to the Crimea to sketch events at the front. Their sketches were then converted into engravings for the weekly paper.

### Raglan's role

Raglan was deeply concerned by the situation and worked hard, as did many officers, to remedy matters. But he did not do enough to inform the government of his worries or appeal for more help. Nor did he do much to rouse the mood of his men. His reluctance to show himself to the troops, to acknowledge their cheers or even to say a few words of encouragement did not help declining morale. His manner gave the impression he was unaware of, or unconcerned about, the welfare of his men. So his men complained about him. Many thought the problem was the lack of command of the commander.

### The result

The Crimean winter was a battle waged against misery, disease, cold, ignorance, incompetence, mismanagement and the absence of foresight. It was a battle lost. Consequently many brave men died. By the end of January, the British army was only 11,000 strong. The sick and wounded totalled 23,000. The French army, 80,000 strong, coped with the rigours of the winter far more efficiently. Britons, informed of the suffering and bureaucratic muddle by Russell and other war correspondents, were appalled. It seemed inconceivable that the richest country in the world could not provide its army with basic necessities. Aberdeen was blamed. He fell from power in February 1855 and was replaced by Palmerston (see pages 52–4).

An example of Fenton's work: officers of the 4th Light Dragoons in February 1856.

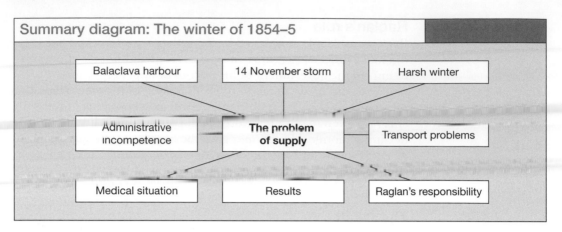

Summary diagram: The winter of 1854–5

- Balaclava harbour
- 14 November storm
- Harsh winter
- Administrative incompetence
- **The problem of supply**
- Transport problems
- Medical situation
- Results
- Raglan's responsibility

## 5 | The War 1855–6

As spring approached, the administrative chaos in the Crimea lessened. Provisions were located in separate depots on the plateau above Balaclava, the railway line was completed, more Turkish labour was recruited and the confusion in Balaclava was tackled. After the third week of February, there was a marked decline in the deaths of soldiers in the military hospitals: 3168 died in January; 1409 in March; 582 in April. By March 1855, as troops received huge supplies of food and clothing, the morale of the army was largely restored.

### The diplomatic situation

Military setbacks induced Tsar Nicholas to accept the Four Points (see page 20) in November 1854. However, Britain now insisted on stiffer terms regarding the Black Sea. Thus peace negotiations never got off the ground. An Austrian-sponsored peace conference met at Vienna from March to June 1855. It collapsed when Russia refused to agree to neutralisation of the Black Sea.

Diplomatically, the allies had some success in 1854–5:

- In December 1854, Austrian Foreign Minister Buol persuaded Francis Joseph to sign a treaty with Britain and France. Although it was called an alliance, the treaty did not mean that Austria had to fight.
- In January 1855, Piedmont, anxious to gain support for its ambitions in Italy, agreed to join Britain and France.

The death of Tsar Nicholas in March 1855 offered some hope of peace. His successor Alexander II did not have the same personal commitment to the war.

### Sevastopol

Over the winter of 1854–5 allied operations against Sevastopol had virtually ceased. However, by March 1855 the allies were ready to try again. By the late spring there were some 175,000 allied troops in the Crimea, only 32,000 of whom were British; 20,000 Turks arrived in April and 15,000 Piedmontese in May. There were also

**Key question**
Why did it take the allies so long to capture Sevastopol?

10,000 foreign mercenaries: Germans, Swiss and Poles. The rest were French.

The allies still faced problems:

- Sevastopol was not encircled and could thus be easily supplied and reinforced.
- Sevastopol's defences – a series of earthwork fortresses – remained strong.

However, Russian problems were greater than those of the allies:

- There were no railway lines south of Moscow. It took three months for men and supplies to get from Moscow and St Petersburg to the Crimea.
- The corrupt Russian administrative system made supply a lottery.
- Fearing and facing attacks on a number of fronts, Russia failed to concentrate its military effort in the Crimea. Instead it tried to protect all possible points of attack, including stationing many troops on the Austrian border to guard against a 100,000-strong Austrian army of 'observation'.

On 9 April 1855, the allies began a second great bombardment of Sevastopol. Five hundred and twenty allied guns poured 165,000 rounds into the town. The bombardment continued for 10 days. The Russians sustained heavy casualties – 6131, compared with 1587 French and 263 British casualties – but maintained their defences. Raglan was keen to launch an attack but the French were less enthusiastic. As the junior partner in the alliance, Raglan had to go along with whatever Canrobert decided.

## General Pelissier and the Kertch expedition

Threatening to come personally to the Crimea to lead his armies, Napoleon III peppered Canrobert with a spate of instructions. In mid-May Canrobert asked Napoleon to relieve him of command. He was replaced by General Pelissier. Tough and aggressive, Pelissier was strong enough to resist directives from Paris.

On 22 May, disobeying orders from Napoleon, Pelissier gave permission for the British-devised Kertch expedition to go ahead. This aimed to cut off Russian supplies from the Sea of Azov area. The 15,000-strong expedition was successful: Kertch captured, the Sea of Azov raided, 100 guns taken, thousands of tons of corn and flour destroyed, Russian boats sunk and arsenals demolished. The British forces lost just one man.

## The death of Raglan

Pelissier now prepared for an assault on Sevastopol. On 7 June, the French captured the Mamelon fortress while British forces took the Quarries. On 18 June, after another great cannonade, British forces hoped to take the Redan and the French the Malakhov, regarded as the key to Sevastopol's defensive system. But the allied attacks failed, the British losing 1500 men and the French 3500. The defeat heightened the tensions and widened the divisions between allied forces, the British blaming the French and the French the British for the debacle.

On 28 June, Raglan, overworked and dispirited, died of dysentery. Florence Nightingale was 'thunderstruck' by news of his death. He was not a very great general, she thought, 'but he was a very good man'. The 63-year-old Sir James Simpson, who had little recent military experience, replaced him. (He had no wish to command and resigned four months later.)

## The capture of Sevastopol

On 16 August 1855, the new Russian commander Gorchakov (who had replaced Menshikov in February) launched a major attack across the Chornya river. The 00,000-strong Russian army was decisively defeated by French and Piedmontese troops. This was the Russians' last effort to break the allied siege. On 8 September, French forces captured the Malakhov (losing 7500 casualties in the process). A British attack on the Redan was a disaster, made all the more painful by the French success. Britain suffered 2500 casualties. But even as the British army licked its wounds, the Russians abandoned Sevastopol. Its fall, while a serious setback for Russia, was not a total defeat. Russian guns to the north still dominated the city, preventing the allies from occupying it in safety. For the remainder of the war the armies in the Crimea sat and watched one another.

Fall of Sevastopol: 1855

**Key date**

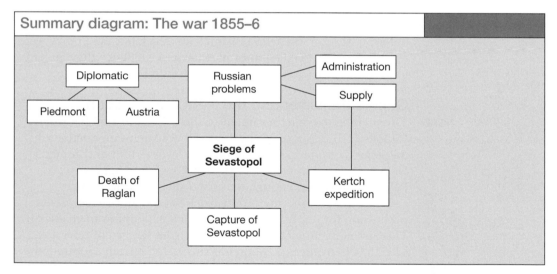

Summary diagram: The war 1855–6

6 | The Wider War

While a considerable part of the fleet was sent to the Black Sea to support allied land forces, the Royal Navy was able to wage a wider war against Russia.

**Key question**
How important was the wider war?

## The Baltic

In 1854, the Admiralty gathered together a scratch force to sail to the Baltic. Command was given to 68-year-old Sir Charles Napier. His fleet, undermanned and short of ammunition, was initially much smaller than that of the enemy. Yet he was ordered to seal the Baltic, destroy the Russian fleet and protect Danish and Swedish shipping from Russian attack. He first established a base south of

Copenhagen. Then, reinforced by British and French ships, he went on the offensive, sailing to the Gulf of Finland. He considered attacking the following:

- Kronstadt, a fortified island barring the approaches to St Petersburg
- Sveaborg, a fortress guarding the entrance to Helsinki (Finland was a province within the Russian Empire).

Deciding that both places were too strong, he attacked and captured the fortress of Bomarsund in mid August. After maintaining his blockade on the Russian coast until the end of October 1854, Napier withdrew. Back in Britain, he faced a grilling from an Admiralty unimpressed with his performance. In fact he had been remarkably successful, bottling up the Russian fleet, tying down 30,000 Russian soldiers, destroying enemy ships and supplies as well as capturing Bomarsund.

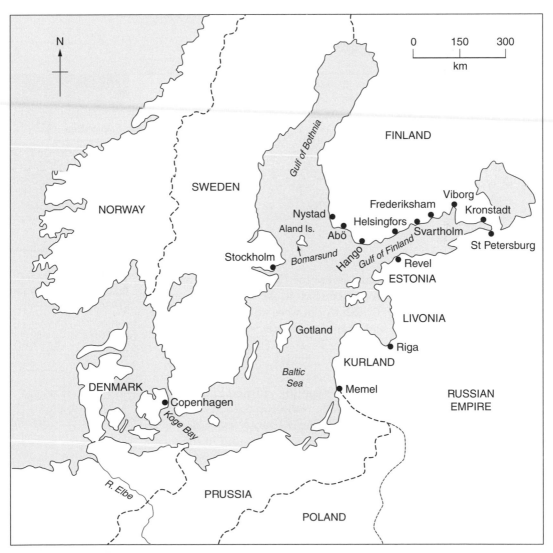

A map of the Baltic.

In 1855, Admiral Dundas replaced Napier and maintained his good
work, blocking Russia's ports, destroying the forts at Svastholm
and Frederiksham and subjecting Sveaborg to a devastating
bombardment. By 1856, the allies had some 250 ships in the
Baltic. Palmerston hoped that this 'Great Armament' would
be strong enough to capture Kronstadt and threaten
St Petersburg

## The White Sea and the Pacific

A small squadron of British ships maintained a partial blockade of
the White Sea. Further afield in the Pacific allied forces failed to
achieve much. The enemy were either too strong or too elusive to
be dealt with effectively.

## Asia Minor

Russian and Turkish forces waged war in Asia Minor. The main
fighting was around the Turkish fortress of Kars, which was
besieged from June to November 1855. Despite the inspirational
leadership of British Colonel Fenwick Williams, the Turkish
garrison was finally forced to surrender.

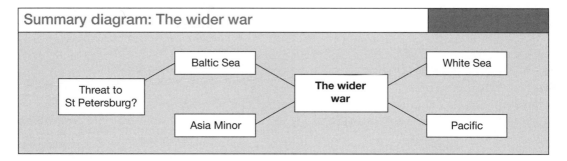

Summary diagram: The wider war

Threat to St Petersburg? — Baltic Sea — The wider war — White Sea, Asia Minor, Pacific

## 7 | Peace

Key question
What were the main
results of the Crimean
War?

With Sevastopol's fall, the campaign in the Crimea petered out.
The winter of 1855–6 was an odd contrast to the year before. As
a result of lessons learned, British troops were well supplied. The
French army, by contrast, had a far worse winter, some 40,000
soldiers dying of disease.

## The end of the war

French opinion felt that Sevastopol's capture satisfied France's
honour and wanted an end to the war. Napoleon agreed. By
contrast, Palmerston, anxious to 'confine the future extension
of Russia', advocated fresh campaigns in the Baltic and in the
Caucasus. He claimed that the British army was about to reach a
peak of strength and was confident of thrashing Russia.

Palmerston's hopes did not come to fruition. In December 1855,
Austria issued an ultimatum threatening Russia with war if it did
not negotiate on the basis of the Four Points (see page 20). The

Russians were aware that this was bluff: the Austrian army was actually in the process of demobilising. Russia's main concern was the Baltic, where the allied naval blockade was damaging Russia's economy, endangering domestic stability. The 'Great Armament' posed a threat to their capital and the Russians also feared Swedish intervention. Therefore, Tsar Alexander II accepted the Austrian ultimatum as the basis of peace talks. Palmerston, unable to fight Russia alone, had no choice but to agree to an **armistice** in February 1856.

## The Treaty of Paris

The Treaty of Paris was signed on 30 March:

- The existing rights and privileges of the Balkan Christians were guaranteed by a new edict issued by the Sultan.
- Turkey's territorial integrity and independence were agreed.
- Kars was returned to Turkey.
- Southern Bessarabia was restored to Turkey and incorporated into Moldavia.
- Turkish sovereignty over the Principalities was guaranteed but the provinces were to be united as a new state of Romania.
- Sevastopol was returned to Russia.
- The Black Sea was neutralised. Russia and Turkey were prohibited from maintaining warships or naval arsenals there.

## The results

The allies could claim that they had achieved most of their objectives. The Ottoman Empire had survived. More importantly, Russia was seriously weakened, its Balkan ambitions checked and its navy kept out of the Mediterranean. The war ended the generally accepted view (pre-1854) that Russia was Europe's dominant power. Russia's efforts to remove the restrictions imposed on its naval power in the Black Sea was not achieved until 1870.

Although emerging victorious, Britain's military reputation had been damaged by the war. However, if the British army had not covered itself in glory, the Royal Navy had performed well. No other state could rival it in size, modernity and technical skill.

France was seen as the real victor of the Crimean War since it seemed to have played a more important military role than Britain. Given the perception of French power, Napoleon was able to pursue his own agenda after 1856, especially the cause of Italian nationalism.

The Crimean War marked the demise of the **Concert of Europe** established in 1815. The period from 1856–70 was a chaotic period of diplomacy. There were no stable alignments between the great powers: all sought to further their own interests rather than acting in the interests of Europe as a whole. The war, preceded by almost 40 years of peace, was followed by 14 years of intermittent warfare. Two hugely important developments took place during this period: the unification of Italy and the creation of the German Empire.

**Key date**

Treaty of Paris: 1856

**Key terms**

**Armistice**
An agreement to suspend fighting.

**Concert of Europe**
The various efforts by the great powers to co-operate in settling possible causes of conflict between themselves in order to maintain peace between 1815 and 1854.

## The military implications

In many respects the Crimean War was a midway point between Waterloo and the First World War. Generally, the armies employed Napoleonic uniforms and tactics but fought with improved weapons. The war emphasised the overriding importance of logistics, entrenchments and firepower, anticipating the experience of the American Civil War (1861–5). It saw the first military use of new technologies: iron-clad warships, **breech-loading** guns and submarine mines. However, it was probably not a turning point in the history of warfare. By no means a **total war**, it did not cause much disruption to civilian life.

## The casualties

The Crimean War involved far heavier casualties than any other European war fought between 1815 and 1914. Some 22,000 British soldiers died (98,000 Britons fought in the Crimea). France lost 95,000, Turkey some 150,000 and Russia at least half a million dead. Most died of disease; less than one in five was killed in battle.

**Key question**
Was the Crimean War the first modern war?

**Key terms**

**Breech-loading**
A firearm loaded at the side instead of the muzzle (the mouth of a gun).

**Total war**
A conflict in which a nation utilises all its resources in an effort to secure victory.

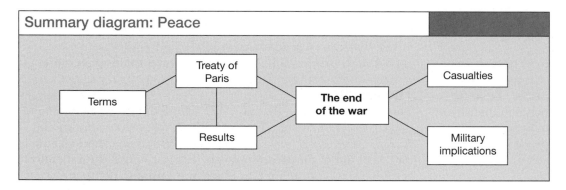

Summary diagram: Peace

Terms — Treaty of Paris — Results — The end of the war — Casualties — Military implications

---

**Some key books in the debate over the Charge of the Light Brigade**

M. Adkin, *The Charge; The Real Reason Why the Light Brigade Was Lost* (Leo Cooper, 1996).

T. Brighton, *Hell Riders: The True Story of the Charge of the Light Brigade* (Penguin, 2004).

C. Hibbert, *The Destruction of Lord Raglan* (Penguin, 1963).

## Study Guide

### In the style of Edexcel

How far do Sources 2 and 3 support the impression of the Charge of the Light Brigade given in Source 1? Explain your answer using the evidence of Sources 1, 2 and 3.                         (20 marks)

### Source 1

*From: The Charge of the Light Brigade by William Howard Russell, a dispatch sent from the Crimea and published in The Times newspaper, 14 November 1854.*

HEIGHTS BEFORE SEBASTOPOL, OCTOBER 25 – If the exhibition of the most brilliant valour, of the excess of courage, and of a daring which would have reflected lustre on the best days of chivalry can afford full consolation for the disaster of today, we can have no reason to regret the melancholy loss which we sustained in a contest with a savage and barbarian enemy.

### Source 2

*From: Timothy Gowing,* Voice from the Ranks: A Personal Narrative of the Crimean Campaign, *published in 1895. Here he describes the Charge of the Light Brigade. Gowing was a sergeant serving in the Crimea in 1854.*

There was a lot of excitement on the hill-side when we found the Light Brigade was advancing, first at a steady trot, then they broke into a gallop. Someone (an officer) said: 'What on earth are they going to do? Surely they are not going to charge the whole Russian army! It's madness!' But, madness or not, they were simply obeying an order. And this noble band pressed on towards the enemy, sweeping down the valley at a terrific pace, in all the pride of manhood. The enemy's guns – right, left and front – opened on this devoted band. A heavy musketry fire was likewise opened; but still they pressed on. The field was soon strewn with the dead and wounded. It was a terrible sight to have to stand and witness without the power of helping them.

We could see the enemy formed up to cut off all retreat; but it was now do or die. In our fellows went with a ringing cheer, and cut a road through them; and now, to our horror, the brutish enemy opened their guns upon friend and foe, thus involving all in one common ruin.

### Source 3

*From:* Mrs Duberly's War: Journal and Letters from the Crimea, *1854–6, published in 1856. Mrs Duberly was the wife of an officer and had accompanied her husband to the Crimea. Here she describes events of 25 October 1854.*

Now came the disaster of the day – our glorious and fatal charge. But so sick at heart am I that I can barely write of it even now. It has become a matter of world history, deeply as at the time it was involved in mystery. I only know that I saw Captain Nolan galloping; that presently the Light Brigade, leaving their position, advanced by themselves, although in the face of the whole Russian force, and under a fire that seemed pouring from all sides, as though every bush was a musket, every stone in the hillside a gun. Faster and faster they rode. How we watched them! They are out of sight; but presently come a few horsemen, straggling, galloping back.

---

### Exam tips

This is an example of your first question (**a**). It is a short answer question, and you should not write more than three or four paragraphs. Note that you are only required to reach a judgement on the evidence of these sources. The question does not ask you to write what you know about the Charge of the Light Brigade. However, you will apply your own knowledge to help you comprehend the sources and the issues they raise.

This question asks you to cross-refer Sources 2 and 3 with the impression created by Source 1. Your first task is to analyse that impression. It is written for publication. What image of the day does it conjure up? Choose two or three adjectives which convey impression and select just a few words from Source 1 to support your analysis.

Then use Sources 2 and 3 to explore whether the impression is confirmed, developed or modified by their evidence.

Finally, you should reach a conclusion about how far the impression given in Source 1 is supported. To do this, you should take into account not only the content of Sources 2 and 3 but also their nature. Before you come to an overall judgement, you will need to explore any elements of the origin or purpose of the source which add weight to it, or cause you to treat it with caution. For example, you might take into account that both Sources 2 and 3 were published in the knowledge of the furore Russell's own account created when it was read in 1854 and may be influenced by that. You could also take into account the attitudes of both of the authors: Source 2, from a serving soldier, is more concerned to emphasise valour, while Source 3 emphasises loss.

# 3 The Impact of the Crimean War on Britain

**POINTS TO CONSIDER**

From a British perspective, the Crimean War was a limited war. Britain relied on naval power, economic blockade, allies, a relatively small army and industrial output to secure its aims. The war had a minimal impact on civilian life. Nevertheless, it did have some important results. It brought Palmerston to his first premiership. It established the reputation of Florence Nightingale. It was also the first 'modern' media war, typified by *The Times* correspondent William Russell. His reports caught the attention of the public and played a large part in bringing down Aberdeen's government in 1855. The war also led to calls for greater efficiency in military and government management. However, reforms were late in coming and limited in practice. This chapter will consider the impact of the war on Britain by considering the following themes:

- Political developments
- Financing the war
- Social change
- Military reform

**Key dates**

| | |
|---|---|
| 1852 | Aberdeen became Prime Minister |
| 1855 | Palmerston became Prime Minister |
| 1856 | Introduction of the Victoria Cross |
| 1857–8 | Indian Mutiny |
| 1865 | Death of Palmerston |
| 1869–72 | Cardwell's military reforms |

# 1 | Political Developments

The political situation in the 1850s was somewhat confused. There were four main groups:

- Liberals and **Whigs** who represented the urban middle classes, and stood for religious liberty, **free trade** and moderate reform.
- Conservatives who represented English county seats and stood for the established Anglican Church and for **protectionist** policies.
- Peelites who had supported the Conservative leader Sir Robert Peel in 1846 when he split his party over the Repeal of the Corn Laws. They stood for free trade, reduction of government spending and administrative competence.
- Radicals who favoured more widespread social and economic reform.

## Lord Aberdeen

In the 1852 general election, Liberals, Whigs and Radicals won 323 seats, the Conservatives 291 and the Peelites 40. Although they were a distinct minority, the Peelites (who included a number of talented men – Gladstone, Herbert, Graham and Aberdeen himself) held the balance of power. Unwilling to return to the Conservative fold, the Peelites agreed to form a coalition with the Liberals. They played the political game skilfully. Aberdeen became Prime Minister and no fewer than six of the 13 cabinet posts were held by Peelites.

On taking office, Aberdeen announced a programme of moderate reform. From 1852 to 1855 there was a great deal of minor although useful legislation on employment, prisons, education and health. However, the Crimean War was to be the keynote of Aberdeen's administration. Aberdeen, who had not wanted war (see page 19), was the one who was blamed as the public outcry grew over conditions in the Crimea during the winter of 1854–5.

## The impact of the press

Newspaper coverage of the war, aided by the electric telegraph, which enabled news to travel across Europe in hours not weeks, ensured that the public was able to read about the reality of warfare with immediacy for the first time. Thanks to new technology and the abolition of various duties, the cost of daily newspapers was falling. That said, newspapers remained too expensive for most of the population and many Britons were unable to read one, even if they could afford one. Daily newspapers in the 1850s (and for the next three decades) largely catered for the literate middle and upper classes.

## The impact of William Howard Russell

The single most influential reporter was William Howard Russell (1820–1907) of *The Times*. He was described by one soldier as 'a vulgar low Irishman [who] sings a good song, drinks anyone's brandy and smokes as many cigars as a Jolly Good Fellow. He is just the sort of chap to get information, particularly out of youngsters.' Russell's reports – sharp, clear, sometimes funny, often moving, always vivid – were hugely significant, 'eagerly awaited and avidly read by almost the entire literate population of London' (according to historian Christopher Hibbert). Russell invariably paid credit to the bravery of the British troops. Although he initially avoided criticising Raglan, he asked awkward questions and when he saw problems, he wrote about them. He was not the only influential reporter, Thomas Chenery, *The Times'* correspondent in Constantinople, was the first to report the dreadful conditions in the hospitals at Scutari.

## The press attack on Raglan

The army's plight stirred John Delane, *The Times'* editor, to attack Raglan and his staff for gross incompetence. On 23 December 1854, *The Times* told its readers that:

> The noblest army ever sent from these shores has been sacrificed to the grossest mismanagement. Incompetency, lethargy, aristocratic hauteur, official indifference, favour, routine, perverseness, and stupidity reign, revel and riot in the Camp before Sevastopol ... We say it with extreme reluctance, no one sees or hears anything of the Commander-in-Chief.

Having opened fire, *The Times* maintained its attack on both Raglan specifically and the army's aristocratic and privileged leadership in general.

Raglan, who had a poor opinion of the press in general, considered the personal attacks on him as unworthy of response. His main concern was that press's uninhibited reporting might give the Russians useful information about the army's dispositions. (The Tsar was reported as saying: 'We have no need of spies, we have *The Times*'.) Nevertheless, Raglan made no efforts to get rid of the correspondents. Nor did the British government impose press censorship. It feared that if it did so this might be interpreted as a means of hiding from public view its responsibility and guilt for what was happening in the Crimea.

## How much impact did the press have?

The horrors brought so vividly to light by *The Times* and other papers (for example, the *Daily News* and the *Morning Herald*) shattered the patriotic complacency of opinion at home. Instead there was a bitter outcry and a search for scapegoats. From Britain's point of view there was probably no greater inefficiency than at the start of most wars: but thanks to newspaper correspondents it appeared as though there was.

However, in some respects newspapers exercised less influence on policy than is often claimed, not least because many ministers (particularly Palmerston) manipulated the press more successfully than the press manipulated them. Although Palmerston distrusted journalists, he was prepared to make the most of any political opportunity that came his way.

## The fall of Aberdeen

In January 1855, the Radical MP John Arthur Roebuck gave notice of a Commons motion for appointing a committee to inquire into the conduct of the war. Lord John Russell, Lord President of the Council, feeling that he could not defend the government, resigned from the cabinet. On 29 January, Roebuck's motion was carried by 305 votes to 148, with more than 80 Liberals voting in the majority. The vote stunned Aberdeen, who resigned the following day.

## Palmerston

The collapse of Aberdeen's government led to a political crisis. The Conservative leader, the Earl of Derby, and Lord John Russell both tried and failed to construct administrations. Their failure ensured that 71-year-old Palmerston became Prime Minister.

Benjamin Disraeli, the Conservative leader in the Commons, remarked in February 1855: 'He [Palmerston] is really an imposter, utterly exhausted, and at best only ginger-beer, and not champagne, and now an old painted pantaloon, very deaf, very blind, and with false teeth, which would fall out of his mouth when speaking if he did not hesitate and halt so in his talk'. Richard Cobden, a radical, proclaimed that 'to call in an exploded sham to master a crisis like this is merely proof that we as a nation are in a state of collapse'.

**Key question**
How great a war leader was Palmerston?

**Key date**
Palmerston became Prime Minister: 1855

'At best only ginger beer' – Lord Palmerston (1784–1865) photographed in about 1860.

But that was not the way most Britons saw things. As a highly visible Foreign Secretary (from 1830 to 1841 and again from 1846 to 1851), Palmerston had never been shy to lecture autocratic regimes, which gave him a reputation for sympathy with liberal causes. His spasmodic bombast, usually directed against minor powers that could be bullied by the Royal Navy, engendered a good deal of popular support. Most Britons liked his 1850 statement that 'as the Roman, in days of old, held himself free from indignity, when he could say *Civis Romanus sum* [I am a Roman citizen]: so also a British subject, in whatever land he may be, shall feel confident that the watchful eye and the strong arm of England will protect him against injustice and wrong'. His foreign policy – apparently freedom-loving, adventurous, proudly British and contemptuous of foreigners, particularly non-Protestants – captured the imagination of most Britons. (In reality Palmerston was an arch-pragmatist and far less warmongering than he sometimes appeared.)

With his progressive rhetoric abroad and his support for moderate reform at home, Palmerston embodied a wide spectrum of opinion both within and outside the restricted government circles of the time. In many ways, he was the most modern politician of his day: cultivating the press, appealing to public opinion on grounds of national pride, and taking his policies to 'the people' by speaking in many of Britain's main cities.

## Palmerston's leadership 1855–6

While Palmerston was popular in the country (despite – or perhaps because of – his numerous love affairs), his position in parliament was far from secure. He survived partly by luck, partly because of his own political skills and partly because his opponents were disunited. At first he led an almost unchanged ministry. However, within a month, the main Peelites in his cabinet – Graham at the Admiralty, Gladstone at the Treasury and Herbert at the Colonial Office – resigned. The ostensible reason was Palmerston's refusal to veto the appointment of a committee of inquiry into the war. In reality, the Peelites were having second thoughts about attaching themselves to a politician whom they had long disliked. Palmerston found replacements: Russell became Colonial Secretary, Cornwall Lewis became Chancellor of the Exchequer while R.V. Smith went to the Admiralty. This ensured that Palmerston's administration no longer looked like Aberdeen's coalition. Most Liberal MPs were delighted at the changes. Moreover, the Peelites, by resigning when they did, associated themselves with the chaotic phase of the war.

The war situation was quickly rectified. Lord Panmure, an energetic Scot, replaced the Duke of Newcastle as Secretary of War in February 1855. Panmure sniped at Raglan and sent General Sir James Simpson to report on Raglan's staff. (Simpson reported that they were doing a good job.) While injecting some energy into the war effort, Panmure and Palmerston benefited from the fact that much had already been done to remedy matters.

To the public Palmerston appeared an excellent war leader. In reality, his administration made only modest changes to the war effort:

- A sanitary commission was sent out to the Black Sea and helped to improve conditions both at Scutari and in the Crimea.
- A special transport department was established which helped the problem of supply.
- Some of the most inefficient administrators in the Crimea were sacked.

## Administrative reform

As criticisms in parliament and the press of military mismanagement increased, there were demands for reform of the Civil Service. Many assumed that the problems stemmed from the aristocracy's monopoly of power in all areas of government. In 1855, the Administrative Reform Association mounted an intensive campaign:

**Key question**
Did the Crimean War lead to major Civil Service change?

- contrasting aristocratic administrative bungling with the triumphs of commerce
- urging that business-like procedures be applied to government and administration
- claiming that competitive exams would allow the middle classes to take over the running of the state.

Palmerston, the recipient of so much middle-class adulation, pointed out that the most serious breakdowns had taken place 'not where the gentry were, not where the aristocracy were, but where there were persons belonging to other classes of the community – in the medical department, the Commissariat department, the transport service, which have not been filled by the aristocracy or the gentry'.

The much-vaunted Civil Service reforms of 1855 were not particularly significant. Nor had they much to do with the Crimean War. Sir Stafford Northcote and Sir Charles Trevelyan's report recommending changes to the Civil Service had been presented in 1853 – before the war. Its main recommendations – for competition in recruitment, promotion by merit and a clear separation between 'intellectual' and 'mechanical' work – were only very partially implemented. A Civil Service Commission was established but departments continued to arrange their own standards for entry. Early competitions were largely artificial. Of the 9826 certificates of competence issued by the Commission between 1855 and 1868, 7033 related to men appointed without any competition at all, 2763 to entrants subjected to very limited forms of competition and 28 to those who had emerged from competitions open to all. Those with power still came from the aristocracy.

Nor did the Civil Service provide much dynamism after 1856. The social reforms of the middle third of the nineteenth century had depended on the energy and influence of a small number of civil servants, men like Edwin Chadwick and James Kay-Shuttleworth who were prepared to engage in disputes of an openly political nature. But by the 1850s there was a growing assumption that civil servants should be administrators, not politicians. This may have reduced the extent to which senior civil servants could make a creative impact on events.

Key question
To what extent did the Crimean War affect politics in the decade after 1856?

## The political repercussions 1856–65

The Crimean War brought Palmerston to power. With the exception of a short period, 1858–9, he remained Prime Minister until his death in 1865. He excelled at turning things to his advantage, not least the war. Depending on almost precisely the same body of support as Aberdeen had done in a parliament notable for political instability, he avoided measures that might cause disruption. (The Marquess of Salisbury claimed in 1864 that Palmerston deserved praise for encouraging parliament to do 'that which it is most difficult and most salutary for a parliament to do – nothing'.)

### The political situation 1857–9

Nevertheless, Palmerston's position was never totally secure. This was shown in 1857. In October 1856, Chinese authorities at Canton (Guangzhou) had arrested a vessel – the *Arrow* – even though the ship had been flying the British flag (as it later turned out improperly). The British Governor of Hong Kong demanded compensation and an apology. When these were not forthcoming, he ordered the bombardment of Canton. News reached London in February 1857. Most cabinet ministers were uneasy about the situation but agreed with Palmerston that Britain's prestige was now so much at stake that there could be no turning back. Palmerston's enemies – Conservatives, Radicals and disgruntled Peelites – had a cause around which they could rally and a motion of censure in the Commons produced a government defeat: 263 to 247. After the vote, Palmerston obtained a dissolution of parliament and in the ensuing general election attacked the Chinese 'barbarians' who had violated the British flag and the Britons who supported them. But, although belligerent patriotism was one of his political assets, not everyone approved of his policies overseas and there were other issues besides China. In the event, Palmerston was returned with a modestly increased majority but was still far from secure.

The Indian Mutiny (see page 66) had a negligible effect on domestic politics. Whereas the Crimean War crisis had transformed itself into a political one, no such thing happened over India. There were no demands for a commission of inquiry into the cabinet's handling of the situation.

In February 1858, Palmerston's government introduced a bill to extend existing Irish legislation throughout Britain by making conspiracy to murder a crime punishable by penal servitude, regardless of where the intended crime was to be committed. This followed an attempt to kill Napoleon III in Paris by the Italian nationalist Felice Orsini. Orsini's plot had been hatched in Britain, where he had also obtained weapons and explosives. Given that the French government had demanded that Palmerston take action, the great jingoist was attacked for 'truckling' to foreigners and selling short Englishmen's free-born liberties. His bill was defeated and he resigned. Derby formed a Conservative minority administration.

## The political situation 1859–65

A Conservative bill to extend the electorate was defeated in March 1859. Another general election followed. The Conservatives made some gains but still remained in a minority. Derby clung to power for a few more weeks. In June, 274 Liberals, Whigs, Peelites and Radicals attended a meeting at Willis's Rooms in London. Putting aside their differences, they agreed to unite against the Conservatives. (Some historians regard this meeting as the formal beginning of the Liberal Party.) Palmerston and Lord John Russell more or less agreed that each would serve under the other, as the queen chose. Five days later Derby's government was defeated along clear party lines. Queen Victoria, desperate to avoid the 'dreadful old men' as she called Palmerston and Russell, eventually asked Palmerston to form an administration. Russell became Foreign Secretary while Gladstone became Chancellor of the Exchequer. In some respects Palmerston's 1859 cabinet looked much like that of Aberdeen's, nine of its 16 members having served in Aberdeen's cabinet. The crucial difference lay in the fact that the new administration was not a coalition but a Liberal government with former Peelites now fully on board.

Palmerston was strongly entrenched after 1859, not so much because of a large majority in the Commons, but because he managed to keep his cabinet and his 'party' happy. He was careful to avoid involvement in the American Civil War and took no action to help Denmark when it was threatened by Prussia in 1863. At home, his government passed a modest amount of useful legislation and avoided the contentious issue of franchise reform. Taxes were reduced and trade increased. Palmerston remained popular. In the general election of July 1865 his government gained about a dozen seats. He died in October 1865. 'Tho[ugh]' he made a joke when asked to do the right thing, he always did it', said Florence Nightingale. There can be few better epitaphs.

**Key date**

Death of Palmerston: 1865

Summary diagram: Political developments

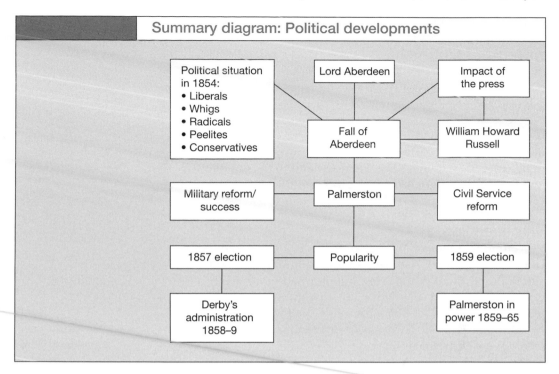

**Key question**
How did Britain pay for the war?

## 2 | Financing the War

The Crimean War had to be paid for. Given that it was relatively short and limited in scope, and Britain was at the height of its economic power, this was not a serious problem. Nevertheless, the cost of the war did have some repercussions.

### William Gladstone

In 1854, Peelite William Gladstone was Chancellor of the Exchequer. A man of great seriousness, he believed in financial probity and the need to reduce taxes, especially income tax and duties which got in the way of free trade. In 1853, he put forward plans for a total repeal of the income tax by 1860 by means of successive reductions from the existing rate of 7d. in the pound. However, his 1854 budget, introduced as Britain was about to declare war on Russia, forced him to backtrack. Income tax rates were doubled, at first for six and then for 12 months, and additional revenue was raised from increases in stamp duty and in duties on spirits, sugar and malt. Gladstone announced that the military costs should be entirely met out of revenue rather than borrowing. That such a hope could even be entertained showed how rich a country Britain had become. But in the event Gladstone was soon forced to backtrack yet again, increasing the government debt by offering **government bonds** for sale. Shortly before his resignation from Palmerston's ministry in 1855, he was obliged to draw up plans for another war loan, twice as large as in 1854.

**Key term**

**Government bonds**
Securities issued by the government, allowing it to borrow money. Those who bought the bonds were guaranteed a return of their money in the future.

## Cornewall Lewis

Sir George Cornewall Lewis replaced Gladstone as Chancellor. His budgets of 1855, 1856 and 1857 showed a greater creativity in dealing with the problems of war finance than Gladstone's. Unlike Gladstone, Lewis did not regard the budget as an instrument of political and economic morality. He saw it simply as a practical business. Nor was he particularly concerned about the need to balance the budget. Convinced that heavy taxation was more damaging to the economy than state borrowing, he was prepared to increase the national debt. The early end to the war allowed him in 1857 to reduce income tax to 7*d*. in the pound and even to reintroduce Gladstone's plan for abolition in 1860.

## War spending

Peacetime spending on the armed forces in 1853 amounted to £15.3 million – 27.7 per cent of total central government expenditure. By 1855, the army and navy had more than doubled in size and cumulative war expenditure had reached around £70 million, of which just under half was eventually met by additions to public borrowing (for example, by the sale of government bonds).

## Gladstone 1859–65

As Chancellor again in 1859, Gladstone determined to restore financial probity. But his return to office coincided with a revival of hysteria about a possible French invasion. There was thus great pressure from all quarters, not least from Palmerston, for additional military expenditure. Although Gladstone fought a series of dogged rearguard actions on behalf of reducing government spending, a higher proportion of central government expenditure (39.4 per cent) was devoted to defence during the years 1861–5, higher than at any other time of peace during the whole of the nineteenth century. Nevertheless the economy was buoyant and with increasing revenues Gladstone was able to bring down income tax to 4*d*. in 1866. In 1860, he cancelled tariffs on a vast range of articles and abolished the paper duty – the last of the '**taxes on knowledge**'.

## The impact of the war on the British economy

Although the British economy suffered a major recession in 1857–8, the commercial crisis was short lived. Overall, the Crimean War had little impact on the economy. For two decades after 1856 Britain remained the world's leading industrial and commercial power.

**Taxes on knowledge**
Taxes on items (like paper) that put up the cost of books, journals and newspapers.

Key term

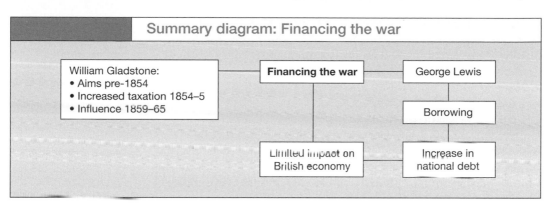

Summary diagram: Financing the war

Key question
What impact did the war have on British society?

## 3 | Social Change

The war had a very limited social impact on Britain. Its main effect came in the field of nursing, the result of the work of Florence Nightingale.

### The social impact of the war

The landowning class remained dominant: socially, economically and politically.

The 1850s and 1860s were essentially decades of consensus and conservatism. Broadly speaking the middle classes had been won to the '**establishment**', or at least to faith in gradual reform. Working-class militancy existed but was much less threatening than in the days of **Chartism** (which fizzled out after 1848). This was probably because there was an improvement, albeit modest, in the prosperity of the mass of the population. Radicals often bemoaned the fact that they could no longer arouse public enthusiasm. 'We live in anti-reforming times', wrote Gladstone (who was by no means a Radical) in 1860.

### Women and nursing

Florence Nightingale's work in the Crimean War has long been recognised. However, there was nothing new in women helping wounded and sick soldiers. Soldiers' wives had long tended soldiers and nuns had often acted as nurses.

Nightingale was by no means the only woman to serve in the Crimea:

- Russian women from all walks of life went to care for Russian sick and wounded.
- Many French nuns served as nurses.
- An Irish Catholic nun, Mother Francis Bridgeman, went to the Crimea in December 1854 to aid the British army. Her nuns worked in hospitals at both Scutari and Balaclava.
- Elizabeth Davis, having quarrelled with Nightingale, served at the hospital at Balaclava with 10 other volunteers.
- Mary Stanley, a convert to Catholicism, took out a predominantly Catholic group of nurses to work at the hospital at Koulali.

Key terms

**Establishment**
The group or class in a community that holds power. Members of this group or class are usually linked socially and usually hold conservative opinions and conventional values.

**Chartism**
A working-class movement for political reform, strong in Britain at various times in the 1830s and 1840s.

- Frances Margaret Taylor worked at Koulali. She wrote a book of her experiences, *Eastern Hospitals and English Nurses*, published in 1856. The book included an impassioned appeal for reform of the nursing system.
- Mary Seacole's work is well known (see page 64).

## Florence Nightingale

Convinced she was doing God's work, Florence Nightingale devoted her life to nursing. Her decision was remarkable. Women of her background were expected to marry and bear children: they did not become nurses. (She never married and had no children.) She was fortunate that her wealthy father:

Key question
How important was
Florence Nightingale?

- believed women should be educated: he personally taught her a range of subjects
- gave her a large annual income, allowing her to live comfortably while pursuing her vocation.

When reports began to filter back to Britain about the horrific hospital conditions in the Crimea, she volunteered to go out to help. On 21 October, she and 38 volunteer female nurses were sent (under the authorisation of War Secretary Sidney Herbert) to the Black Sea. Arriving in November at Selimiye Barracks in Scutari (modern-day Uskudar in Istanbul), they found sick and wounded soldiers being badly cared for by overworked medical staff – all male. Medicines were in short supply and hygiene was neglected.

In the army, there was a deep prejudice against women's involvement in medicine. Dr John Hall, the Inspector General of Hospitals and Raglan's Principal Medical Officer, tried to have Nightingale shipped back to Britain. Although he failed, Hall and his military doctors initially allowed her nurses to undertake only menial duties. But the flood of men who poured into the hospitals in 1854–5 forced officialdom's hand and Nightingale's influence grew accordingly. With a fund of £30,000 to manage, she was able to purchase some of the necessities so badly needed. She also worked with energy and devotion, ensuring that wards were cleaned, fresh bed linen was available and special diets were prepared.

For all Nightingale's zeal, 52 per cent of patients at Scutari died in February 1855. At this stage, she had no better understanding of the hazards of polluted water, overcrowding, lack of ventilation and poor hygiene than army doctors. Nevertheless, she became a national heroine and gained the nickname 'The Lady with the Lamp', derived from a phrase in *The Times*:

> She is a 'ministering angel' without any exaggeration in these hospitals, and as her slender form glides quietly along each corridor, every poor fellow's face softens with gratitude at the sight of her. When all the medical officers have retired for the night and silence and darkness have settled down upon those miles of prostrate sick, she may be observed alone, with a little lamp in her hand, making her solitary rounds.

In many ways Nightingale was – and is – wrongly depicted. Rather than the caring 'Lady with the Lamp', she was more a tough-minded administrator.

## The Royal Commission on the Health of the Army

Nightingale's Crimea experience was only the prelude to her more important post-war career. On returning to Britain, she was determined to improve the health of British troops. Through her efforts, and with the support of Queen Victoria and Prince Albert, a Royal Commission on the Health of the Army was appointed in 1857, chaired by Herbert. When she began collecting evidence for the Commission, Nightingale realised that most of the soldiers at Scutari died as a result of poor hygiene and sanitation. Henceforward, she energetically promoted the thorough overhaul of the health of the army in general and the cause of improved sanitary conditions in particular. Shrewd and forceful, she manipulated her fame to masterly effect for her own ends.

### Army improvement

As a result of the Royal Commission's findings and Nightingale's pressure, sanitation, diet and leisure facilities in army barracks and military hospitals were improved. An Army Medical School was also established.

'The Lady with the Lamp.' The public image of Florence Nightingale, doing her rounds at Scutari. A painting of about 1855.

## Hospital design

Nightingale made extensive efforts to identify the best types of hospitals and to improve hospital design:

- She highlighted sanitary arrangements, cleanliness of wards, overcrowding, heating, deficiency of natural light and administrative arrangements as crucially important.
- She was impressed by a Paris hospital which had a number of separate units (or pavilions). Realising that such units minimised the spread of infection, she promoted this design in Britain.

Nightingale's research culminated in her book *Notes on Hospitals* in 1859. This book, which addressed many issues with regard to hospital construction, provision and management, had considerable effect on hospital design, not just in Britain but across Europe.

## The Nightingale Training School

In November 1855, while Nightingale was still in the Crimea, a public meeting to give recognition to her work led to the establishment of the Nightingale Fund for the training of nurses. With £45,000 at her disposal, she was able to set up the Nightingale Training School at St Thomas' Hospital in London in 1860, the first secular nursing school in the world. Its mission was to train nurses to work in hospitals and with the poor. The first trained Nightingale nurses began work in 1865 at the Liverpool Workhouse Infirmary.

### Notes on Nursing

In 1859, Nightingale published *Notes on Nursing*, a book that served as the cornerstone of the curriculum at the Nightingale and other nursing schools, although the book was written specifically for the education of those nursing at home. The book, the first of its kind to be written, dealt with topics of vital importance for patients' well-being. She continued to produce influential books, for example, *Notes on Matters Affecting the Health, Efficiency and Hospital Administration of the British Army*.

## Statistics

As Nightingale continued to campaign for the improvement of care and conditions in military and civilian hospitals, she made extensive use of graphical representation of statistics. Her methods ensured that her statistics were read and understood by MPs and civil servants. In many respects, she was as much a statistician as a nurse.

## Nightingale's influence abroad

In 1858–9, she successfully lobbied for the establishment of a Royal Commission into the health of soldiers in India. It completed its study in 1863. Thereafter, as a result of sanitary reform, mortality among soldiers in India declined considerably. She later made a comprehensive statistical study of sanitation in Indian rural life and helped to improve medical care in India generally. Her work served as an inspiration for nurses (like Clara Barton) in the American Civil War.

## Profile: Florence Nightingale 1820–1910

| | |
|---|---|
| 1820 | – Born into an upper-class family |
| 1844 | – In spite of opposition from her family, she announced her decision to enter nursing |
| 1847 | – Met Sidney Herbert, who had been Secretary at War (1845–6), a position he held again in the Crimean War. She and he became lifelong friends |
| 1853 | – Became superintendent at the Institute for the Care of Sick Gentlewomen in Upper Harley Street, London |
| 1854 Oct. | – Went to help the Crimean army, largely as a result of Herbert's influence |
| 1854 Nov. | – Arrived at Scutari |
| 1855 | – Made hospital inspections in the Crimea |
| 1857 | – Suffered from depression, probably the result of an infection picked up in the Crimea. Despite being intermittently bedridden, she continued to promote the development of nursing and hospital reform |
| 1860 | – Set up the Nightingale Training School |
| 1910 | – Died |

Florence Nightingale is often seen as the saviour of sick and wounded soldiers in the Crimea. Until recently it was often asserted that Nightingale managed to reduce the death rate in the hospitals at Scutari from 42 per cent to two per cent by making improvements in hygiene. Unfortunately, the truth is very different. Despite the unstinting efforts of Nightingale and her team, death rates did not drop: on the contrary they continued to rise. Indeed, the death count at Nightingale's own hospital at Scutari was the highest of all the hospitals in the region.

Over the winter of 1854–5 over 4000 soldiers died at Scutari. (Ten times more died from illnesses such as typhus, cholera and dysentery than from battle wounds.) According to historian Hugh Small, she effectively presided over 'a death camp'. While she helped her patients to die in greater comfort, she did not save their lives. Not until a Sanitary Commission was sent out by the government in March 1855 was there a marked improvement. It effected the flushing out of the sewers and improvements to ventilation. Thereafter death rates were sharply reduced. Nightingale herself never claimed credit for helping to reduce the death rate at Scutari. During the war she believed the high death rates were due to poor nutrition and supplies rather than poor hygiene. Once she realised her mistake after 1856, she worked incessantly to improve matters in army and civilian hospitals.

## Nightingale's influence as a role model

Nightingale's achievements are all the more impressive when they are considered against the background of social restraints on women in Victorian England. Few women pursued professional careers. Interestingly, she did not assist, nor was interested in, the cause of equal rights. (She opposed women's suffrage.) She seems to have had little respect for women in general, preferring the friendship of powerful men. She saw herself as 'a man of action'. Nevertheless, she undoubtedly inspired many women to devote their lives to nursing. The pioneer of modern nursing, she set an example of compassion, commitment to patient care and diligent and thoughtful hospital administration.

## Mary Seacole

Mary Seacole (1805–81), daughter of a Scottish army officer and a Jamaican woman, has recently become almost as well known as Nightingale for her work in the Crimea. Taught herbal remedies by her mother, she helped to treat sick people (especially cholera victims) in Jamaica and Panama in the 1840s and 1850s. Hearing of the poor medical provision for British soldiers, she travelled to London and applied to the War Office, hoping to be sent as an army assistant to the Crimea, but without success.

**Key question**
How important was Mary Seacole?

Borrowing money, she went out to Turkey. When Nightingale declined her offer of help, she continued her journey to Balaclava. Building a 'hotel' from salvaged materials, she provided a canteen business at the same time as nursing sick soldiers. Nightingale was ambivalent about Seacole. She later wrote that Seacole 'kept – I will not call it a "bad house" – but something not very unlike it … She was very kind to the men and, what is more, to the officers – and did some good – and made many more drunk'. Russell in *The Times* was more complementary. In September 1855, he wrote that she was a 'warm and successful physician, who doctors and cures all manner of men with extraordinary success. She is always in attendance near the battle-field to aid the wounded and has earned many a poor fellow's blessing'.

In 1856, Seacole returned to Britain, in poor health and bankrupt. Her plight was highlighted in the press and as a result a Testimonial Fund was set up for her, to which many prominent people contributed (including Nightingale), indicating the regard with which she was held. An autobiographical account of her travels was published in 1857: the first such work written (or rather **ghost-written**) by a black woman in Britain. Honoured in her lifetime, Seacole was forgotten for almost a century after her death. Recently there has been a resurgence of interest in her achievements, not least because she overcame the racial and gender prejudices of many sections of Victorian society.

## The health of the nation

Nightingale's good work did not have much immediate impact on Britain's health. Between the 1840s and the mid-1870s the annual death rate hovered around 22 per 1000 people in every five-year period. Before the 1880s, the chief causes of death among those who survived childhood were infectious diseases, especially typhus, typhoid, **tuberculosis**, **diphtheria** and cholera (until the 1860s).

Mid-nineteenth-century experts were divided between those who believed that such diseases sprang from corruptions of the atmosphere caused by earthly vapours or bad smells (the miasma

**Key terms**

**Ghost-written**
A book written by someone on behalf of another who is credited as the author.

**Tuberculosis**
A disease which affects the lungs. It is characterised by fever, lack of energy, weight loss and breathlessness.

**Diphtheria**
A bacterial infection which produces a membrane across the throat that can choke a child.

theory) and those who looked to diseases spreading as a result of direct contact with an infected person, insect or animal. Many of the big 'names', like Nightingale, were on the miasmic side. Not until Pasteur and Lister's work in the 1860s was germ theory accepted. This was to have a massive impact on the nation's – and the world's – health.

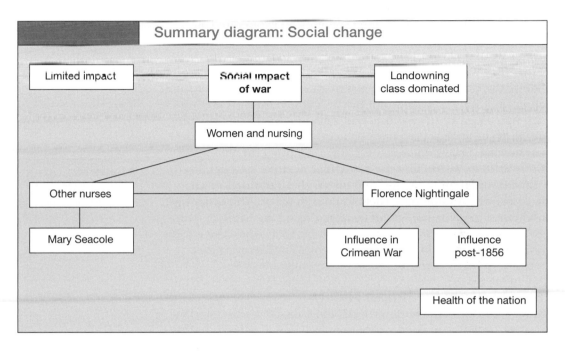

Summary diagram: Social change

### 4 | Military Reform

Key question
Why was there so little military reform both during and after the Crimean War?

During the Crimean War, army affairs commanded unprecedented public and parliamentary interest. Although found wanting in many respects, the army survived largely unchanged and after 1856 the progress of military reform resumed its former unhurried pace.

### Administrative reform 1854–6

Some changes were made in 1854–5, simplifying the bureaucratic structure and improving the army's support services:

- The military duties of the Colonial Secretary were transferred to the War Office, which also took over the Commissariat from the Treasury.
- The Board of Ordnance was abolished, its responsibilities shared between the new Secretary for War and the Commander-in-Chief.
- A land transport corps was formed.
- A new medical corps was set up.

The select committee to investigate the conditions of the army, secured by Roebuck (see page 52), reported in June 1855. It criticised the arrangements for transport, provisioning and hospital care and condemned ministers for having sanctioned an expedition which was ill-prepared for a protracted war. However, by the summer of 1855, the feelings of indignation had cooled and little action followed.

The final surge of parliamentary interest in Crimean mismanagement came in 1856 with the report of a commission appointed to inquire into the working of the Commissariat. The criticisms of five senior officials provoked heated exchanges in parliament. But when an ensuing commission exonerated all concerned, the campaign to expose military bungling expired.

## The Victoria Cross

Before the Crimean War there was no official standardised system of recognition of valour within Britain's armed forces. Given that other European countries had gallantry awards that did not discriminate against class or rank, many felt that a British award was needed. Queen Victoria officially constituted the Victoria Cross in 1856, instructing the War Office to strike a medal that would be awarded to officers and men without distinction who had performed some signal act of valour in battle. The order was backdated to recognise acts of courage during the Crimean War. The first award ceremony was held in June 1856, when the queen invested 62 of the 111 Crimean recipients. The Victoria Cross remains Britain's highest decoration for gallantry.

> **Key dates**
>
> Introduction of the Victoria Cross: 1856
>
> Indian Mutiny: 1857–8

## The impact of the Indian Mutiny

In the years immediately after 1856, the army performed well in a rash of imperial actions, not least in India. In May 1857, Indian troops at Meerut mutinied in support of fellow **sepoys** who had been disgraced and imprisoned for refusing to use cartridges greased with beef and pork fat. (Eating pork offended Muslims and eating beef offended Hindus.) The mutiny spread and was accompanied by rebellion among the civilian population, alienated by the disruptive effects of modernising policies on traditional society. For a few months many Britons feared that the uprising might succeed, especially since only 45,000 of the 277,000 British and East India Company troops in India were Europeans.

> **Key term**
>
> **Sepoys**
> Indian soldiers who fought for Britain.

The army managed to put down the revolt remarkably quickly. The military leaders – Havelock, Neill, Nicholson, Campbell and Rose – became heroes in Britain. But while the press contrasted the skills of 'professional' military leadership in India with the 'aristocratic' failures of the Crimea, the truth was less reassuring. After all, the campaigns mounted in India were precisely those for which the army had been prepared. The forces involved were small: often no more than 2000 British troops with some loyal sepoys in support. Had generals been obliged to conduct affairs on a Crimean scale their success would have been less certain. Moreover, despite British success, there was a good measure of military incompetence. British victories seemed greater than they were thanks to some creative accounting which made it seem as if miniscule British forces were defeating vast hordes. In fact the estimates of the rebel armies were greatly exaggerated.

## Lack of demand for military change

Military success in India (and elsewhere) and the waning of public disquiet over army affairs undermined the cause of reform. In the period 1856–68 no fewer than 17 royal commissions, 18 select committees, 10 internal War Office inquiries and 35 committees of officers dealt in some manner with military administration. But precious little was actually done. Parliament, once more preoccupied with economy, displayed only sporadic attention to the army while the press lost interest in a subject that had disappeared from the national agenda. Complacency and conservatism at the **Horse Guards** did not help matters. The Duke of Cambridge, Commander-in-Chief from 1856 to 1895, was sceptical of most aspects of change, fearing it might damage the *esprit de corps* of the army.

The American Civil War provoked a good deal of interest in British military circles but little effective analysis. Most experts dismissed the novel tactics and techniques developed in the USA as aberrations arising from unique circumstances. While Prussia's success against Austria (1866) and France (1870–1) left a deep impression on some British officers, few politicians looked to Germany as a model for reform. Most Britons assumed they would never again be involved in a major continental war.

## Military reform 1856–68

There were some reforms in the dozen years after the Crimean War:

- Florence Nightingale and her disciples kept up a vigorous campaign to improve the health of soldiers.
- A major programme of barrack construction was launched in 1859–60. But ministers soon shrank from the high spending needed.
- Military authorities set up a Staff College at Camberley to raise training standards. But controversy continued to centre on whether all officers should have to undertake courses of professional study and pass examinations as a prerequisite for obtaining commissions and promotion. Many officers continued to scorn military education, regarding the acquisition of professional qualifications as less valuable than qualities of character and gentlemanly breeding.
- The army was generally provided with the best available weapons.

## The problem of recruitment

Army authorities and successive governments did little to enhance the appeal of service life:

- Soldiers remained poorly paid.
- Marriage was discouraged.
- Scant provision was made for recreation.
- Military discipline remained harsh: flogging was not abolished until 1881.

Consequently the army rarely met its recruitment targets.

---

**Key terms**

**Horse Guards**
The army's main administrative headquarters in Whitehall, London.

*Esprit de corps*
Morale.

---

**Key question**
Why did the army find it difficult to obtain recruits?

## Cardwell's reforms

In 1868, Edward Cardwell was appointed Secretary of State for War in Gladstone's first ministry. Cardwell, who retained his post until 1874, undertook comprehensive reform of the organisation of the army:

- He reorganised the War Office, establishing clear divisions of duties.
- Short-term enlistments were introduced. Infantry had an initial engagement of six (later seven) years and then joined the army reserve. Although soldiers could extend their period of service to 21 years, it was expected that most would quit the army at the end of the minimum period. Cardwell hoped that short-term enlistments would reduce the pension list, help to form a reserve, ensure that the army contained men in the prime of life, induce a better class of man to enlist, enhance the appeal of service life and improve recruitment.
- Cardwell determined to abolish the purchase system, whereby officers bought their commissions. Although he managed to overcome the **filibustering** of the 'Colonels' in the Commons in July 1871, he failed to secure the passage of the Bill through the Lords. The government resolved the impasse by announcing the abolition of purchase by Royal Warrant from 1 November 1871.
- The Localisation Bill (1872) divided the country into 66 territorial districts and based two regular battalions, two militia battalions and a quota of volunteers in each district with a depot to receive recruits. The scheme was designed to foster local connections, to improve the efficiency of the auxiliary forces, and to induce men from the militia to enter the regular army. One of the two regular battalions was to be based at home while the other served abroad. The home-based battalion was to train recruits and to supply drafts and reliefs for the battalion overseas.

### How effective were Cardwell's reforms?

The desire for economy underlay most of Cardwell's measures. His reforms promised far more than they delivered:

- Despite the reorganisation of the War Office, responsibilities remained confused. No planning department was established and no chief of staff appointed to set out the purpose and strategy of the army as a whole.
- The army lost more men than it gained by the introduction of short-service enlistments. Moreover, the men it lost were trained men. Recruitment thus remained a major problem.
- The abolition of the purchase of commissions did little to alter the social composition of the officer corps. Officers came from broadly the same classes in 1900 as they had done in 1870. Without a large private income, few officers could survive financially, so poor was their army pay.
- The localisation of forces did not transform the army. The constant need for men to serve overseas put great strain on the

**Key question**
How significant were Cardwell's reforms?

**Key date**
Cardwell's army reforms: 1868–72

**Key term**
Filibustering
Trying to obstruct new legislation by making lengthy speeches, hoping that there will not be enough time for the legislation to pass.

home battalions. By the Zulu War (1879), there were only 59 battalions at home supporting 82 abroad. For the rest of the century, the home battalions were essentially 'squeezed lemons', supplying men for a larger number of battalions abroad.

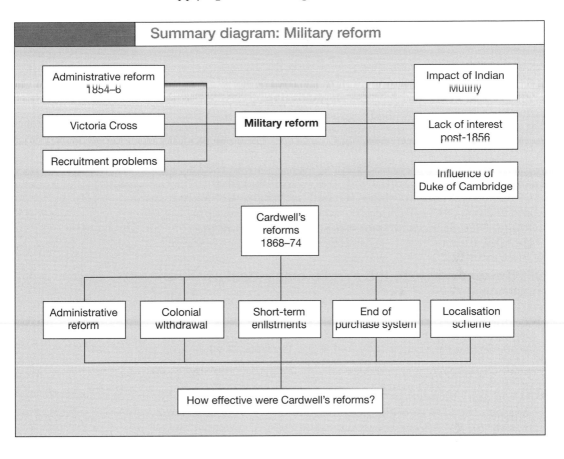

**Summary diagram: Military reform**

- Administrative reform 1854–6
- Victoria Cross
- Recruitment problems

**Military reform**

- Impact of Indian Mutiny
- Lack of interest post-1856
- Influence of Duke of Cambridge

Cardwell's reforms 1868–74

- Administrative reform
- Colonial withdrawal
- Short-term enlistments
- End of purchase system
- Localisation scheme

How effective were Cardwell's reforms?

## 5 | Key Debate

What was the significance of the Crimean War?

A case has recently been made by Orlando Figes, in *Crimea: The Last Crusade*, that the Crimean War was one of the most significant events of the nineteenth century. While a case can be made to that effect, an equally good – indeed probably better – case can be made to suggest that the war, from Britain's perspective, was relatively unimportant.

### Did the war shape national consciousness?
The argument for:

- The war was fought when Britain's national identity was being fixed in the new mass media of the Victorian age.
- Most Britons had the notion of gallant Britain standing firm against the Russian Bear to defend liberty: a simple fight of right against wrong. Britons thereafter saw their country's role in the world as helping the weak against tyrants and bullies.

- The idea of Britain as a godly land of 'Christian soldiers' fighting righteous wars became integral to the country's imperial mission. Many of the ideas of this myth were embodied in the cult of **muscular Christianity**: a concept expressed in *Tom Brown's Schooldays*, written in the wake of the war, and its sequel, *Tom Brown at Oxford*, where sport is extolled as a builder of manly character, teamwork and moral fortitude.

> **Muscular Christianity**
> A vigorous combination of Christian living with devotion to athletic enjoyments.
>
> *Key term*

The argument against:

- The war did not last long enough to have much effect on national identity.
- The notion that Britain had a responsibility to help the underdog preceded the Crimean War. The sense of John Bull going to the rescue of weak Turkey against the Russian bully was one of the reasons why Britons supported the war in 1854.
- The cult of muscular Christianity had little to do with the Crimean War. This movement is mainly associated with author and clergyman Charles Kingsley (who repudiated the term). Kingsley was propounding his views before the start of the Crimean War.

## Did the war advance the middle-class ideal of meritocracy?

The argument for:

- American writer Nathaniel Hawthorne wrote in his *English Notebooks* that the year of 1854 had 'done the work of 50 ordinary ones' in undermining aristocracy and promoting the professional ideal.
- The military blunders by the army's aristocratic leadership – most famously the Charge of the Light Brigade but also the failure to provide for the troops over the winter of 1854–5 – appalled most Britons. The mismanagement stimulated a new assertiveness in the middle classes, which rallied round the principles of professional competence and meritocracy in opposition to the privilege of birth.
- It was a sign of middle-class triumph that in the decades after the war, Conservative and Liberal governments alike introduced reforms promoting middle-class ideals: the opening of the Civil Service to talent and a new system of merit-based promotion in the armed services.
- Florence Nightingale symbolised the new confidence of the professional classes. The legend of the 'Lady with the Lamp' contained the basic elements of the middle-class Victorian ideal: a Christian narrative about good works, self-sacrifice and self-improvement.

The argument against:

- The landed classes continued to exert huge power in Britain for decades after the mid-1850s, maintaining their grip on parliament and most other citadels of power.

- Reform of Civil Service recruitment procedures remained limited. Competitive exams for the Civil Service were not introduced until 1870.
- The aristocratic nature of the army did not change until the First World War.
- By the 1850s, large elements within the middle class had had enough of reform. There were no longer clear lines of demarcation at Westminster between aristocratic and middle-class politicians with regard to most issues.
- Florence Nightingale came to symbolise many things, but not the new confidence of the professional classes.

## Was the war the first 'modern' war in the age of mass communications?

The argument for:

- It was the first war to be photographed.
- It was the first to use the electric telegraph, enabling news to travel quickly.
- It was the first 'newspaper war'.
- War became much more immediate to ordinary Britons.

The argument against:

- Photographs had been taken in the American–Mexican War (1846–8).
- Fenton took relatively few photographs and these were seen by relatively few people.
- The war was far from a modern war. Wellington and Nelson would have felt at home with most of the means and methods of fighting.
- News was not always immediate.

## Did the war bring about a change in Britain's attitudes towards its fighting men?

The argument for:

- Previously the military hero had been a gentleman, like the Duke of York, son of George III, whose column was erected in Waterloo Place in London in 1833.
- The heroes who returned from the Crimea were the common troops. Their deeds were recognised for the first time in 1856 with the introduction of the Victorian Cross, awarded to gallant servicemen regardless of class or rank.
- In 1861, the collective sacrifice was commemorated with the unveiling of a Guards Memorial. Standing opposite the Duke of York's column, the three bronze guardsmen symbolised a fundamental shift in values. Britain's military heroes were no longer dukes but ordinary soldiers who fought courageously and won Britain's wars in spite of the blunders of its generals.
- Nightingale embodied a national concern for the suffering of ordinary troops.

The argument against:

- Generals remained the heroes of war. Most British cities have statues to colonial generals who won campaigns in India and Africa post-1856, not statues to the ordinary soldiers who fought the battles.
- After 1856, few people put ordinary soldiers on a pedestal. Despite the popularising of the army's imperial role, many families regarded it as a disgrace if any of their members enlisted.
- Despite all Nightingale's efforts, conditions in the army did not improve much after 1856.

## Did the war have a significant effect on British foreign policy?

The argument for significance:

- By 1856, Britain's military weakness was obvious to all. Britain had ceased, in any real sense, to be a great European power.
- After 1856, Britain avoided continental entanglements and adopted a policy of 'splendid isolation', focusing on imperial expansion rather than on European affairs.

The argument against significance:

- After 1856, Britain still considered itself – and was perceived by others to be – a great European power. Britain had never had a large army. Its power, pre- and post-1856, lay in the Royal Navy and in its economic strength.
- Britain had no permanent European allies before 1854. So-called 'splendid isolation' was not the result of the Crimean War.
- British imperial policy did not change as a result of the Crimean War.
- Palmerston, who had a huge influence on foreign policy in the two decades before 1854, continued to have a huge influence thereafter. His aims remained much the same.

## Conclusion

It is hard to believe that the Crimean War had a hugely significant impact on Britain domestically. The fact that the war ended in victory, a victory immediately followed by success on the Indian subcontinent (see page 66), was enough to sustain a belief that the heart of the British system was sound. As soon as peace was restored, the army was starved of money, as hitherto. Cardwell's army reforms (see page 68) had more to do with the Franco-Prussian War than the Crimean War. The pioneering work of Florence Nightingale apart, it seems likely that Britain would have continued on a similar course, with or without the Crimean War.

---

**Some key books in the debate**

Eric Evans, *Shaping of Modern Britain: Identity, Industry and Empire 1780–1914* (Longman, 2011).

Orlando Figes, *Crimea: The Last Crusade* (Allen Lane, 2010).

K. Theodore Hoppen, *The Mid-Victorian Generation 1846–1886* (Clarendon Press, 1998).

---

## Study Guide

### In the style of Edexcel

Do you agree with the view that Florence Nightingale made a significant contribution to improvements in military and civilian hospital care in the years 1855–61? Explain your answer, using Sources 1, 2 and 3 and your own knowledge.          (40 marks)

#### Source 1

*From: a report by John MacDonald published in The Times February 1855. At the time MacDonald was in the Crimea, administering the fund collected by* The Times *for use in support of sick and wounded soldiers. He is writing about Florence Nightingale.*

Wherever there is disease in its most dangerous form, and the hand of the spoiler distressingly nigh, there is that incomparable woman sure to be seen; her benign presence is an influence for good comfort even amid the struggles of expiring nature. She is a 'ministering angel' without any exaggeration in these hospitals, and, as her slender form glides quietly along each corridor, every fellow's face softens with gratitude at the sight of her.

#### Source 2

*From: R.E. Foster,* Florence Nightingale: Icon and Iconoclast, *published in 2010.*

If the insalubrities of the Barrack Hospital did contribute to mortality, it should be remembered that she had no control over the choice of site. Mortality rates did fall at Scutari, down to 20 per cent by March 1855. Even if based on misplaced theory, her hospital initiatives did help combat disease. Her example helped change the public perception of nursing for the better …

Nightingale's work after 1856 went on, as she put it 'off the stage' and has thus tended to be overlooked by posterity. [She successfully lobbied] for a royal commission into army hospital and sanitary conditions. This began sitting in May 1857 and she assisted its efforts by compiling an unofficial 230,000 word report on the subject (*Notes on matters affecting the Health and Efficiency and Hospital Administration of the British Army*), as well as submitting 33 pages of formal evidence. The resulting report of February 1858, with its conclusion that poor sanitary conditions were principally to blame for the death rate, led to a raft of reforms. These included the creation of a statistical department for the army and an army medical school, as well as a programme to create sanitary barracks. By 1861, Nightingale was able to claim that army mortality rates had halved.

## Source 3

*From: Alan Farmer,* Access to History: The Experience of Warfare in Britain: Crimea, Boer and the First World War 1854–1929, *published in 2011.*

Florence Nightingale is often seen as the saviour of sick and wounded soldiers in the Crimea. Until recently it was often asserted that Nightingale managed to reduce the death rate in the hospital at Scutari from 42 per cent to two per cent by making improvements in hygiene. Unfortunately, the truth is very different. Despite the unstinting efforts of Nightingale and her team, death rates did not drop: on the contrary they continued to rise. Indeed the death count at Nightingale's own hospital at Scutari was the highest of all hospitals in the region … Not until a Sanitary Commission was sent out in March 1855 was there a marked improvement. It effected the flushing out of the sewers and improvements to ventilation. Thereafter death rates were sharply reduced.

---

### Exam tips

*The cross-references are intended to take you straight to the material that will help you to answer the question.*

This is an example of a (**b**) question, worth two-thirds of the marks for the unit. You should expect to write a substantial answer to this question, leaving yourself about 35–40 minutes to write up your answer after you have analysed the sources and planned a response.

Examiners will award you a maximum of 16 marks for making use of the provided sources and 24 marks for deploying your own knowledge. You must identify points raised by the sources, and then you can use your own knowledge to develop those further and to introduce new and relevant points that the sources do not contain. But you should start your plan with the sources. This makes sure that you don't get so carried away with planning and writing a standard essay answer that you forget to use the sources properly. For the highest marks, you should develop techniques that enable you to use your own knowledge in combination with material from the sources – integrating the two.

Try working with a set of columns that allows you to plan in an integrated way where your own knowledge can extend a point found in the sources. In this answer, you will need to balance points that suggest Nightingale's contribution was significant and those that suggest her work made little improvement. Some examples are given on page 75.

| Significant (evidence from sources) | Significant (evidence from own knowledge) | Not significant (evidence from sources) | Not significant (evidence from own knowledge) |
|---|---|---|---|
| Source 2: praises her nursing ability | The publicity given to her in *The Times* led to the development of the Nightingale Fund, which in turn enabled nurse training to be developed in England under her influence (page 62) | | |
| Source 2: Her example helped change the public perception of nursing | Her image and influence were significant in changing the role of nursing in England. The Nightingale training school for nurses set new standards of professionalism (page 62) | | |
| | | Source 3: The praise for her work at Scutari is based on myth and misinformation | |

Additional points are given below. Try slotting these remaining points into the plan. You will need to decide into which column they should go and how they should be grouped. Do some of them add to points in the plan above, or are they new points? What other points or information can you add from the sources or your own knowledge?

- Her insistence on cleanliness helped to combat disease.
- Her influence was increased by her effective use of statistics which were carefully collected and graphically represented.
- She published *Notes on Nursing* and *Notes on Hospitals*.
- Her evidence to the royal commission on army hospital and sanitary conditions led to a number of reforms.
- The death rate in her own hospital at Scutari was the highest in the region before March 1855.
- The reduction in death rates in the hospital at Scutari was the result of the work of the Sanitary Commission.

And what is your overall conclusion? Is her importance exaggerated and based on myth, or did she make a significant contribution? Reread pages 60–65 before you decide.

# 4 The Boer War 1899–1902

## POINTS TO CONSIDER

The Second Boer War (1899–1902) is sometimes called the Anglo-Boer War, the South African War or simply the Boer War. The biggest 'small war' of the late Victorian period, it was fought between Britain and two independent Boer republics: the Transvaal and the Orange Free State. Britain, at the height of its power, was to be seriously embarrassed, first by Boer success and then by tenacious Boer resistance. Nevertheless, British forces eventually triumphed. This chapter will consider the key issues of the war by examining the following themes:

- The causes of the war
- The British army in 1899
- The first phase of the war, October–December 1899
- The second phase of the war, January–September 1900
- Guerrilla war, September 1900 to May 1902
- The end of the war

## Key dates

| | | |
|---|---|---|
| 1880–1 | | First Boer War |
| 1886 | | Discovery of gold in the Transvaal |
| 1895 | | Jameson raid |
| 1899 | May–June | Bloemfontein conference |
| | October | Start of Second Boer War |
| | December | Black Week |
| 1900 | January | Roberts took command of British forces |
| | January | Battle of Spion Kop |
| | February | Relief of Kimberley |
| | February | Relief of Ladysmith |
| | May | Relief of Mafeking |
| | November | Roberts returned to Britain – Kitchener left in command |
| 1901 | | Concentration camp scandal |
| 1902 | | Treaty of Vereeniging |
| 1910 | | Creation of Union of South Africa |

# 1 | The Causes of the War

The war resulted from decades of dispute between Britain and the **Boers**.

## The situation to 1880

In 1815, Britain formally acquired Cape Colony, captured from the Dutch in 1806. It was a crucial naval base on the trade route to India and the Far East. The Dutch colonists, called Afrikaners or Boers, had settled in the area from the late seventeenth century. Most were fiercely independent farmers. In the 1830s some 5000 Boers, who disliked many aspects of British rule, especially the decision to abolish slavery in the Empire in 1834, chose to migrate northwards. Their Great Trek was initially towards Natal. After Britain annexed Natal in 1843, Boer families headed into the interior where they founded the Orange Free State and the Transvaal. The Boer republics enshrined their Protestant identity and their language in their constitutions, excluding black Africans (and anyone else who was not Boer) from voting.

The Boers' desire for land created a great deal of antagonism with black African peoples, especially the Zulus. In 1877, Britain, pursuing a **policy of confederation**, took control of the Transvaal and proceeded to defeat the Zulus in 1879.

## The First Boer War

Soon after the Zulu defeat, the Transvaal asked Britain to restore its independence. When Britain refused, the Boers rebelled. In the First Boer War (1880–1), British forces were defeated, most heavily at Majuba Hill. Gladstone's government, unwilling to fight

**Key question**
What were the main causes of the Second Boer War?

**Key terms**

**Boer**
The Dutch word for farmer.

**Policy of confederation**
Britain hoped to unite its southern African colonies, plus the Orange Free State and Transvaal, into one country, under British supremacy.

**Key question**
To what extent were the Boer republics independent states after 1881?

**Key date**
First Boer War: 1880–1

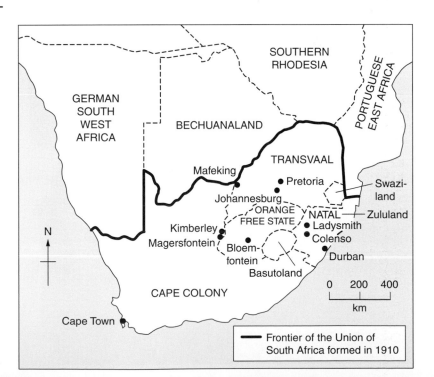

Map of southern Africa in the late nineteenth century.

an expensive war for little obvious benefit, agreed to restore partial independence to the Transvaal. In 1882, Britain recognised the Transvaal and the Orange Free State as self-governing nations under the '**suzerainty**' of the British Crown. It was not altogether clear what this meant. The London Convention (1884), by omitting the word 'suzerainty', meant it became even more unclear exactly what powers Britain retained over the republics, save that of supervising their foreign policies. While Boers chose to believe that they were fully independent, this was not Britain's understanding of the situation.

## The discovery of gold

In 1871, diamonds were discovered at Kimberley, prompting a **diamond rush** and an influx of foreigners to the borders of the Orange Free State. Then, in 1886, gold was discovered in the Transvaal. Gold made the Transvaal the richest nation in southern Africa. This situation threatened to tilt the balance of power between Britons and Boers in the region in favour of the Boers. It was possible that the Transvaal might try to take over the whole of southern Africa. The fact that thousands of Boers still lived in Cape Colony and Natal made this a feasible proposition.

**Key terms**

**Suzerainty**
Overlordship: ultimate power.

**Diamond rush**
A surge of miners, hoping to discover diamonds.

**Key question**
Why was the discovery of gold in the Transvaal a problem for (a) Britain and (b) the Boers?

**Key date**

Discovery of gold in the Transvaal: 1886

President Kruger (1825–1904), a man who seemed to typify Boer stubbornness, photographed in about 1900.

### The problem of the *uitlanders*

The Transvaal lacked the manpower and the industrial base
to develop the goldmines on its own. Consequently, waves of
immigrants – *uitlanders* – mainly from Britain poured into the
Transvaal hoping to make their fortune. Some did. Indeed,
much of the Transvaal's new wealth was soon in the hands of
a few British and German mineowners. By the mid-1890s, the
*uitlanders* outnumbered the Boer inhabitants. This caused
unrest. Determined to maintain Boer supremacy, the Transvaal
government, led by President Kruger, insisted that *uitlanders* had
to reside for 14 years in the Transvaal before they could apply for
naturalisation.

Kruger's denial of voting rights to the *uitlanders*, coupled
with irksome – some thought oppressive – taxation gave the
British government a pretext for interference in the Transvaal,
whose independent behaviour it was anxious to stop. Britain was
particularly angry in 1894–5 when the Transvaal government
proposed building a railway through **Portuguese East Africa**,
thereby bypassing British-controlled ports in Natal and Cape
Colony. This would undermine the prosperity of the British
colonies.

### Lord Salisbury

In 1895, Lord Salisbury became Conservative Prime Minister.
He was also Foreign Secretary. His aims were to protect Britain's
essential interests – security, India, the sea lanes – by preserving
peace. Salisbury's tenure of the Foreign Office is usually associated
with 'splendid isolation', the idea that Britain did not need to make
binding alliances with any other power.

Lord Salisbury
(1830–1903),
splendidly bearded
and isolated, in this
engraving from about
1895.

Parliament had little influence over Salisbury's foreign and imperial policy. Such disagreements as there were took place within the Liberal Party, where '**Little Englanders**' denounced Britain's imperial ambitions, which necessitated high military expenditure, and were critical of the exploitation of native peoples. But Liberal leaders generally supported Salisbury's policies. Salisbury disliked the encroachment of democratic pressures into the diplomatic process and feared popular excitements, fanned by newspapers. But he knew that public opinion could not be entirely ignored. Thus, he sometimes found himself being pushed in directions he did not wish to go. Joseph Chamberlain was one of those who pushed him.

## Joseph Chamberlain

Chamberlain, with other Liberal Unionists (see pages 105–6), had transferred his allegiance to the Conservatives because he opposed Irish Home Rule. In 1895, Chamberlain became Colonial Secretary. Over the previous years he had advocated the notion of forging a more cohesive Empire, bound together by economic interest and with a viable imperial parliament. Chamberlain liked to give the impression of being an 'outsider', bringing to the stuffy Westminster establishment the no-nonsense approach of an experienced businessman. In practice, he was not particularly efficient or 'businesslike'. But he gave the impression of dynamism – an impression fostered by his press admirers. He quickly enhanced his own authority and raised the profile of the Colonial Office. His aggressive defence of British interests sometimes collided with Salisbury's quieter conduct of policy.

## Cecil Rhodes

Cecil Rhodes played a crucial role in southern Africa. Arriving at the Cape in 1870, aged 17, he quickly made a fortune from diamond mining. In 1887, he established a powerful goldmining company in the Transvaal and in 1890 became Cape Prime Minister. Convinced that the British were 'the first race in the world and that the more of the world we inhabit the better it is for the human race', he dreamed of greatly expanding the Empire. Standing in the way of Rhodes' ambitions in Africa were the two Boer republics.

Through the British South African Chartered Company, Rhodes sent men north of the Limpopo river into Mashonaland in 1890. He hoped that they would discover gold, which would cancel out the Transvaal's advantage. Rhodes' action led to the annexation of territories which became known as **Southern and Northern Rhodesia**. However:

- no gold was discovered north of the Limpopo
- the Transvaal still stood in the way of Rhodes' imperial ambitions.

## The Jameson raid

**Key question**
Why did the Jameson raid fail?

Jameson raid: 1895

**Key date**

In the early 1890s, Rhodes encouraged *uitlanders* to agitate for voting rights. The Transvaal government correctly saw this as a deliberate plot to undermine its independence. In 1895, Rhodes hatched a scheme to seize control of the Transvaal. Several hundred men, mainly comprising Rhodes' Rhodesian policemen, would seize Johannesburg, trigger an uprising by the *uitlanders* and overthrow Kruger's government. Rhodes left the planning to Dr Jameson, a key administrator of the Chartered Company.

In December 1895 Jameson led a column of 600 armed men into the Transvaal. Unfortunately for Jameson, Boer authorities had advance warning of the raid and tracked it from the moment it crossed the border. Four days later, the column was surrounded within sight of Johannesburg. After a brief skirmish in which the column suffered 65 casualties (the Boers lost just one man) Jameson's men surrendered. The uprising of *uitlanders* never materialised.

## The repercussions of the Jameson raid

**Key question**
What were the main results of the Jameson raid?

- Chamberlain and Salisbury denied any knowledge of the raid. (Chamberlain had apparently approved Rhodes' plans on the assumption that his men would cross into the Transvaal only in the event of a 'spontaneous' rising of the *uitlanders*.)
- Rhodes was severely censured at both the Cape inquiry and the London parliamentary inquiry and was forced to resign as Prime Minister of the Cape and as Chairman of the Chartered Company. However, because Rhodes accepted full responsibility for the raid, Chamberlain's career survived the parliamentary inquiry.
- The Transvaal government handed their prisoners over to the British authorities and they were put on trial in Britain. Jameson, regarded as a hero by the British public, was sentenced to 15 months' imprisonment.
- The raid alienated many Cape Afrikaners from the British.
- The raid drew the Transvaal and the Orange Free State (led by President Steyn) together in opposition to the British threat. In 1897, the two republics signed a military pact.
- Convinced that a future war with Britain was highly likely, Kruger purchased the best European rifles and artillery for the Transvaal's armed forces.

## British action 1896–9

**Key question**
What were Britain's aims in southern Africa in the late 1890s?

The British government, which still claimed rights of suzerainty over the Boer republics, was now drawn more directly into southern African affairs. In 1897, it sent out Alfred Milner as High Commissioner. A passionate imperialist, Milner told a friend that he was going to 'teach those bloody Boers a lesson'. Milner worked to mobilise pro-British elements throughout southern Africa and constantly exerted pressure on behalf of the *uitlanders*. In his dealings with Kruger he took an uncompromising stance, demanding that the *uitlanders* be granted full citizenship within five years.

Many organised groups supported Milner's efforts to uphold what were perceived to be Britain's interests in southern Africa. These included:

- Unionists at all levels
- the Primrose League
- many influential newspapers.

However, by no means all Britons were jingoistic. Even Chamberlain felt some disquiet at Milner's 'forward' policy, believing that war with Transvaal, 'unless upon the utmost and clearest provocation', would be 'entirely unpopular in the country'.

## The coming of war

In a last-ditch effort to resolve Anglo-Transvaal problems, President Steyn invited Milner and Kruger to attend a conference in Bloemfontein on 31 May 1899. At the meeting, Milner made several demands, including the enactment by Transvaal of a law that would immediately give *uitlanders* the right to vote. As Milner expected, Kruger rejected these demands. All Kruger was prepared to offer the *uitlanders* was full citizenship within seven years – in return for British recognition of the Transvaal's independence in domestic matters. Despite encouragement from Chamberlain to continue the talks, Milner walked out of the conference on 5 June.

Milner remained confident that Kruger would 'bluff up to the cannon's mouth' and then accept Britain's demands. As tension mounted, Salisbury's government, against the advice of its generals, did not send substantial reinforcements to southern Africa. War Secretary Lord Lansdowne feared that such action would strike too aggressive a posture and might encourage a Boer attack rather than help to bring about a negotiated settlement. This suggests that the British government did not want war.

Nevertheless, by the summer of 1899 the cabinet, the majority of MPs and the British press were all of the view that the Boers needed 'teaching a lesson'. In September, Chamberlain sent an ultimatum demanding full equality for British citizens resident in the Transvaal. Kruger, regarding war as inevitable, issued his own ultimatum on 9 October, giving Britain 48 hours to withdraw all its troops from the Transvaal border, otherwise the Transvaal, allied with the Orange Free State, would declare war. News of the ultimatum reached London on the day it expired. Most newspaper editorials shared the sentiment of the *Daily Telegraph*, which declared: 'there can only be one answer to this grotesque challenge. Kruger has asked for war and war he must have'. The Boers declared war on 11 October.

**Primrose League** *Key term*

**Primrose League**
A patriotic organisation which campaigned on behalf of Britain's imperial interests.

**Key question**
Did Britain want war in 1899?

**Bloemfontein conference: May–June 1899**

**Start of Second Boer War: October 1899**

*Key dates*

## Key question

Which British statesman was most responsible for the war?

**Radical Liberal**
Radical Liberals sympathised with the underdog, whether in Britain or abroad, and supported social reform.

## Who was responsible?

The **Radical Liberal** J.A. Hobson claimed that the war was caused by a 'conspiracy of financiers' for whom the *uitlander* issue was a cloak to hide a desire for private profit. Thomas Pakenham, in *The Boer War* (1979), agreed, claiming that leading mineowners were 'active partners' with Milner in the making of the war. This overstates the case. Most historians now reject the view that the British government was the puppet of the mining magnates.

Salisbury did not want war and had misgivings about Milner's obduracy at the Bloemfontein conference. Nevertheless, he believed that the Transvaal, the Orange Free State and the Cape Boers aspired to a Dutch South Africa, and that the creation of such a state would damage Britain's interests. In the last analysis, he shared Milner's view that what was at stake was a struggle to make sure that 'we not the Dutch are Boss'.

Chamberlain had long expressed concerns about the dangers for British interests of an independent Transvaal. After 1895, he soured Anglo-Boer relations in several ways (for example, he appointed Milner as High Commissioner). Yet it is unlikely that Chamberlain did this as part of a deliberate plan to instigate war.

The leading candidate for 'warmonger' is Milner. He believed that there was 'a greater issue than the grievances of the *uiltanders* at stake … our supremacy in South Africa … and our existence as a great power in the world is involved'. Nevertheless, he too did not expect war. He thought Kruger would ultimately accept British overlordship.

Kruger must share responsibility for the war. Convinced that Britain wanted to end the Transvaal's independence and unwilling to concede rights to the *uitlanders*, he believed war to be inevitable. He thus prepared for it. His resolve was stiffened by the fact that his leading generals were convinced that the Boers would win and that the outcome would be a United States of Southern Africa under Transvaal leadership. Kruger's actions in October 1899, as Salisbury said, 'liberated us from the necessity of explaining to the people of England why we are at war'.

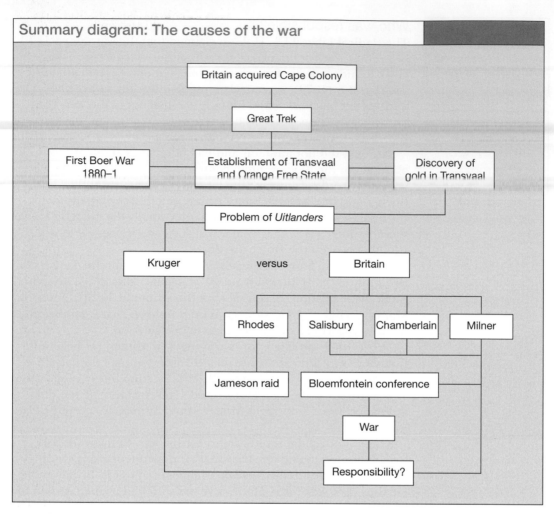

Summary diagram: The causes of the war

Britain acquired Cape Colony

Great Trek

First Boer War 1880–1

Establishment of Transvaal and Orange Free State

Discovery of gold in Transvaal

Problem of *Uitlanders*

Kruger          versus          Britain

Rhodes    Salisbury    Chamberlain    Milner

Jameson raid    Bloemfontein conference

War

Responsibility?

## 2 | The British Army in 1899

Most Britons expected an easy victory. Salisbury was more realistic. He told a surprised Queen Victoria that 'We have no army capable of meeting even a second-class Continental Power'.

### Problems of military reform

The British army remained small, with fewer than 135,000 men (excluding India). In the last two decades of the nineteenth century the main aim of military reformers was not so much to boost numbers as to bring the army up to a higher level of professionalism. But there were formidable obstacles in their way:

- The government was not anxious to spend extra money on the army.
- The army had performed well in colonial wars in the 1880s and 1890s. There was thus little pressure for change.
- The Commander-in-Chief of the army from 1856–95 was the Duke of Cambridge, who was a stubborn defender of traditional practices.

**Key question**
To what extent was the British army prepared for war?

**Key question**
Why was the British army so small?

In 1895, Cambridge was finally dislodged and replaced by Lord Wolseley. Wolseley and the young officers whom he favoured realised the need for reform. But, deprived of money by an economically minded government, there was not much they could do. Wolseley chaffed at civilian control and scarcely bothered to conceal his contempt for his superior, War Secretary Lord Lansdowne.

Key question
What problems did the British army face in 1899?

## British preparedness in 1899

George Wyndham, Under Secretary at the War Office, claimed in October 1899 that the army was 'more efficient than at any time since Waterloo'. There was some truth in this view:

- Many officers and men had been hardened in a succession of colonial wars. This success had been due in part to the fact that army leaders had responded well to scientific and technological innovation.
- Army leaders appreciated the danger of underestimating opponents and local conditions.
- Wolseley had driven home the importance of supply and transportation.
- Once war was declared in 1899, mobilisation went like clockwork and the Admiralty transported men and supplies over a distance of 6000 miles (9500 km) without a hitch.

Key terms

**Veldt**
Open, unforested grass-country.

**Khaki**
A dull-brownish cloth used for military uniforms. It provided better camouflage than red tunics.

**Commando**
An armed group of Boers, varying in size from a few dozen men to several hundreds.

Nevertheless, there were problems:

- In 1899, there was an almost total absence of maps of southern Africa.
- There was a shortage of ammunition.
- The army had piles of red, white and blue uniforms (quite useless for action on the **veldt**) but an inadequate supply of **khaki**.
- Several auxiliary departments, for example, the Royal Army Medical Corps, were seriously understaffed.
- Intelligence and staff work were inadequate.
- British officers failed to recognise the impact of destructive fire from trench positions and the mobility of cavalry raids, both of which had been developed in the American Civil War.

Key question
Why did the Boers pose a serious challenge?

## The Boer army

On paper, the Boer army looked no match for the British:

- The Boers could put fewer than 60,000 men in the field. (The total white population of the two Boer republics, women and children included, was 300,000.)
- The Boer republics had no regular army units, apart from a few artillery troops.

The Boer army was essentially a civilian militia. When danger loomed, all the adult male citizens (aged 16–60) in a district were expected to form a military unit called a **commando**, which elected officers. Each man brought his own weapon, usually a hunting rifle, and his own horse. Those who could not afford a gun were given one by the authorities.

Boer civilian-soldiers – men who proved to be dangerous opponents. Photographed in about 1900.

But the Boers should not have been underestimated:

- The First Boer War suggested that the Boers were likely to be tough opponents.
- Excellent horsemen and hunters, they were expert mounted infantry.
- They were armed with Europe's best weapons: smokeless Mauser rifles and the latest Krupp field guns from Germany, and French Creusot siege guns.
- They had a greater familiarity with the terrain than British officers.
- Boer morale was strong and was sustained by the belief that they were engaged in a life-and-death struggle to preserve their distinctive culture.
- Many Boers in Cape Colony and Natal sympathised with the Transvaal and the Orange Free State Boers.

## Summary diagram: The British army in 1899

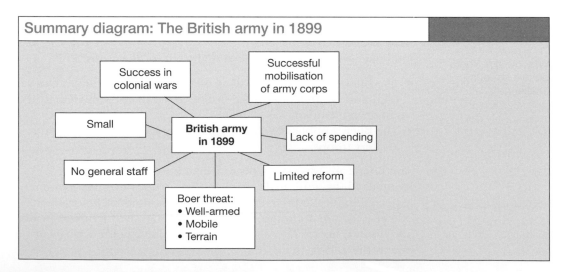

## 3 | The First Phase of the War, October–December 1899

Salisbury's government had failed to ensure that adequate troops and supplies were in place for the conflict. Lansdowne must take much of the blame for what went wrong.

### Boer superiority

**Key question**
Why were the Boers so successful in the first few weeks of the war?

The Boers struck first at Kraaipan on 12 October, an attack that heralded the invasion of Cape Colony and Natal. Fortunately for Britain, Sir George White, with 10,000 men from the Indian army, had been shipped over to Natal, arriving on 7 October in the nick of time to prevent the Boers marching unimpeded on Durban. But the Boers, with some 35,000 men in the field, still decisively outnumbered the British. Britain's First Army Corps, earmarked for service in southern Africa, did not sail from Southampton until 12 October.

### Ladysmith

White established his main base at Ladysmith and unwisely allowed General Penn-Symons to send a brigade forward to the town of Dundee. This became the site of the war's first battle. Boer guns began shelling the British camp from Talana Hill at dawn on 20 October. Penn-Symons immediately counterattacked. His men drove the Boers from the hill, but at a cost of 446 British casualties. Penn-Symons himself was fatally wounded.

Another Boer force had occupied Elandslaagte, which lay between Ladysmith and Dundee. General John French and Colonel Ian Hamilton managed to clear the line of communications to

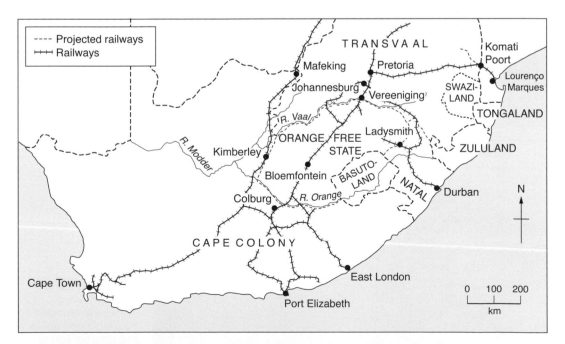

South Africa 1899–1902.

Dundee. However, fearing that more Boers were about to attack, White retreated to Ladysmith. The town was surrounded by Boers who bombarded it with siege guns. White ordered a major sortie against the enemy artillery positions. The result – the battle of Modderspruit – was a British disaster, with 140 men killed and over 1000 captured. White was now trapped in Ladysmith.

## Mafeking and Kimberley

Colonel Robert Baden-Powell had raised some 1200 local men at Mafeking, hoping to lead raids against the enemy. But, instead of being the aggressor, Baden-Powell found himself the defender when 7000 Boers commanded by Piet Cronje attacked Mafeking. The town held out and the Boers besieged the place, hoping to starve it into surrender.

In early November, 7500 Boers laid siege to the diamond-mining town of Kimberley, defended by 5000 men. Despite Boer shelling, the 40,000 inhabitants (including Rhodes) were under little threat as the town was well stocked with provisions.

The Boers' decision to commit themselves to sieges handed the initiative back to the British, who were given time to recover. Other than a single attempt to storm Ladysmith, the Boers made no attempt to capture the besieged towns.

## The situation in the Cape

In November, Boers crossed into the Cape, which was defended by only 7000 British troops. Since the electoral defeat of Rhodes' party in 1898, the Cape government had been headed by the Afrikaner

British soldiers in southern Africa. The Royal Munster Fusiliers open fire in this photograph of about 1900.

William Schreiner, whose administration adopted a neutral stance on the war. Even when some 10,000 Cape Dutch joined the invading commandos, it was only with great difficulty that Milner secured permission to declare martial law in the most disaffected districts.

## General Buller's strategy

General Sir Redvers Buller, Wolseley's protégé, arrived in Cape Town on 31 October, followed on 18 November by the first contingent of the First Army Corps. The balance of power had now changed. Buller initially intended an offensive straight up the railway line leading from Cape Town via Bloemfontein (capital of the Orange Free State) to Pretoria. But fearing the political repercussions of abandoning White to his fate and losing Kimberley, Buller decided to split his army into three widely spread detachments:

- General Lord Methuen, with 20,000 men, set out to relieve Kimberley and Mafeking.
- General Gatacre, with 3000 men, headed towards Stormberg to secure the Northern Cape from Boer raids and rebellion by Boer inhabitants.
- Buller led the main force to relieve Ladysmith.

## Black Week

Methuen won two small but costly victories at Belmont (23 November) and at Graspan (25 November). He then walked into a trap set for him by the Boer commander de la Rey at the Modder River (28 November) and suffered some 500 casualties before the Boers retreated to Magersfontein.

In 'Black Week' (10–15 December), the British suffered a series of defeats:

- On 10 December, Gatacre's attempt to take Stormberg ended in defeat, with over 700 casualties.
- On 11 December, Methuen launched an ill-judged attack at Magersfontein. The Highland Brigade were pinned down by accurate Boer fire from well-positioned trenches. After suffering from intense heat and thirst for nine hours (and being accidentally shelled by their own side), the Scottish troops broke in ill-disciplined retreat. Methuen's forces suffered over 900 casualties and failed to relieve Kimberley.
- On 15 December, Buller with 21,000 men tried to cross the Tugela River at Colenso to relieve Ladysmith. Eight thousand Boers, led by Louis Botha, repelled all British efforts to cross the river. Buller retreated, his troops' having suffered nearly 1400 casualties. (The Boers lost only eight dead.) As a result of a communications' breakdown, Buller also lost a whole battery of artillery, despite heroic attempts to save its 10 guns.

By mid-December, British forces had been defeated at every turn. Buller, a competent subordinate but a failure in high command, lost his nerve. After Colenso he signalled by **heliograph** to White in

Ladysmith that he should fire off his ammunition and surrender. This action convinced the British government that Buller must be replaced. Lord Roberts, hero of the 1880 Afghan War, was sent to command the British forces with Kitchener, hero of the 1898 Sudan campaign, as his chief of staff. Roberts' delight was marred by the news that his only son was one of those killed trying to save the guns at Colenso.

## The situation in December 1899

The Boers, fighting on the defensive, had the advantage of prepared positions. Adept at siting trenches, their marksmanship was also superior to that of the British. British troops experienced for the first time the difficulties of crossing battlefields swept by smokeless, **magazine rifles** which could kill at 2000 yards. The Boers were helped, too, by unimaginative British command. 'Our generals', remarked Liberal MP Herbert Asquith, after reading one despatch, 'seem neither able to win victories nor to give convincing reasons for their defeats'.

To meet the emergency, Britons rushed to join the colours. Among the most famous detachments was the City Imperial Yeomanry, which included 34 MPs and peers. Even so, volunteers who fought in southern Africa comprised only 0.76 per cent of British men of military age. (Just eight per cent of males, aged 18–40, did some kind of military service between 1899 and 1902, including involvement in home defence formations.) Some 30,000 men from British South Africa came forward as volunteers, as did men from Australia, Canada and New Zealand in a display of imperial solidarity. By 1902, 16,310 Australians, 6051 Canadians and 6416 New Zealanders had seen service in southern Africa.

**Magazine rifles**
Rifles from which a succession of shots can be fired without reloading.

**Key term**

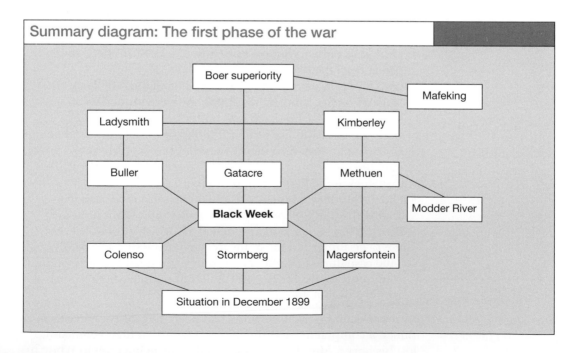

Summary diagram: The first phase of the war

Boer superiority — Mafeking

Ladysmith — Kimberley

Buller — Gatacre — Methuen — Modder River

**Black Week**

Colenso — Stormberg — Magersfontein

Situation in December 1899

## 4 | The Second Phase of the War, January–September 1900

With the sieges still continuing, two more divisions were sent to fight the Boers. By January 1900, 180,000 British and colonial troops, the largest force Britain had ever sent overseas, were in southern Africa. British forces now easily outnumbered the Boers.

### Lord Roberts

Roberts (known affectionately as 'Bobs') arrived at the Cape in January 1900. He headed a Field Force of over 40,000 men and 108 guns. He issued new tactical guidelines, insisting on careful reconnaisance before an attack, the avoidance of frontal attacks in mass formations, and more use of cover by infantry and artillery. Like Buller, he first intended to attack directly along the Cape Town–Pretoria railway. But again like Buller, he decided he must relieve the beleaguered garrisons. Leaving Buller in command in Natal, Roberts massed his main force near the Orange River behind Methuen's force at the Modder River and prepared to make a wide outflanking move designed to relieve Kimberley and then take Bloemfontein. Kitchener improvised a transport system of wagons, unshackling British troops from dependence on the railway lines.

### Spion Kop

With fresh reinforcements, Buller made another bid to relieve Ladysmith. General Warren successfully crossed the Tugela west of Colenso but then faced a Boer defensive position centred on a hill known as Spion Kop. In the resulting battle, British troops captured the summit during the early hours of 24 January 1900. But as the morning fog lifted they realised that they were overlooked by Boer gun emplacements on surrounding hills. The rest of the day was a disaster for British arms, largely caused by poor communications between Buller and his commanders. Between them they issued contradictory orders, some officers ordering men off the hill, while others ordered reinforcements to defend it. The result was 1350 casualties (243 dead) and a retreat back across the Tugela. The Boers suffered 300 casualties. Widely publicised photographs of dead soldiers strewn across Spion Kop's ridge brought home to the British public the reality of modern war. On 5 February, Buller attacked Botha again, this time at Vaal Krantz, and was again defeated.

### Kimberley relieved

Further west, Roberts and Kitchener launched their offensive on 10 February, intending to outflank the Boers defending Magersfontein. To ensure greater mobility, they doubled the number of their mounted infantry but skimped on supplies needed to sustain them – a problem aggravated by loss of the ox-wagon convoy containing medicines and food at Waterval Drift (15 February). This setback was overlooked when on the same day

**Key question**
Did Roberts make any real difference to the British war effort?

**Key dates**

Roberts took command of British forces: January 1900

Battle of Spion Kop: January 1900

**Key question**
Why were British forces successful from February to September 1900?

The dead of Spion Kop, later commemorated at Anfield (Liverpool) and other football grounds where one end of the ground was called 'Spion Kop'.

news came through that French's cavalry had made a successful dash to relieve Kimberley, ending its 124 days' siege.

Roberts, pursuing Cronje, who had abandoned Magersfontein, succeeded in trapping the Boer army at Paardeberg. On 17 February, a pincer movement, involving French's cavalry and Robert's main force, failed to take the entrenched Boer position. Roberts now resorted to bombarding Cronje into submission. On 28 February, the Boer leader surrendered with 4000 men.

Relief of Kimberley:
February 1900

Relief of Ladysmith:
February 1900

Key dates

## Ladysmith relieved

On 14 February, Buller made another attempt (his fourth) to relieve Ladysmith: the battle of the Tugela Heights. His progress was painfully slow. But on 26 February Buller, using all his forces in one all-out attack, at last succeeded in crossing the Tugela and defeating Botha's forces north of Colenso. After a siege lasting 118 days, Ladysmith was relieved.

## British problems

Roberts advanced into the Orange Free State from the west, putting the Boers to flight at Poplar Grove (7 March) and capturing Bloemfontein unopposed on 13 March. However, Roberts was then forced to delay for six weeks:

- His army was short of supplies and horses.
- There was an outbreak of typhoid, partly caused by troops drinking from the Modder River at Paardeburg, which had been polluted by the corpses of men and horses. Almost 1000 troops died in the epidemic with which the Hospital Field Service was unable to cope.

### Mafeking relieved

Despite the problems at Bloemfontein, Roberts was able to send a small force towards Mafeking. The place was relieved on 17 May after a 217-day siege, provoking huge celebrations in Britain. Its defender Baden-Powell became a national hero, with good cause. He had tied down 7000 Boers, almost a fifth of their total forces, at a crucial period in the war when Cape Colony was almost denuded of defenders.

### British success

In May, Roberts was able to continue his advance. Given the overwhelming superiority of British numbers, the Boers could only retreat. On 28 May, the Orange Free State was annexed. Meeting little Boer resistance, Roberts captured Johannesburg on 31 May and Pretoria on 5 June. Both places were abandoned without a fight.

General Hunter, meanwhile, set out to mop up the last major Boer force in the Orange Free State. Although he failed to capture President Steyn, Hunter trapped the main Boer army, led by General Pretorius, forcing 4500 men to surrender.

Kruger and what remained of his government retreated to eastern Transvaal. Roberts, joined by Buller, advanced down the railway line leading to Portuguese East Africa, reaching Komati Poort on 21 July, so cutting the Boers off from the outside world. Roberts finally broke the Boers' defensive position at Bergendal on 26 August. Kruger fled to Europe, dying in exile in 1904. But Botha led the remains of the Boer army through the Drakensberg mountains into the Transvaal high veldt.

### The end of the war?

After the capture of Bloemfontein, Johannesburg and Pretoria and the flight of Kruger, most British observers, including Roberts, believed the war was all but over. On 3 September 1900, the Transvaal was formally annexed. Many troops returned home to a heroes' welcome. In November 1900, after handing over to Kitchener, Roberts set sail for England, where he replaced Wolseley as Commander-in-Chief and was voted a sum of £100,000 by a grateful parliament. All that remained to be done in southern Africa, it seemed, was to mop up small pockets of resistance.

---

**Key dates**

Relief of Mafeking: May 1900

Roberts returned to Britain – Kitchener left in command: November 1900

---

**Key question**
Why did many observers believe the war was over by September 1900?

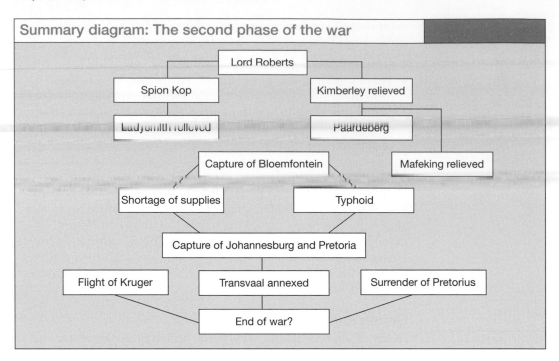

Summary diagram: The second phase of the war

Lord Roberts

Spion Kop

Kimberley relieved

Ladysmith relieved

Paardeberg

Capture of Bloemfontein

Mafeking relieved

Shortage of supplies

Typhoid

Capture of Johannesburg and Pretoria

Flight of Kruger

Transvaal annexed

Surrender of Pretorius

End of war?

## 5 | Guerrilla War, September 1900 to May 1902

By September 1900 British forces were nominally in control of both Boer republics. But the hard core of the Boer armies (some 20,000 men) and their most determined leaders remained at large.

### Boer tactics

Boer commandos were sent to their home districts where they could rely on local support and had personal knowledge of the terrain. Ordered to act against the British whenever possible, their tactics were to strike fast and hard, causing as much damage as possible, and then to withdraw and vanish before British reinforcements could arrive. This resulted in a disorganised pattern of scattered engagements. The vast size of the republics made it difficult for the 250,000 British troops to control territory effectively. As soon as a British column left a district, British authority faded away.

### Boer leaders

De Wet, who led Boer resistance in the western part of the Orange Free State, inspired a series of attacks. In January 1901, he led a renewed invasion of Cape Colony. While there was considerable sympathy for the invaders, there was no general uprising among the Cape Boers and De Wet's men, hampered by bad weather and relentlessly pursued by British forces, narrowly escaped across the Orange River. De Wet left forces under Cape rebels Kritzinger and Scheepers to maintain a guerrilla campaign in the Cape Midlands area. The result was bitter civil war, with intimidation by both sides of each other's civilian sympathisers. British forces, tracking down a Boer commando, wiped it out at Groenkloof. Several captured

Key question
Why did the British find it hard to deal with the continued Boer challenge?

rebels, including Scheepers, were executed for treason or for crimes such as the murder of prisoners and civilians.

Boer forces under Jan Smuts, joined by the surviving rebels, made another attack on the Cape in September 1901. Hard-pressed by British columns, they escaped after routing some of their pursuers at Elands River. Until the end of the war, Cape rebels continued to join Smuts' army but no general uprising took place.

Boer forces, under Botha and Viljoen, fought in Eastern Transvaal. Botha's forces, in the south, were particularly troublesome, raiding railways and supply columns and even invading Natal in September 1901. After defeating British troops at Blood River Poort, heavy rains forced Botha to withdraw. Back on Transvaal territory, he successfully attacked a British column at Bakenlaagte. Pursued by British troops, Botha was forced to retreat to a narrow enclave bordering Swaziland. Viljoen, less active in the north, was eventually captured.

Boer commandos, under de la Rey, in Western Transvaal fought a number of battles between September 1901 and March 1902. In March 1902, the Boers attacked the rear guard of a British column at Tweebosch, capturing Lord Methuen (the British second-in-command). In April at Rooiwal a Boer commando attacked a superior British force and suffered severe casualties. This proved to be the last major battle of the war.

## Blockhouses

**Key question**
How successful was Kitchener's strategy 1900–2?

Kitchener, endeavouring to restrict the movement of Boer raiders and to protect his supply routes, built 8000 fortified blockhouses, each housing six to eight soldiers. Costly to construct, the blockhouse system was also costly to maintain. The British eventually linked the blockhouses with barbed wire fences, stretching over 4000 miles and parcelling the veldt into small areas. British columns were then able to conduct a series of 'sweeps' across these areas in an attempt to trap the enemy. British forces deployed the latest technology, maintaining communications through the telephone and the cable, and using electric lights to protect buildings.

## Raiding columns

Kitchener established mounted raiding columns in support of the larger sweeper columns. These were used to rapidly follow and harass the Boers, hoping to delay them or cut off their escape, while the main columns caught up. The British also used armoured trains to deliver rapid reaction forces to incidents or to drop men off ahead of retreating commandos.

## Scorched earth

Before leaving South Africa, Roberts initiated a policy of burning farms thought to be giving support to commandos. Kitchener continued this 'scorched earth' policy, targeting everything that could give sustenance to Boer guerrillas. As British troops swept the countryside, they destroyed property and crops, salted fields and poisoned wells.

## Concentration camps

Concentration camps were set up as refugee camps for families who had been forced to quit their homes. While following naturally from the scorched earth policy, the moving of Boer women and children into camps was also intended to prevent civilians assisting the commandos. In military terms the concentration camp policy may have been a mistake. Although in the long run it perhaps undermined the Boers' will to resist, in the short term it freed them from responsibility for their families and thus had the opposite effect of that intended. In humilitarian terms the policy was illustrous. Inadequate food, poor shelter, bad hygiene and sanitation, shortage of medical facilities and overcrowding led to diseases such as measles, typhoid and dysentery to which children were particularly vulnerable. Over 20,000 Boer women and children died in the 40 camps; about one in four of the inmates.

Tens of thousands of black Africans were also forcibly removed from Boer areas and placed in separate camps. Conditions in these camps were probably worse than in the Boer camps. Few records were kept but over 12,000 black inmates probably died.

The high death rate in the camps was the result of incompetence and lack of foresight on the part of British military authorities. It was not a deliberate policy of extermination. Kitchener argued that to turn the people held in the camps out on to the ransacked veldt would have been even worse cruelty.

## Criticism of the camps

In early 1901, Radical Liberals, led by David Lloyd George, denounced the concentration camps. War Secretary, St John Broderick, defended the policy by claiming that the camps were 'voluntary' and that the interned Boers were 'contented and comfortable'. When this claim proved untenable, he resorted to the 'military necessity' argument.

Liberal leader Henry Campbell-Bannerman did not initially support the Radical Liberals:

- He saw it as his duty to support the government in time of war.
- The Radicals only made up about a third of Liberal MPs. Aware that many Liberals supported the war, he was reluctant to press a matter which was certain to divide his party.

However, **Emily Hobhouse**'s description of camp conditions in June 1901 created an international outcry. German Chancellor von Bülow denounced Britain's treatment of the Boers as 'brutal and inhuman'. Campbell-Bannerman now attacked 'the methods of barbarism' being used in southern Africa.

## The Fawcett Commission

Concerned by the public outcry, the government called on Kitchener for a detailed report. His statistical returns confirmed that death rates in the camps were very high. The government responded by appointing a (uniquely) all-woman commission, headed by Millicent Fawcett, a Liberal Unionist. Between August and December 1901, the commission conducted its own tour of the camps,

**Key question**
Were concentration camps a military necessity?

**Key date**
Concentration camp scandal: 1901

**Key figure**
**Emily Hobhouse**
Sister of a leader-writer for the *Manchester Guardian*, she visited some of the concentration camps in early 1901.

confirming everything that Hobhouse had said. It recommended a long list of measures, including the need for increased rations and more nurses. In November 1901, Chamberlain ordered Milner to ensure that 'all possible steps are being taken to reduce the rate of mortality'. Civil authorities now took over the running of the camps. By early 1902, the death rate for white inmates dropped to two per cent, a lower rate than that which pertained to many British cities. But by then the damage had been done.

## A change of policy

Given the uproar over the camp conditions, Kitchener in December 1901 instructed all column commanders not to bring in women and children when they 'cleared' the country. This was a shrewd move. While seeming to appease his critics, it also handicapped the guerrillas, who now had to care for their desperate families.

## Peace efforts

Kitchener sought a speedy end to the war. A prolongation of the war, he warned Milner, was futile since eventually Boers and British settlers would have to share the running of the country. In February 1901, Kitchener had informally met Botha to discuss peace terms. But Milner and the British cabinet would make no concessions. Denied the compromise peace that he favoured, Kitchener continued to pursue his scorched earth policy.

## A white man's war?

Boers and British alike feared the consequences of arming black Africans. The memories of the Zulu War and other tribal conflicts were still fresh and there was recognition that whoever won would have to deal with the consequences of a mass militarisation of the black population. At first there was an unwritten agreement that the war would be a 'white man's war'. But as the war continued, the British increasingly used armed black people as scouts, watchmen in blockhouses and auxiliaries.

By 1902, some 30,000 black people had served in the British army. Black Africans, almost without exception, were pro-British.

## A gentleman's war?

**Key figure**

**J.F.C. Fuller**
An experienced soldier and distinguished military writer who served in both the Boer War and the First World War.

The Boer War was described by **J.F.C. Fuller** as 'the last of the gentlemen's wars'. By this, Fuller meant the war was essentially a civilised conflict. There is some truth in this claim:

- Both sides took (white) prisoners and did what they could to keep them alive.
- Many British soldiers, including Kitchener, came to respect the Boer enemy.

However:

- The concentration camp deaths were, for many people, 'barbaric'.
- A number of atrocities were committed by both sides. (Boers, for example, shot black prisoners.)
- A tenth of the white population of the Transvaal and Orange Free State died during the war.

## Summary diagram: Guerrilla war

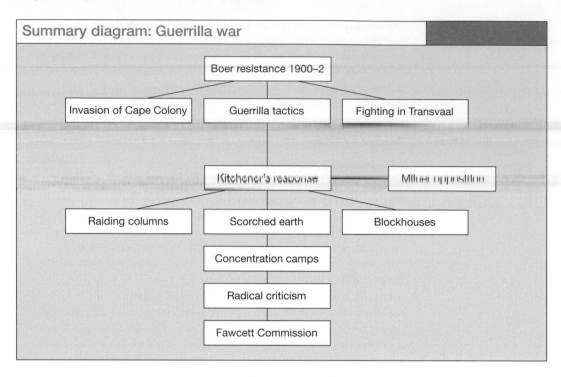

## 6 | The End of the War

So successful were Kitchener's tactics of containment and harassment that many Boer 'joiners' threw in their lot with British authorities. By early 1902, it was obvious, even to Boer 'bitter-enders', that further resistance was futile.

### Peace

The war ended with the Treaty of Vereeniging, signed on 31 May 1902. Boer commandos, except for a few 'irreconcilables', pledged their allegiance to Britain and recognised Britain's annexation of the two republics. Britain, in return, was generous:

- The Boers were given £3 million for reconstruction purposes.
- Britain agreed to restore self-government at the earliest opportunity.

### The cost of the war

The war cost around 60,000 lives: 22,000 British soldiers died (7792 were killed in battle, the rest though disease, especially typhoid) and 100,000 British troops were wounded or incapacitated by disease. Some 7000 Boer soldiers died. Over 20,000 Boer civilians and perhaps 12,000 black Africans died in the concentration camps.

The scale of the war exceeded all expectations. It required the services of 450,000 British and colonial troops and cost the British taxpayer £217 million. (By 1901 it was costing the Treasury £140 to knock out a single Boer combatant.) In Lloyd George's view, 'every shell fired amounted to the cost of a pension for an old person in Britain'.

**Key question**
How successful was British peace-making?

Treaty of Vereeniging: 1902

Key date

## The results of the war for South Africa

Post-war reconstruction was presided over by Milner. Anxious to
destroy Boer influence, Milner soon realised this was impossible.
Britain, for all its sacrifices, had not secured total predominance in
southern Africa.

In 1906–7, Britain restored self-government and free elections
(for whites) to the Transvaal and the Orange Free State. The
Liberal government in Britain portrayed this as an act of
reconciliation, designed to win the allegiance of former enemies,
by extending to them the hand of trust and friendship. In reality,
ministers were not so confident that their policy would succeed.
But it did, in the short term:

- In the 1907 elections, the Afrikaner *Het Volk* Party, committed
  to both a Union of South Africa and racial segregation, won
  a sweeping victory with the support of the newly enfranchised
  *uitlanders.*
- The South African Act united the Transvaal, the Orange Free
  State, Cape Colony and Natal in a Union of South Africa, which
  came into existence in 1910. Botha became its first Prime
  Minister.
- When Botha took South Africa into the First World War on
  Britain's side in 1914 it seemed as though the Liberal gamble
  had been vindicated. South Africa was to prove a valuable ally to
  Britain during the First and Second World Wars.
- The price for this achievement was the sacrifice of the black
  peoples of South Africa. Only whites could sit in the Union
  Parliament and vote in the Transvaal and the Orange Free State.

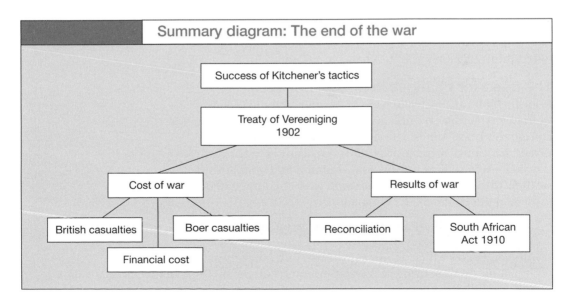

**Summary diagram: The end of the war**

Success of Kitchener's tactics

Treaty of Vereeniging
1902

Cost of war

Results of war

British casualties

Boer casualties

Financial cost

Reconciliation

South African
Act 1910

## 7 | Key Debate

What lessons did Britain learn from the Boer War?

In his poem *The Lesson*, Rudyard Kipling wrote of the Boer War. 'We have had no end of a lesson, it will do us no end of good'. But the lessons of the war proved to be ambiguous.

- Different people drew different conclusions.
- Arguably the war simply confirmed contemporaries' long-held views about the value of Empire.

## The nature of warfare?

The Boer War gave insights into the grim nature of war. There was little that once lent war some glamour: no bright uniforms, no bands playing men into battle, no flags – just killing. British and European military academies did not subsequently use the war as a case study because most soldiers believed it had little relevance for armies preparing for great power conflict in Europe. But there were lessons to be learned, not least that barbed wire and trenches gave huge advantages to the defender.

## The need for reform of the British army?

The humiliations suffered in the first months of the war indicated that the British army needed to be reformed (despite the fact that the army had waged war very professionally, and in difficult circumstances, after 1899). The war led to full-scale government investigations into military planning, the military needs of Empire, recruitment, army and navy organisation and home defence. However, there was no consensus about what changes were necessary. The only thing that most Britons agreed on was that less money should be spent on the army. Thus reform proved to be a difficult business (see pages 124–8).

## The need for changes in foreign policy?

Prior to 1899 Salisbury had been associated with the policy of 'splendid isolation': no military alliances with other major powers. During the Boer War, isolation had seemed far from splendid. Britain had been stripped bare of troops, leading to fears of invasion (especially as international opinion had sympathised strongly with the Boers). This situation gave encouragement to those seeking an escape from isolation.

- In 1901–2, Chamberlain's efforts to secure an agreement with Germany resulted only in a series of bad-tempered exchanges with von Bülow which achieved nothing. Indeed, the war contributed to a souring of Anglo-German relations. By 1902, the British public had become increasingly anti-German. This was, in part, because German leaders (and newspapers) were strongly pro-Boer. Germany's imperial and naval ambitions also posed serious challenges.

- The British government was worried by the threat posed by the Russian fleet in the Far East. It thus decided to enlist the support of Japan. The Anglo-Japanese Alliance (1902) seemed to be the start of a major change in foreign policy.

## National inefficiency?

The fact that it took an imperial army of 450,000 men 32 months to defeat (at most) 60,000 Boers was a source of concern. The war shattered national complacency and created an intensified sense of danger. Many believed that the British Empire might be brought down – like the Roman Empire – by decadence and incompetence. There was much talk of the need for 'national efficiency'. Some thought that military failure suggested that Britain was conducting its affairs by reference to a false system of values. Public schools came under fire for elevating 'character' over scientific 'intelligence'. The upbringing and education of all children, rich and poor, was seen as crucial if Britain was to remain a great imperial power.

## The need for modernisation?

For some, the Boer War underlined the need for modernisation. But for others it encouraged nostalgia for a rural past. Many army officers, for example, admired the military prowess of their Boer adversaries and the vigour of the colonial troops. These impressions reinforced their belief that urbanisation had damaging consequences on physical well-being and character.

## The impact of the war on the Empire?

Some regard the Boer War as the first nail in the coffin of the Empire. The war certainly damaged the view that the Empire spread peace and prosperity around the world. However, imperial enthusiasm survived the war and after 1902 there were fresh demands for tighter imperial union (see page 116).

---

**Some key books in the debate**
J. Charmley, *Splendid Isolation: Britain and the Balance of Power 1874–1914* (Hodder & Stoughton, 1999).
J. Gooch (editor), *The Boer War: Direction, Experience and Image* (Cass, 2000).
D. Judd and K. Surridge, *The Boer War* (John Murray, 2002).
B. Nasson, *The South African War 1899–1902* (Arnold, 1999).
G.R. Searle, *A New England? Peace and War 1886–1918* (Oxford, 1980).

---

## Study Guide

### In the style of Edexcel

How far do these sources suggest that the British treatment of Boer civilians was barbaric? Explain your answer using the evidence of Sources 1, 2 and 3.

(20 marks)

### Source 1

*From: a speech by the Liberal Party leader, Sir Henry Campbell-Bannerman, to Liberal supporters in 1901. He is referring to conditions in the camps into which Boer civilians were placed.*

A phrase is often used that war is war in relation to the conditions in the camps. But when one asks what is going on in South Africa the government says there is no war, it is a local dispute. So I ask when is a war not a war? When it is carried on with the methods of barbarism now used in South Africa.

### Source 2

*A cartoon, 'Sending the innocents to Heaven', published in* Ulk, *a German satirical magazine, in 1901. Kitchener, shown on the right, was in command of the British forces in South Africa from November 1900.*

Source 3

*From: a letter by Emily Hobhouse to a family member in 1901. She is writing about her visit to the camp for civilians at Bloemfontein in January 1901. Hobhouse was an opponent of the war and was Secretary of the Women's Branch of the South African Conciliation Committee.*

Tho authorities are at their wits' end and have no more idea how to cope with the difficulty of providing clothes for the people than the man in the moon. Crass male ignorance, stupidity, helplessness and muddling. I rub as much salt into the sore places of their minds as I possibly can, because it is good for them; but I can't help melting a little when they are very humble and confess that the whole thing is a grievous mistake and gigantic blunder and presents an almost insoluble problem and they don't know how to face it.

---

### Exam tips

This is another example of a compulsory **(a)** question. The format is different from the example given at the end of Chapter 2. This question asks you to test a claim against the evidence of the three sources you are given. Again, it does not require you to introduce additional own knowledge in order to answer the question, but you should use your knowledge to contextualise the sources when you consider how much weight the evidence has.

For example, when using Source 2, you should factor in what you know about German attitudes to British involvement in the area and the conflict since this could have a bearing on the strength of criticisms. This collection of sources introduces a cartoon. When analysing a cartoon, keep in mind that every element of it – the visual images and the caption – have been deliberately created for impression. In this case, the two figures, Chamberlain and Kitchener, have been given devil-like images to convey an image of evil acts carried out on 'innocents'. The cartoon's message is that atrocities are deliberate and the responsibility of both the British government and the army in South Africa.

Campbell-Bannerman's reference to 'barbarism' conveys a similar message, but how far does the evidence of Source 3 support the charge of deliberate cruelty? Note the evidence of Source 3, which does support Sources 1 and 2 in relation to the suffering of civilians in the camps, but note also the evidence which challenges the idea that it was planned or deliberate policy – it points to inefficiency rather than cruelty. In coming to an overall conclusion, you should take into account the origin of all three sources: Source 1 from the Liberal opposition, Source 2 from Germany and Source 3 from a war opponent. Hobhouse's position lends all the more weight to her evidence which goes some way to challenge the charge of barbarism, while confirming the suffering in the camps.

# 5 The Impact of the Boer War on Britain

**POINTS TO CONSIDER**
The Boer War had a considerable impact on British public opinion and on political and (ultimately) social developments. While most Britons supported the war, there were some who bitterly opposed it. The war led to a serious debate about the value of Empire and Britain's imperial role. Problems raised by recruitment to the army led to concerns about national efficiency. This, in turn, impacted on the need for social reform. This chapter will consider these issues by examining the following:

- The political impact of the war
- The economic impact of the war
- The social impact of the war
- Reorganisation of imperial defence
- The debate on Empire

**Key dates**
1896    *Daily Mail* launched
1900    Khaki election: Unionist victory
1902    Balfour replaced Salisbury as Prime Minister
1903    Chamberlain launched his tariff reform campaign
1904    Anglo-French *entente*
1906    Liberal victory in general election
1907    Territorial Army created
1908    Boy Scout movement founded

## 1 | The Political Impact of the War

In 1899, the British public seemed united in its support of the Boer War. Most people expected a short and successful conflict. However, the fact that the war initially went badly, and then dragged on for three years, led to increased political divisions.

### British 'democracy'
Britain was more democratic in 1899 than it had been in the mid-nineteenth century. The 1884 Parliamentary Reform Act had increased the franchise by nearly two million new electors. However:

> **Key question**
> What were the main political results of the war?

- Only about 60 per cent of adult males had the vote.
- Women could not vote.

The House of Lords still had considerable power while the House of Commons was drawn from a scarcely less narrow social constituency. In the 1880s and 1890s more than half of English, Scottish and Welsh MPs came from aristocratic and landed backgrounds. This class dominated ministerial posts, regardless of which party was in power.

Given that MPs were not paid until 1912, few men from humble backgrounds could afford to entertain parliamentary ambitions. The only exceptions were:

- Irish Nationalists, many of whom were financed by Irish–American sympathisers
- working-class politicians who were sponsored by their trade unions or (after 1900) by the newly formed Labour Party (see below).

## The political parties

The Liberals and Conservatives were the two main parties. The only exception was in Ireland, where Catholics elected Nationalist MPs who demanded home rule while Protestants, strong in Ulster, elected MPs who were committed to maintaining the Union. Religion remained a crucial determinant of voting behaviour in Britain generally. The Liberal Party was closely aligned with nonconformity, the Conservatives with the Church of England. This meant there were considerable regional variations in party support. The Conservatives were usually the strongest party in England while the Liberals were strong in Wales and Scotland, where nonconformist traditions were strong. Class was also an important determinant of voting behaviour. Working-class voters tended to vote Liberal while middle-class voters tended to vote Conservative.

Some workers supported **socialist** movements. Britain's first socialist party, the **Social Democratic Federation** (SDF), was founded in 1883. The **Fabian Society** was less extreme than the SDF, its leaders, for example the **Webbs** and **George Bernard Shaw**, taking a more pragmatic attitude to social problems. The formation of the Independent Labour Party (ILP) in 1893 provided some hope of uniting left-wing voices. Its leaders (like Keir Hardie) realised the necessity of linking with the trade union movement, whose resources in manpower and money were vital. But not all trade unionists – or workers – were won over to the socialist cause. The ILP had little political success. In the 1895 general election it fielded 28 candidates, all of whom finished bottom of the poll.

The key issue dividing the main parties in the last two decades of the nineteenth century was Irish Home Rule. Over the winter of 1885–6, Gladstone committed the Liberal Party to establishing an Irish parliament. However, his government was unable to carry its Home Rule Bill through the Commons since 93 Liberal MPs – a third of the parliamentary party – voted against the measure. These Liberal Unionists entered into an electoral alliance with the Conservatives. The maintenance of Empire was part of the Home

Rule issue. Irish independence, **Unionists** warned, would be fatal to Britain's greatness and security. Colonial subjects and foreign powers alike would assume that Britain had lost the will to protect its territory.

## Unionist dominance

In the 1895 election, the Unionists, led by Salisbury, won a landslide victory. With 341 MPs, the Conservatives possessed an overall majority but the Liberal Unionists also won 70 seats. Now that the Union seemed safe, other issues, apart from Ireland, could come to the fore, not least the need for social reform.

## Support for the Empire

Most Britons felt a sense of pride in the Empire and, whatever their class, derived satisfaction from the thought that they constituted a successful imperial 'race'. Most regarded the superiority of whites over blacks as self-evident. They also placed Britons in the vanguard of the white races. However, the 'Anglo-Saxon' race was not usually thought of in purely biological terms. It was envisaged more as a carrier of a distinct set of values and institutions. In fact the most common justification of Empire rested less upon race than on the concept of 'mission'. When in 1898 Rudyard Kipling spoke of the 'White Man's Burden', he was addressing the Americans who had just assumed responsibility for the Philippino peoples following the **Spanish–American War**. But the phrase was one that well captured the mood of late Victorian imperialism. There was a strong belief that Britain brought education, peace, prosperity and better conditions of life to 'lower races'.

## Support for the war

Most MPs – Conservatives and Liberals – supported the Boer War in 1899. In all likelihood, so did most Britons (although this cannot be quantified). There was undoubtedly a strong sense of patriotism, reflected in the opposition to Irish Home Rule and pride in Empire.

## The impact of the press

The press, as well as encouraging support for both the imperial idea and the war, reflected that support. By the 1890s, more Britons had the money (thanks to rising real wages) to buy daily newspapers. Technical improvements ensured that newspaper costs were falling. Moreover, newspapers were able to sell below cost price, bridging the gap by advertising revenue. Thus some 150 daily papers catered for the tastes of an expanding reading public and the dailies were supplemented by a plethora of weekly papers, monthly periodicals and quarterly reviews. In the absence of other methods of mass communication, the press was the main medium for politicians to put their views to the people and for people to keep themselves informed about public affairs.

**Key question**
How strong was support for the Empire in 1899?

**Key terms**

**Unionists**
Conservatives and Liberals who were united in their opposition to Irish Home Rule.

**Spanish–American War**
A short conflict, fought between Spain and the USA in 1898, which the USA easily won.

**Key question**
Did the press influence or merely reflect British opinion in 1899?

**Key date**

*Daily Mail* launched: 1896

**Key figure**

**Alfred Harmsworth**
A great newspaper magnate, Harmsworth launched the *Daily Mail* and the *Daily Mirror* and acquired the *Observer* and *The Times*. He was made Viscount Northcliffe in 1905.

**Key term**

**Reuters**
An agency which supplied newspapers with international news.

In 1896, **Alfred Harmsworth** launched the *Daily Mail*, selling his paper for a halfpenny when most established papers cost a penny. By 1900, the *Mail* had built up a circulation of nearly one million, far more than all its rivals. This had two effects:

- other papers had to drop their prices to stay competitive
- new papers appeared in imitation of the *Daily Mail*. The *Daily Express*, launched in 1900, daringly printed news on its front page.

The *Mail* was fiercely imperialist. It marketed itself as the voice of Empire and in the first years of its publication devoted huge space to imperial topics. It was hardly surprising that the *Mail* supported the Boer War. So did most papers. Rather than rely on news agencies (like **Reuters**), many sent war correspondents to southern Africa to report the war at first hand. (War reporting throughout the 1890s had been popular with the public and had helped to sell newspapers.) Some, like George Stevens of the *Daily Mail*, became 'stars'. Winston Churchill, who filed reports for the *Morning Post*, used his experiences in southern Africa to launch his political career (see page 108).

War correspondents exercised huge political influence through their access to news and their control over its dissemination. Image could be as potent as reality, particularly when it came to military reputations. General Buller was popular with his men, of whose creature comforts he took great care. But his contempt for pressmen and his heavy-handed methods of censorship cost him dear. Unable to present his own side of the story, he was widely depicted by journalists as a blundering buffoon. Roberts, by contrast, went out of his way to butter up the press corps. He also took care to keep correspondents away from unpleasant scenes such as the typhoid epidemic. A striking example of how heroic status could be achieved through press manipulation was provided by Baden-Powell. His exploits at Mafeking, although not inconsiderable, became magnified in the public's imagination.

## The impact of other media

The war saw an outpouring of stories and poems, some written from the comfort of the armchair by non-participants but many by soldiers on active service, drawn from all ranks. The soldiers' literary efforts suggest that many felt uneasy about the war. The Boers, devout and self-sufficient farmers, seemed to embody religious and moral ideas and values to which many British soldiers themselves subscribed. They had no wish to destroy the Boer way of life, which was effectively what they were doing by the use of scorched earth tactics.

Britons were vicariously caught up in the conflict in two other ways:

- The war was vividly caught in photographs. Troops, as well as journalists, had access to cartridge film first used in the Pocket and Bullet Kodaks of 1896, supplemented from 1900 by the cheap Brownie camera.

## Profile: Winston Churchill 1874–1965

| | |
|---|---|
| 1874 | – Born in Blenheim Palace, Oxfordshire, son of Lord Randolph Churchill and his American wife Jenny |
| 1893–4 | – Trained as a cavalry officer at Sandhurst |
| 1895 | – Obtained a commission from the *Daily Graphic* to write about the war in Cuba between the Spanish and Cuban guerrillas |
| 1897 | – Campaigned on the North West Frontier of India; wrote articles for *The Pioneer* and *The Daily Telegraph* |
| 1808 | – Fought in the Sudan; also worked as a war correspondent for the *Morning Post* |
| 1899 | – Resigned from British army; failed to win a seat in the Oldham by-election; became a war correspondent for the *Morning Post*; captured by the Boers and escaped |
| 1900 | – Elected Conservative MP for Oldham |
| 1904 | – Joined the Liberal Party because he opposed tariff reform |
| 1908–10 | – President of the Board of Trade |
| 1910–11 | – Home Secretary |
| 1911–15 | – First Lord of the Admiralty |
| 1917 | – Minister of Munitions |
| 1919 | – Secretary of State for War |
| 1924–9 | – Conservative Chancellor of the Exchequer |
| 1939–40 | – First Lord of the Admiralty |
| 1940–5 | – Prime Minister |
| 1951–5 | – Returned as Prime Minister |
| 1965 | – Died |

Churchill, at the forefront of the political scene for over 50 years, is best known for his leadership during the Second World War. The Boer War was an important step in his rise to political power. In 1899, he obtained a commission to act as war correspondent for the *Morning Post*. Rushing out to southern Africa, he tried to get as close to the action as possible. Accompanying a scouting expedition in an armoured train, he was captured by Boers (after brave action on his part) and held in a prisoner-of-war camp in Pretoria. Escaping from the camp, he travelled almost 300 miles (480 km) to Portuguese Lourenço Marques (present-day Maputo, Mozambique). This exploit made him a minor national hero. Continuing as a war correspondent, he also gained a commission in the South African Light Horse. He was among the first British troops into both Ladysmith and Pretoria. Returning to England in 1900, he published two books of his Boer War experiences: *London to Ladysmith* and *Ian Hamilton's March*. He was elected as a Conservative MP in the 1900 Khaki election.

**Key term**

**Bioscope**
The first moving film apparatus.

- Through the **bioscope**, invented in 1895, audiences could see moving pictures from South Africa. However 'staged' much of the footage was, it gave the war a sharper immediacy.

The commercial world was quick to exploit the war's drama. Soldiers, throughout the years of imperial expansion, had featured prominently in advertisements but during the war they were used even more to promote every conceivable kind of product.

### Khaki fever

**Key question**
How strong was 'khaki fever'?

In 1899–1900, 'khaki fever' raged throughout Britain. Labour leader, John Burns, thought his fellow countrymen to be 'khaki clad, khaki mad and khaki bad':

**Key figure**

**Arthur Sullivan**
A musician, famous for his popular operas written with W.S. Gilbert.

- There was a spate of popular jingoistic songs. Kipling's 'Absent-minded Beggar', which Mrs Beerbohm Tree recited nightly and to which **Arthur Sullivan** wrote accompanying music, earned at least £250,000 for soldiers' families.
- Half a million people cheered off the First Army Corps as it embarked at Southampton.
- Men rushed to volunteer for the army.
- Hysterical fervour greeted news of the lifting of the siege of Ladysmith and the relief of Mafeking.

Bovril helps the troops. 'For Men of Action,' an advertisement from the *Illustrated London News* of about 1900.

- Patriotic mobs disrupted the lecture tour given in 1900 by the Boer S.C. Cronwright-Schreiner.
- Prominent British 'pro-Boers' who tried to hold public meetings were given a rough ride. When Lloyd George addressed a rally in Birmingham, disorder broke out: one man was left dead, others were injured and Lloyd George had to be smuggled out of the town hall disguised as a policeman.

## Opposition to the Empire

Not all Britons supported imperialism:

- In 1881, the historian J.R. Seeley noted that some Britons regarded the Empire as 'a kind of excrescence' which deprived them 'of the advantages of our insularity' and exposed them to 'wars and quarrels in every part of the globe'.
- 'Little Englanders' insisted that imperial ambitions (and expense) served to distract attention from social problems at home.
- Some attacked the Empire for its exploitation of native races.
- Critics of imperialism saw greed as the motivating force in overseas expansion.
- Imperial issues had driven a wedge between Liberal Imperialists and Radical Liberals throughout the 1880s and 1890s.

## Opposition to the war

A sizeable minority of the population – Liberals, socialists, Irish Nationalists – vehemently opposed the war from the start. They were backed by C.P. Scott's *Manchester Guardian*, the *Morning Star*, the *Daily News* (from 1901 onwards) and assorted socialist journals.

**Key question**
Why did some Britons oppose the Boer War?

### Anti-war groups

There was a number of influential anti-war groups, including the following:

- Stop The War Committee, chaired by a former Methodist minister Silas Hocking, though its main inspirer was W.T. Stead, a former friend of Rhodes
- South African Conciliation Committee
- League Against Aggression and Militarism, which included Lloyd George, C.P. Scott and J.A. Hobson.

### The opposition's case

The opposition's case was stated, at its simplest, in a resolution drafted by Lloyd George in 1900 in which the war was denounced as 'a crime and a blunder, committed at the instigation of irresponsible capitalists'. Opposition to government policy was often accompanied by an idealisation of the enemy, who were seen as living a simple pastoral life, devoted to family and farm. Some pro-Boers sounded an anti-Semitic note. In *The War in South Africa* (1900), Hobson claimed Britain was fighting for 'a small group of international financiers, chiefly German in origin and Jewish in race'. He penned a more sophisticated interpretation of events in *Imperialism* (1900), claiming that the war and imperial expansion generally were fuelled by the export of surplus capital, a view accepted by many socialists.

### Religious opposition?

Most Radical Liberals attacked the war, not so much by subjecting it to an economic critique but simply because they considered it to be morally wrong. In taking this stand, they received little backing from the churches. Most Anglican and Methodist clergymen supported the war. Nonconformists prevaricated. Prior to the outbreak of war, the National Council of Free Churches had held prayer meetings for peace. But in 1900, its organising committee banned all discussion of the war. While some prominent Quakers denounced the war, a significant minority declined to follow this lead. The Primitive Methodists alone were more or less united in opposing the war.

### Labour opposition?

**Key terms**

**TUC**
The Trades Union Congress.

**Leader of the Commons**
Prime Minister Salisbury, a peer, sat in the Lords. Therefore, Balfour led the Conservatives in the Commons.

Organised labour, like mainstream nonconformity, took a cautionary approach. The **TUC** officially maintained a position of neutrality on the war, partly because of the traditional assumption that questions of foreign policy and imperial defence lay outside the TUC's remit, partly because the leadership did not wish to pick a quarrel with numerous trade unionists who had rushed to join the colours. The ILP and the SDF stood by their anti-war convictions. Their members believed that the conflict was a capitalist war. But other labour leaders announced that in a national emergency they were Britons first and socialists second. Socialists' criticism of the war was muted by their unwillingness to rock the boat while engaged in constructing the Labour Representation Committee (LRC). This brought together the main socialist groups: the Fabians, the ILP, the SDF and interested trade unions. The inaugural LRC conference, held in February 1900, did not mention the war at all.

### Irish Nationalist opposition

The most outspoken antagonists of the war were the Irish Nationalists who empathised with the Boers as fellow victims of imperialist aggression. In March 1902, Irish MPs laughed and waved their order papers on being informed of Methuen's capture at Tweebosch, an act which alienated the bulk of MPs and the country as a whole and which was thus probably counterproductive.

**Key question**
Why were the Liberals unable to gain political advantage from the war?

### Liberal divisions

Initially the war seemed to provide the Liberals with some opportunities to increase their popularity. Anger at government mismanagement soon ran high, giving the Liberals much to exploit. Salisbury's failure to provide decisive leadership meant that Balfour, the **Leader of the Commons**, found himself playing a key role. But badly judged speeches in November 1899, when he said he had no more idea than 'the man in the street' of the Boers' military preparedness, led to much criticism. Chamberlain, astonished at the turn of events, momentarily lost much of his fire.

War Secretary Lansdowne was so discredited that some newspapers called for his impeachment.

The Liberal leader, Campbell-Bannerman, accused Chamberlain of precipitating an unnecessary war through a reckless policy of bluff. However, he could not defend the Boers, particularly while they were occupying British territory and when the war was going so badly for the British army. His 'middle of the road' policy did not satisfy either the Radical or Imperialist factions within his party. The depth of Liberal division was apparent in October 1899 when a motion critical of the conduct of negotiations with the Boers led to a three-way split. The motion, supported by 99 Liberals, was easily defeated. Campbell-Bannerman and Asquith along with 40 other Liberal MPs abstained. Fifteen Liberals supported the government. Another three-way split in July 1900 gave Liberal Imperialists (like Haldane and Grey) the hope that Campbell-Bannerman would resign, allowing Asquith to take his place. This did not happen and Liberal strife continued.

## The Khaki election

In September 1900, believing that the war had effectively ended, Salisbury called for a general election, although parliament still had two more years to run. In the campaign Chamberlain, who played a crucial role, declared that 'every vote given against the government is a vote given to the Boers'. The Unionists were returned with a majority of 134 over all their opponents, eight seats fewer than in 1895 but slightly more than they had held on the eve of parliament's dissolution.

Historians struggle to make sense of the so-called 'Khaki election'. In some areas the election was dominated by the war. Elsewhere it took second place to other issues. The Unionist ploy of draping their candidates in the Union Jack similarly achieved mixed success. Some anti-war candidates, for example William Steadman in Stepney, were defeated. Others, for example George Burns in Battersea, held off their assailants by campaigning hard on social reform. In general, the Unionists tended to do best in big cities, dockyard towns and armament centres while the Liberals held their own in smaller market towns. Arguably the election results reflected Liberal disorganisation rather than a vote in support of the war. The Liberals had difficulty fielding candidates because the party was in dire financial straits as many of its wealthy backers, disliking the anti-imperialist stance of many party members, continued to desert it. There were 161 uncontested Unionist victories (as against 22 Liberal ones).

## Unionist problems

Despite winning a decisive electoral victory, the Unionist ministry had problems:

- The press screamed for the replacement of some of the 'old gang' with younger talent.
- The reshuffle when it came was a disappointment. Lansdowne replaced Salisbury as Foreign Secretary while St John Brodrick

**Key question**
Why did the Unionists win the 1900 election?

Khaki election: Unionist victory: 1900

Key date

became War Secretary. Lord Selborne, Salisbury's son-in-law, became First Lord of the Admiralty (one of four close relatives of Salisbury to hold high office). Chamberlain remained at the Colonial Office, admired by many, loathed by others.

- The war continued and there was plenty of evidence of government mismanagement.
- Unionist success in 1900 owed much to Liberal disunity. If the Liberals could put aside their differences they would pose a much greater challenge.

## Liberal disunity

In 1901–2, the Liberal Party seemed close to disintegration. Emily Hobson's revelations of conditions in the concentration camps (see page 90) brought Liberal tensions to a head. In June 1901, Campbell-Bannerman moved closer towards the pro-Boer MPs by using the phrase 'methods of barbarism' to describe Britain's pacification policy. Liberal Imperialists, shocked at this 'treacherous' attack on the army and hopeful of reconciliation with the Liberal Unionists, openly plotted to replace Campbell-Bannerman with Asquith or **Lord Rosebery**. But Campbell-Bannerman had the support of most Liberal MPs. Asquith, at heart a 'centrist' (despite his friendship with Haldane and Grey), remained loyal to the Liberal leader. The Peace of Vereeniging in 1902 removed the main bone of contention among Liberals. Moreover, the Unionists helped to unite their opponents through their Corn Duty (1902) and the 1902 Education Act (see below).

**Key figure**

**Lord Rosebery**
Liberal Prime
Minister 1894–5.

**Key question**
What problems did
Balfour face?

**Key date**

Balfour replaced
Salisbury as Prime
Minister: 1902

## The Unionist government 1900–5

The Unionist government, headed by Salisbury and then by Balfour (his nephew) after Salisbury stepped down in 1902, had some considerable achievements:

- Selborne launched an important series of naval reforms (see page 129).
- In foreign policy important initiatives were taken, including an alliance with Japan (1902) and *entente* with France (1904).
- The 1902 Education Act created Local Education Authorities (LEAs) to organise educational provision at all levels: elementary, secondary and technical. The Act made possible a dramatic improvement in the provision of secondary education.

But Balfour soon faced major problems:

- The 1902 Education Act was a political disaster. Many opposed the abolition of School Boards and the granting of rate aid to Church schools. Campaigning on the education issue, Liberals won a series of by-elections.
- In 1904, Alfred Lyttelton, who had replaced Chamberlain as Colonial Secretary, allowed Milner to import Chinese labourers to work in the Transvaal gold mines. This action, which seemed to confirm the Radical view that the war had been fought for the profits of mineowners not the interests of the *uitlanders*, was

unpopular in South Africa. It soon created a storm of protest in Britain when it emerged that the Chinese were routinely flogged and treated as little better than slaves.

- The Boer War saddled Balfour with a fiscal crisis, which helped to give rise to Chamberlain's tariff reform campaign (see below).

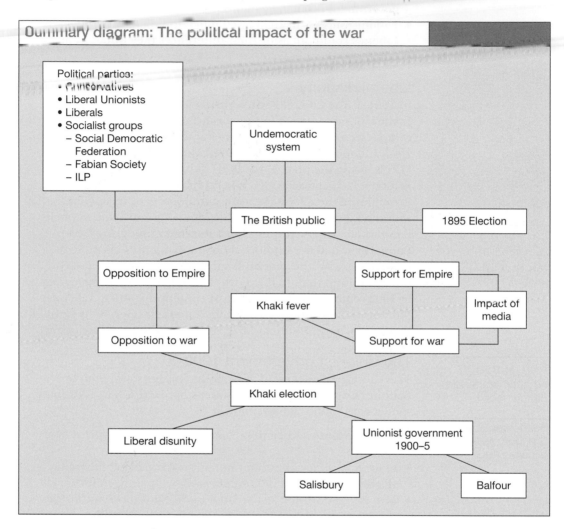

**Summary diagram: The political impact of the war**

Political parties:
- Conservatives
- Liberal Unionists
- Liberals
- Socialist groups
  - Social Democratic Federation
  - Fabian Society
  - ILP

Undemocratic system

The British public — 1895 Election

Opposition to Empire

Support for Empire

Khaki fever

Impact of media

Opposition to war

Support for war

Khaki election

Liberal disunity

Unionist government 1900–5

Salisbury

Balfour

## 2 | The Economic Impact of the War

The rise in public expenditure had been a worry in the 1890s. Then came the Boer War, which cost over £200 million. Given that Britain seemed to be reaching the limits of tolerable taxation, there were issues about how to pay for the war.

**Key question**
Why did the government face fiscal problems?

### Financial problems
Faced by war-related expenditure, Chancellor of the Exchequer Michael Hicks Beach in 1901:

- put a tax on refined sugar
- imposed a levy of 1s. on exported coal
- raised income tax by 2d. to 1s. 2d. in the pound.

To the dismay of traditional economists, only a third of the war's cost was met by taxation. Instead, the government resorted to borrowing. In his 1902 budget, Hicks Beach added another penny to income tax and reimposed the registration duty on corn, abolished in 1869. Although he made it clear he was doing this only for revenue purposes, the announcement of the Corn Duty seemed a danger to free trade.

Financial problems continued after the war's end. Alarm over the state of the armed services meant that government spending

---

### Profile: Joseph Chamberlain 1836–1914

1836 – Born in London, son of a successful manufacturer
1854 – Moved to Birmingham to join his uncle's screw making business; helped to make the firm a commercial success
1866 – Actively involved in Liberal politics in Birmingham
1873 – Became mayor of Birmingham, promoting many civic improvements
1876 – Elected Liberal MP for Birmingham
1880 – President of the Board of Trade
1886 – Resigned from the cabinet over the issue of Irish Home Rule
1892 – Became leader of the Liberal Unionists in the House of Commons
1895 – Appointed Colonial Secretary
1900 – Dominated the Unionist election campaign
1903 – Resigned from government and took up the cause of tariff reform
1906 – Suffered a serious stroke that effectively ended his political career
1914 – Died

Chamberlain has the distinction of being the only individual to have divided both major British political parties in the course of his career. He split the Liberal Party over the issue of Irish Home Rule. Less than 20 years later, his campaign for tariff reform divided the Conservatives. Churchill called Chamberlain 'a splendid piebald: first black, then white, or, in political terms, first fiery red, then true blue'. This is the conventional opinion of Chamberlain's politics: the view that he began to the left of the Liberal Party and ended up to the right of the Conservatives. But arguably he was always a radical in home affairs and an imperialist in foreign affairs. Arguably, too, these views were not in conflict. Essentially, he rejected *laissez-faire* capitalism in favour of government intervention. His enthusiasm for Empire and his support for stronger imperial union are not in doubt. He had long hoped to reform the Empire as a federation of nations with an imperial parliament replacing the House of Lords. Given the growing challenge from Germany and the USA, he believed that imperial unity was vital if Britain was to remain a great power.

looked set to remain high. Balfour's cabinet was divided on what types of measure were necessary. Charles Ritchie, Hicks Beach's successor as Chancellor, favoured retrenchment rather than raising taxation. Chamberlain, by contrast, supported tariff reform.

## Chamberlain and tariff reform

In 1903, Chamberlain proposed that protective duties should be levied on corn and on manufactured goods. Given his main concern – imperial unity – he argued there should be no tariffs on colonial imports. In Chamberlain's view, tariff reform would:

- raise money
- strengthen the Empire
- protect British industry from foreign competition, especially from Germany and the USA, countries that already had high tariffs
- safeguard British jobs
- safeguard British industry against unfair practices like **dumping**
- pay for much-needed social reform
- give the Unionists a constructive programme, now that Irish Home Rule was dormant.

Chamberlain's support for tariff reform split the Unionist coalition wide open. Balfour did his best to preserve unity. But when Chamberlain announced his desire to leave the government to campaign in support of tariff reform, Balfour encouraged him to do so. The Tariff Reform League was created in July 1903. Most of its members were businessmen, attracted by its commitment to 'the defence and development of the industrial interests of the British Empire'.

Free traders fought back. Traditional anti-protectionist arguments still carried resonance:

- Duties on corn would raise food prices.
- Britain exported twice as much to foreign countries as it exported to its colonies.
- High duties might simply protect inefficient British industries.
- Free trade, by keeping food and other costs low, helped to reduce labour costs. Thus many industries derived a competitive edge over their foreign rivals, which in turn generated further profits and employment.

## The 1906 election

By 1905, Balfour's government was bitterly divided on tariff reform. By contrast, the Liberals were strong:

- By defending free trade, the Liberals could claim to be defending working-class interests.
- The 'Chinese slavery' (see page 113) issue helped the Liberals.
- The Liberals had made a secret deal with the LRC to prevent both parties standing in seats that might ensure Unionist victory.

Balfour resigned in late 1905. Campbell-Bannerman, who formed a minority government, called a general election in January 1906.

**Key question**
How realistic was tariff reform as an economic policy?

**Key dates**

Chamberlain launched his tariff reform campaign: 1903

Liberal victory in general election 1906

**Key term**

**Dumping**
Exporting commodities for sale at below the cost of production to ruin overseas competition.

**Key question**
Why did the Liberals triumph in 1906?

The Liberals, with 400 seats, won an overwhelming victory. The Unionists retained only 157 seats. Even Balfour lost his seat. The Irish Nationalists won 83 seats and Labour 30. Interestingly, the Boer War hardly featured in the election. The Unionists did not want to remind voters of their mismanagement of the war while the Liberals wished to forget their past divisions.

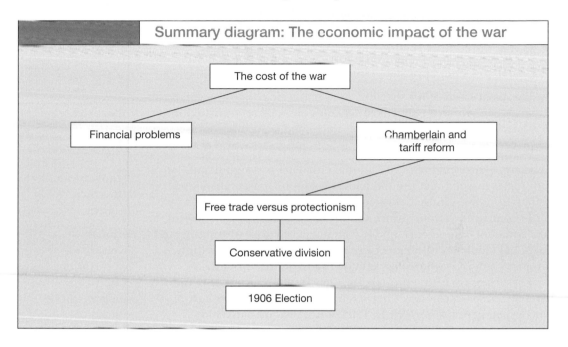

Summary diagram: The economic impact of the war

3 | The Social Impact of the War

**Key question**
What impact did the Boer War have on Britain's social development?

The Boer War's immediate effect was to divert political attention and potential economic resources from several areas of activity. These included old-age pensions and subsidised working-class housing, for which there had been some pressure in the 1890s. However, the national efficiency movement, arising from the war, encouraged social reform. More specifically, the rejection rate among would-be volunteers for the army reinforced concern over demographic trends and over the condition of the mass of the population.

## National efficiency

**Key question**
What was the national efficiency movement?

Early failure in the war seemed symptomatic of a deep malaise, analysis of which preoccupied the political class for years to come under the guiding rule of national efficiency. The national efficiency 'movement' was mainly held together by an informal network of friends and acquaintances. Its only institutional legacy was a dining club, the 'Co-Efficients', established in 1902, whose original 12 members (including Haldane, Grey and Sidney Webb) aspired to 'permeate' the state and reshape its policy agenda. Later, the movement became associated with a circle of young men, forming around Milner, who viewed 'efficiency' as a way of escaping from the sterility of adversarial politics through its fusion of imperialism and social reform. National efficiency supporters generally wanted to:

- institute a career system open to talent
- shame the existing élite into modernising itself before it was swept away
- modernise Britain's secondary schooling and higher education systems, particularly by taking science and technology seriously, so that the country retained its economic competitiveness.

National efficiency appealed to many different groups:

- The Webbs and other socialists used it as a cloak behind which to advance their own **collectivist schemes** of social reconstruction.
- Many Liberals and Conservatives welcomed what they saw as a project of modernisation that was both progressive and patriotic.

The cross-party character of national efficiency was significant. Its advocates insisted that the old battles between Conservatism and Liberalism, even those between capitalism and socialism, meant little compared with the more serious battle taking place between the forces of competence and incompetence. Those who supported national efficiency often saw Germany as a model for emulation, and also as a rival whose very efficiency threatened Britain.

The obsession with national efficiency fostered a view of people as a resource – a resource that was being squandered through incompetence and neglect. In 1901, journalist Arnold White claimed that at the Manchester recruiting station three out of five recruits in 1899 had to be rejected because they failed to meet the army's physical standards. (In reality, 33 per cent of men were rejected in 1899, 28 per cent in 1900 and 29 per cent in 1901.) Anxieties about physical deterioration were to influence policy debates long after the Boer War had ended.

National efficiency may well have given a considerable boost to social reform as a concept which politicians (of all parties) could not ignore. But in narrowly political terms, it achieved little of significance. While there was talk about the desirability of establishing a **national government** under Rosebery, this hope was doomed by Rosebery's ineptitude – or inefficiency!

## National inequality

In Britain in 1900 there were huge inequalities of wealth. A quarter of the land belonged to fewer than 1000 individuals, a concentration of ownership more extreme than in any other European country. A tenth of the population owned 92 per cent of the nation's wealth. By contrast, nearly nine-tenths fell below the income tax threshold of £160 a year. Living standards were rising: between 1882 and 1899 average real wages rose by over a third and people, generally, had better diets, better health and more leisure time. Nevertheless, grinding poverty was still a fact of life both in the big cities and in a countryside hit by agricultural depression. Many groups – politicians, trade unionists, Christian organisations – wished to do something to alleviate both poverty and the inequality of wealth.

**Key terms**

**Collectivist schemes**
The idea that industry should be run by workers and the government rather than by big business.

**National government**
A government made up of the most able men from all the political parties.

**Key question**
Why did many Britons support social reform?

## The condition of the nation

- **Charles Booth**'s research in London and **Seebohm Rowntree**'s research in York suggested that nearly a third of people were living in abject poverty, largely due to unemployment, old age and sickness.
- Infant mortality remained high, at around 150 per thousand. Mortality for infants (and for adults) was deeply divided by class. The poor died young.
- Given the marked differences in height between children from different backgrounds, it almost seemed as though Britain's social classes constituted separate races.
- Urbanisation was seen as contributing to the nation's physical (and moral) decay.
- There was evidence that differential fertility was bringing about a situation in which, according to **Karl Pearson**, 'the fertile, but unfit, one sixth' of the population was about to reproduce one half of the next generation, a trend which alarmists believed would lead to 'race suicide'.
- Many Britons believed in **Social Darwinism**. They were convinced that the nations that were 'fittest', both physically and mentally, would inevitably dominate the rest.

Thus imperial needs legitimised government and voluntary action on welfare issues, not least the survival of (fit) babies and the care of children: the next generation.

But there was great disagreement about the best way to help the poor:

- Rowntree favoured a minimum wage.
- Booth wanted an old-age pension and the state to take care of the poorest 10 per cent of the population.
- Socialists wanted a redistribution of wealth and collective ownership of land and large industries like coal, iron and steel, and gas.
- Those who believed in *laissez-faire* still supported **self-help**.

## Unionist action

Unionists were split on the extent to which they should support a programme of social reform. Some Conservatives believed that:

- molly-coddling by the state would damage rather than help individuals
- national welfare reform would be too costly
- reform should be left to local government and to voluntary organisations.

But other Conservatives felt that they had no option but to sponsor reforms. If they failed to take the initiative, the Liberals or the newly formed Labour Party would take advantage. Thus Balfour's government undertook some reform:

- The 1902 Education Act made possible a dramatic improvement in the provision of secondary education. By 1914, over 1000 secondary schools had been created under the Act, 349 of them for girls.

**Key figures**

**Charles Booth**
A Liverpool ship-owner and manufacturer, Booth carried out a series of investigations into poverty in London between 1886 and 1903.

**Seebohm Rowntree**
A Quaker and a member of the York chocolate and cocoa manufacturing family, Rowntree carried out a survey of poverty in York. His findings were published in 1901.

**Karl Pearson**
A strong supporter of the eugenics movement.

**Key terms**

**Social Darwinism**
Social Darwinists believed that only the fittest nations and social systems could thrive and prosper.

**Self-help**
The belief that people are best doing things for themselves without government assistance.

- The Unemployed Workmen's Act (1905) allowed local committees to be set up to provide work for the unemployed, using voluntary subscription.
- A Royal Commission on the **Poor Laws** was set up in 1905. Including experts like Charles Booth and Beatrice Webb, its purpose was to investigate the shortcomings of the Poor Law system and suggest ways of improving it.

**Poor Laws**
The measures passed to help those in severe poverty. Those who were desperate for help found refuge in the workhouse.

Key term

## The Report of the Select Inter-departmental Committee

A Report of the Select Inter-departmental Committee on Physical Deterioration (1903–4) found no evidence of:

- decline in the physical condition of the population
- 'impaired vitality' as a result of urbanisation
- racial degeneration.

Nevertheless, the committee found plenty of evidence of poverty, sickness and squalor, and emphasised that there was much that should be done to improve matters. The committee emphasised the need for an effective system of school medical inspection and for government-sponsored school meals. In addition, it made recommendations on issues such as overcrowding, the distribution and handling of food and milk, work conditions, childcare instruction for mothers, girls' domestic education, adult drinking and state-encouraged physical training. Town planners, educationalists, doctors and social workers could all find material in the committee's report from which to draw encouragement and a spur to action.

## Liberal reform

After 1906, the Liberal government introduced a variety of measures which aimed to provide protection against the harsh vicissitudes of life. Liberal motives were mixed. They included the need to fend off the challenge of Labour, humanitarianism, the search for electoral popularity, considerations of national efficiency and a desire to strengthen national solidarity in a dangerous world. In organisational terms, the reforms were something of a hotch-potch. The cabinet seldom debated social policy and its wider implications. Campbell-Bannerman (who, seriously ill, resigned in 1908) and then Asquith ran their governments on a loose rein, leaving the initiative to individual ministers, the more energetic of whom like Lloyd George and Churchill then presented colleagues with schemes for rubber-stamping. Much was borrowed from abroad, especially Germany. Much was improvised. In embarking on welfare legislation, the government did not have the field to itself; other agencies were at work: private charities, self-help organisations (for example, trade unions) and insurance companies. But the government was aware that a sizeable section of the population, through poverty or irregular earnings, could not get themselves adequately covered from a private source.

**Key question**
Why did the Liberals introduce so much social reform?

### The main Liberal reforms

- In 1907, mother and infant clinics were set up, their work supported by health visitors.
- The 1907 Education Act established school medical inspection. The establishment of school clinics soon followed.
- The 1908 Mines Act introduced a maximum eight-hour working day for miners.
- The 1908 Children's Act empowered authorities to cleanse verminous children and place children deemed at risk into safe custody. It also stopped children from purchasing tobacco or alcohol.
- In 1908, Lloyd George introduced old-age pensions.
- In 1909, Churchill set up a national network of Labour Exchanges.
- The 1910 Housing and Town Planning Act introduced slum clearance schemes and gave local councils the power (but not the cash) to build council houses.
- In 1911, Lloyd George introduced a National Insurance scheme.

### The results

**Key question**
What were the main results of the Liberal social reform measures?

In the nineteenth century, the lives of British citizens had been affected more by what happened in local government than by events at Westminster. Local decisions determined whether baths, washhouses and libraries were built, needy children were helped, slum housing was cleared, and public health measures were vigorously prosecuted. School Boards decided the physical as well as the educational fate of many children while the dignity of the old was often at the mercy of the Boards of Guardians. The Liberal reforms ensured that national government would now play a major role in welfare provision. If the Liberals had not created the Welfare State, they had at least laid down its foundations.

The reforms were costly. Initially the Liberals had hoped to finance the welfare initiatives by cutting military spending. However, the naval arms race with Germany (see below) drove up expenditure. The government thus had no option but to increase taxation. Lloyd George's 'People's Budget' (1909) raised taxes on the rich, increasing income tax and death duties and introducing a new supertax.

The Liberal government was not responsible for all welfare initiatives. For example, voluntary bodies, in association with local authorities, continued to take the lead in promoting the health of women and children. In 1905 (prior to government legislation), 48 LEAs in England and Wales were already making provision for medical inspection or supervision of school children and 55 of 71 county boroughs were organising school meals. This pattern of activity continued after 1907. The government did not offer grants in support of maternity and child-welfare services to local governments until 1914.

## Health improvement?

In 1914, the percentage of army volunteers rejected as physically unfit was almost as high as it had been in 1900. This might suggest that the various social reforms had had little effect. However, there was bound to be a time-lag before the benefits of the new state aid made themselves felt. Moreover, there is some evidence that the nation's health, particularly the health of children, was improving. There was a fall in infant death rates between 1890 and 1914: down from 163 to 105 per thousand births, a 35 per cent fall. (This probably owed more to a weakening in the ferocity of certain diseases than it did to infant clinics and prenatal care.)

## Eugenics

Not everyone was convinced that welfare reform would have a positive effect. The scientist Sir Francis Galton stressed the need for eugenics, which he defined as 'the study of the agencies under social control that may improve or impair the racial quality of future generations either physically or mentally'. Eugenics stressed the successful application of the science of agricultural breeding whereby farmers had improved their livestock. The movement was influential. The Eugenics Education Society, founded in 1907, had nearly 1000 members by 1914, including many doctors. It supported:

Key question
How influential
was the eugenics
movement?

- 'positive eugenics', encouraging the 'fit' to have large numbers of children
- 'negative eugenics', hoping to arrest the 'multiplication of the unfit', preferably by persuasion but if need be by bringing defective adults into custodial care so they could not reproduce.

Many eugenics supporters feared welfare reform might encourage the 'unfit' to breed and that increased taxes (to pay for welfare) might encourage the 'fit' to limit their families.

Leading Liberals gave eugenics a wide berth. Nevertheless, the Mental Deficiency Act (1913) allowed the 'feebleminded' to be brought into custodial care and to be sexually segregated. Churchill even considered the possibility of sterilising mental defectives.

## Motherhood and the cult of maternalism

On the left, the Fabians called for the 'endowment of motherhood', claiming it was woman's central vocation. On the right, those who supported the cult of maternalism saw women as 'the guardians of an imperial race'. Subjects – household affairs, hygiene and nutrition – were inserted into the school curriculum with a view to turning out good, stay-at-home wives. Some women supported the new emphasis on the importance of mother and child. At the same time, others were campaigning for equal rights for women, especially the right to vote in parliamentary elections.

## The Boy Scouts

A range of youth movements flourished in Edwardian Britain. Many propagated their own particular version of 'manliness', complementing the fostering among girls of skills of motherhood and home-making. However, the older youth movements struggled to become mass organisations.

Into this gap moved Baden-Powell, the hero of Mafeking. Between 27 July and 9 August 1907, 'B-P' held his first experimental camp on Brownsea Island in Poole Harbour, trying out the various rituals, pastimes and organisational structures which would characterise his Boy Scout movement, founded in 1908. In 1910, B-P retired from his post as commander of the Northumbrian Division of the Territorial Army to devote himself full-time to the training of youth. By 1914, the Scouts had over 150,000 members, nearly two and a half times as many as the **Boys' Brigade** – the next most successful youth movement.

'Scouting' possessed some obvious military features, especially in its early years before it surprised its founder by mushrooming into an international movement:

- B-P was a professional and patriotic soldier.
- The original editions of *Scouting for Boys* preached a message of honour, duty, loyalty and self-control. Boys were told to learn from the example of the 'young Romans who lost the Empire of their forefathers by being wishy-washy slackers without any go or patriotism in them'. B-P exhorted the scouts to 'BE PREPARED to die for your country … so that when the time comes you may charge home with confidence, not caring whether you are to be killed or not'.
- Many early scoutmasters were serving or retired army officers.

However, the success of the scouts owed much to the avoidance of emphasis on military drill. Instead, B-P encouraged interest in outdoor life and activities, his high-minded desire to improve the nation's health. An eclectic thinker, B-P drew heavily upon Ernest Thompson Seton's romantic woodcraft movement, itself loosely based on the lore and rituals of American Indians. B-P had an instinctive understanding of what boys and youth enjoyed: the camaraderie of the camp, games and the open air. The militaristic undertones of the scouting movement were soon played down. Even so, the emphasis on patriotism, loyalty and comradeship – all soldierly virtues – remained.

## Girl Guides

Characteristically, B-P, in launching his movement, overlooked the fact that half of all youth were female. Many girls found the outdoor activities of the scouts exciting and initially they were allowed in as members, only for B-P to find himself accused by the editor of the *Spectator* of sponsoring a 'mad scheme of military co-education'. His sister Agnes was promptly drafted in to organise the Girl Guides on suitably feminine lines. If anything, the patriotic elements in the guides were even more pronounced than in the to mobilise, the Schlieffen Plan's success was endangered. Thus, Germany demanded that Russia cease all military activities within 12 hours. In the absence of a reply, Germany declared war on Russia on 1 August. France was asked for a promise of neutrality. When no such promise was received, Germany declared war on France on 3 August. Meanwhile, on 2 August, Germany demanded free passage for its troops through Belgium. When this 'request' was refused, German troops invaded Belgium.

## Britain declares war

As Europe lurched into war, the British government was divided on what to do. Prime Minister Herbert Asquith, Sir Edward Grey, Winston Churchill and others were committed to supporting France. But within the cabinet a majority opposed intervention, as did the Liberal press and many Liberal MPs. The violation of Belgium's neutrality, guaranteed by Britain in 1839, decided the issue. For centuries, it had been a prime objective of British policy to ensure that no strong power controlled the Low Countries. Virtually all the cabinet agreed that Britain should fight to defend Belgium. Britain thus demanded the withdrawal of German troops from Belgium. Receiving no reply, Britain declared war on Germany on 4 August.

Although there had been some opposition to war prior to 4 August, once it was declared, all the major political parties, including the Irish Nationalists, supported the war. King George V declared war on Germany in the name of the entire Empire. The governments of the self-governing colonies – Australia, New Zealand, South Africa and Canada – were not consulted. Nor were 250 million Indians and 50 million Africans. Although there was a short-lived Afrikaan revolt in South Africa, the white populations of the Empire rallied eagerly to Britain's defence.

**Key question**
Why did Britain declare war on Germany?

Britain declared war on Germany: August 1914

Key date

**Table 6.1:** The balance of power in 1914

|  | Great Britain | France | Russia | Germany | Austria-Hungary |
|---|---|---|---|---|---|
| Population | 46,407,037 | 39,601,509 | 167,000,000 | 65,000,000 | 49,882,231 |
| Soldiers available on mobilisation | 711,000[1] | 3,500,000 | 4,423,000[2] | 8,500,000[3] | 3,000,000 |
| Merchant fleet (net steam tonnage) | 11,538,000 | 1,098,000 | 486,914 | 3,096,000 | 559,784 |
| Battleships (built and being built) | 64 | 28 | 16 | 40 | 16 |
| Cruisers | 121 | 34 | 14 | 57 | 12 |
| Submarines | 64 | 73 | 29 | 23 | 6 |
| Annual value of foreign trade (£) | 1,223,152,000 | 424,000,000 | 190,247,000 | 1,030,380,000 | 198,712,000 |
| Annual steel production (tons) | 6,903,000 | 4,333,000 | 4,416,000 | 17,024,000 | 2,642,000 |

[1] Including the Empire.
[2] Immediate mobilisation.
[3] Emergency maximum.

## Summary diagram: The start of the war

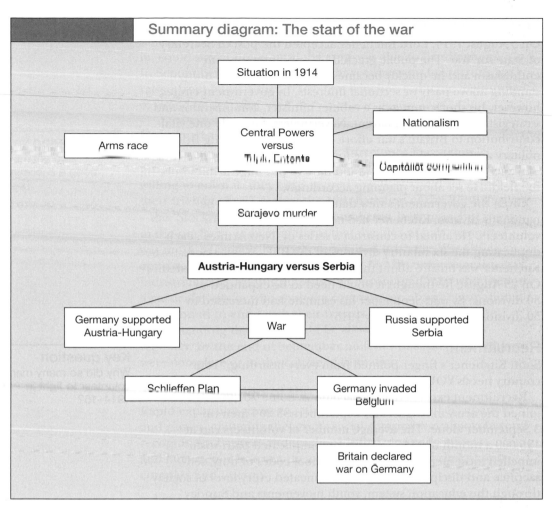

Situation in 1914

Arms race — Central Powers versus Triple Entente — Nationalism — Capitalist competition

Sarajevo murder

**Austria-Hungary versus Serbia**

Germany supported Austria-Hungary — War — Russia supported Serbia

Schlieffen Plan — Germany invaded Belgium

Britain declared war on Germany

**Key question**
How well prepared was the British army in 1914?

## 2 | The British Army's Readiness for War

In 1914, the British Expeditionary Force (BEF), in the view of the official history, was 'incomparably the best trained, best organised and best-equipped British army which ever went forth to war'. But the army was unprepared for a protracted campaign in Europe.

### The British army in 1914

On 4 August 1914, the regular army consisted of 247,432 officers and men, about one-third of whom were in India. Most of its officers came from traditional sources of supply: the peerage, the landed classes and military families. Most of its recruits came from the urban working classes. The part-time territorial force, with 268,777 men, attracted a broader spectrum of society. Its primary role was regarded as home defence. While Britain was now committed to fighting in Europe, the implication of that commitment had not been thoroughly explored. Crucially, all British plans were based on the war being short. In the event of a long war, little thought had gone into how to raise a mass army or increase munitions' output.

- Temporary commissions were granted to suitable men, a major source of applications being the Officers' Training Corps (OTC). Between August 1914 and March 1915, 20,577 current or former OTC members were commissioned.

## High command

The BEF was commanded by Sir John French. Aged 62, he had seen ample active service in Egypt and South Africa. Unfortunately, French, his staff at **GHQ** and his divisional and corps commanders had little practice or training at their respective levels of command. Nor had the Staff College prepared senior commanders very well for modern war. The Russo-Japanese War (1904–5) had provided clear indications of the impact of firepower. But since the aggressive Japanese had defeated the defensive-minded Russians through costly attacks with the bayonet, the wrong lessons were drawn. The British army had developed no particular doctrine pre-1914 except that of the offensive under almost all circumstances. Senior staff expected to overcome the enemy's firepower through mobility, discipline and moral force.

## Munition problems

The army was woefully deficient in modern technology. In 1914:

- each battalion had only two machine guns
- the entire army had only 80 motor vehicles
- all guns and supplies were drawn by horses
- there were no field telephones or wireless equipment.

Worse still, in August 1914 barely 6000 rifles and 30,000 rounds of shells a month were being produced and the stock of munitions was grossly inadequate. Rather than spreading munition production, the War Office concentrated orders in the hands of government ordnance factories and long-established contractors (insisting that only experienced firms knew how to produce munitions of satisfactory quality). This limited industry's ability to respond to the new demands. So did the fact that indiscriminate recruiting had led to the enlistment of many skilled engineers who were not easily replaced.

**Key term**

**GHQ**
General Head Quarters, comprising military staff officers who advised the Commander-in-Chief on policy and administration and helped him to carry out his plans.

**Key question**
How serious were British munition problems in 1914?

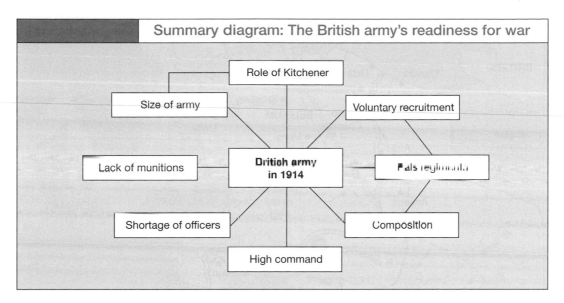

## Summary diagram: The British army's readiness for war

Role of Kitchener

Size of army

Voluntary recruitment

Lack of munitions

British army in 1914

Pals regiments

Shortage of officers

Composition

High command

## 3 | The War in 1914

In accordance with the Schlieffen Plan, 1.5 million German troops marched through Belgium, aiming to encircle Paris and crush France within six weeks. Meanwhile, the French hurled their main armies into Lorraine where they were mown down by enemy machine guns and artillery. In three weeks France incurred 300,000 casualties.

### Mons and Le Cateau

**Key question**
How well did the BEF fight in 1914?

The 120,000-strong BEF was sent to Mauberge on the French left, according to pre-war plans. This decision placed the BEF smack in the path of the advancing German armies. On 23 August, 75,000 troops of the BEF II Corps under General Smith-Dorrian faced 300,000 men of the German 1st Army at Mons. British troops demonstrated their proficiency at rifle fire, checking the enemy advance. Learning that the French 5th Army on his right was pulling back, Smith-Dorrien was forced to retreat. On 26 August, he stood and fought at Le Cateau, stopping three German corps but losing 8000 men. He and the rest of the BEF then continued their retreat. By the start of September, Sir John French contemplated withdrawing the BEF to below the River Seine (or even leaving France altogether) to refit. Kitchener rushed to Paris and ordered French to keep his place in the Allied line.

### The Battle of the Marne

**Key date**
Battle of the Marne: September 1914

On 28 August, General von Kluck changed his line of advance. Instead of sweeping around Paris from the west, he moved east. On 5 September, the French commander, General Joseph Joffre, attacked the exposed German right flank. The fighting, which lasted over the next week, is known as the Battle of the Marne. Sir John French joined the attack, promising Joffre that 'we will do all that men can do'. In fact the BEF did very little. It simply and driving deep into Galicia before being halted by German intervention.

## Stalemate

By December the expectation of a short war had proved false. On the Western Front a line of trenches ran for over 475 miles from the Channel to Switzerland – a thin line by later standards but solid enough to prevent a war of movement. British forces held about 35 miles of this line, including the Ypres **salient**. The BEF, despite its small size and shortage of munitions, had fought well. Had it not done so, the Germans might well have captured Paris and won the war. The most serious problems had been at high command level. French and his GHQ had maintained only tenuous control of the BEF at critical points. Exuberant one moment, depressed the next, French often operated more by intuition than by rational calculation.

## The naval war

At the start of the war, the elderly Lord Fisher (see page 129) was recalled as First Sea Lord. Command of the Grand Fleet was transferred from Prince Louis of Battenberg (whose German origins made him unacceptable) to Admiral Sir John Jellicoe. The Grand Fleet, with 20 Dreadnoughts (see page 129) and 26 pre-Dreadnought battleships, was stationed at Scapa Flow in the Orkneys. To the disappointment of the British public, the German High Seas Fleet, with 13 Dreadnoughts and 12 pre-Dreadnoughts, remained in port. However, the containment of the German fleet was an important strategic victory. It ensured that Britain did not face the threat of invasion, permitted the safe passage of British troops and supplies to France and ensured the equally safe transportation of troops from India, Canada, Australia and New Zealand to Europe, Asia Minor and Africa. Moreover, Britain was able to enforce a blockade of Germany. While Germany was deprived of goods, supplies poured into Britain from all over the world.

The main danger to the Royal Navy came from **U-boats** and from mines. On 22 September, three British cruisers were sunk by a single U-boat. A month later a battleship was sunk by a mine. Scapa Flow was not secure from U-boats. Thus, Jellicoe led his fleet first to the west of Scotland and then to Ireland, not returning to Scapa Flow until its U-boat defences were completed in mid-1915. Thereafter, Jellicoe, acutely conscious that he was 'the only man on either side who could lose the war in an afternoon', remained cautiously in harbour.

Meanwhile German ships mounted a series of bombardments on east coast towns, killing a number of people at Bridlington, Scarborough and Hartlepool, hoping – without success – to lure out and ambush small British squadrons. British battlecruisers, based at Rosyth in the Firth of Forth, under the command of Sir David Beatty, caught German battlecruisers at Dogger Bank in January 1915 (see page 163) but, thanks to the inefficiency of British gun crews, the outnumbered German fleet managed to escape.

**Key terms**

**Salient**
A narrow area pushing into enemy lines which can thus be attacked from several sides.

**U-boats**
German submarines.

**Key question**
Why did Jellicoe pursue a cautious naval policy 1914–16?

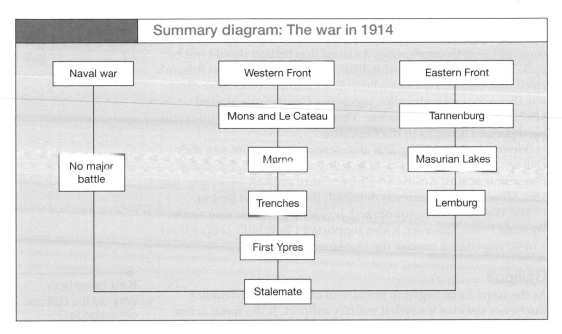

Summary diagram: The war in 1914

- Naval war
  - No major battle
- Western Front
  - Mons and Le Cateau
  - Marne
  - Trenches
  - First Ypres
  - Stalemate
- Eastern Front
  - Tannenburg
  - Masurian Lakes
  - Lemburg

## 4 | The War in 1915

With the failure of the Schlieffen Plan, the Germans had no option but to fight a war on two fronts. In 1915, the German general staff determined to hold ground in the west and concentrate its main efforts in the east. Given that the Germans remained in occupation of most of Belgium and large parts of northern France, France's strategic objective was self-evident: the liberation of its national territory. Kitchener was concerned. The German lines, he believed, had become a fortress 'which cannot be taken by assault'. But what should Britain do instead?

### The British army in 1915
- In January 1915, the BEF was 250,000 strong. It was still composed mainly of regular troops, a fifth of whom were from the Indian army.
- In March 1915, the first Territorial division reached the Western Front.
- Britons continued to volunteer in huge numbers. (The lowering of the height standard back to 5 feet 3 inches in November 1914 helped recruitment.)
- Munition shortage remained a serious problem.
- Kitchener's New Armies would not be ready for battle until late 1915 at the earliest.

### Easterners versus Westerners

Key question
Was the Gallipoli expedition a sensible idea?

In October 1914, the Ottoman Empire joined the Central Powers and declared war on Britain. The widening of the war presented Britain with new opportunities.

In a series of War Council meetings in January 1915, ministers debated British strategic options. 'Easterners', like Lloyd George, favoured pulling out from France and Belgium and launching called off, British troops had sustained some 13,000 casualties, double those of the enemy.

On 22 April, the new German commander, Falkenhayn, launched an offensive (the second Battle of Ypres) using chlorine gas for the first time. The British held firm but suffered 60,000 casualties, the Germans 35,000. While the use of gas as a killing agent was greeted by the British with indignation, they quickly followed suit. A British gas unit was created which soon developed the far more deadly phosgene.

In early May, British forces attacked at Aubers Ridge. The opening artillery bombardment left the enemy barbed wire uncut and British troops were mown down. The attack was aborted. This pattern was repeated at Festubert in mid-May. The British suffered 165,000 casualties for little purpose.

French cloaked his failure by complaining about a shell shortage. There was some truth in the claim. Despite Lloyd George's promptings, Kitchener had refused to extend the list of authorised firms and had deluged these firms with orders which they could not fulfil. Northcliffe (see page 107), the greatest of the press lords, resolved to launch an outcry against the 'shell scandal' which would drive Kitchener and possibly Asquith's government from office.

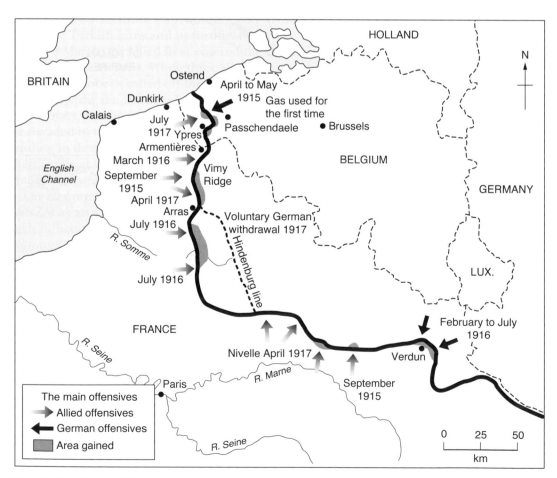

The Western Front 1915–17.

**Key question**
Why was a national government formed in 1915?

**Key date**

Formation of national government: May 1915

## National government

In May 1915, Asquith's government, blamed for Gallipoli and the shell shortage and embarrassed by Fisher's resignation (in protest at 'the further depletion of our Home resources for the Dardanelles'), faced a crisis. On 17 May, the Conservative leader, Bonar Law, met Lloyd George, who declared that 'the situation was altogether intolerable'. Agreeing on the necessity of coalition, they presented Asquith with what amounted to an ultimatum. Asquith fell in with their wishes. Thus, a national government came into being on 25 May, almost half the Liberal ministers stepping down to make way for Conservatives:

- Kitchener survived. Despite his many failings, he remained popular.
- Lloyd George became head of a newly created Ministry of Munitions.
- Churchill, blamed for Gallipoli, was replaced at the Admiralty by Balfour.
- Arthur Henderson joined the cabinet, nominally as President of the Board of Education, but in reality as the voice of Labour. Labour thus entered government for the first time.

**Key question**
Why was Lloyd George's work as Minister of Munitions so important?

## Lloyd George as Minister of Munitions

Lloyd George's appointment was crucial. It was from this point that the real transformation of industry began. New munitions factories multiplied, employing growing numbers of women and unskilled men. Thanks to Lloyd George's drive, shell deliveries rose from 5.3 million between July and December 1915 to 35.4 million in the second half of 1916. Machine gun output increased from 287 to 33,507 between 1914 and 1916. The manufacture of heavy artillery similarly soared. Lloyd George also deserves credit for overruling Kitchener on two important issues:

**Key term**

**Mortar**
A short-barrelled gun which lobs shells at the enemy.

- When the War Office rejected Wilfred Stokes' new light **mortar**, Lloyd George persuaded a wealthy Indian prince to finance its production. It proved to be a very effective weapon.
- While Kitchener was unimpressed with the tank, first demonstrated in 1916, Lloyd George supported its production.

## Gallipoli: the second landings

In mid-June, while accepting the primacy of the Western Front, the new cabinet resolved to mount a second landing at Gallipoli. Five raw divisions were sent to reinforce Hamilton. On 6–7 August, troops landed at Suvla Bay, taking the Turks by surprise. But the initial success was not exploited. General Stopford remained on board ship and slept throughout the afternoon. Most of his men bathed on the beach, instead of capturing the surrounding hills. This gave the Turks time to strengthen their defences and create a new trench line. The whole expedition should probably now have been abandoned but the government feared this would lead to the collapse of British prestige throughout the east.

In October, Hamilton was replaced by Sir Charles Monro, who immediately recommended Gallipoli's evacuation. Eventually, in

December, the government decided to abort a venture which had cost nearly 300,000 casualties: 43,000 ANZAC and British dead and 250,000 sick (mostly the result of dysentery) and wounded. The evacuation proved to be the most effective Gallipoli operation: all the beaches were evacuated by January 1916 without loss of life. Although the Gallipoli expedition was a serious blow to Allied morale, the fighting inflicted huge damage on the Turkish army from which it never fully recovered.

## Salonika

In August, Bulgaria entered the war on the side of the Central Powers. This deepened Serbia's plight. Greece, seemingly about to join the Allies, asked Britain and France to send troops to the Balkans. But by the time the force arrived, the pro-Allied Greek government had been overthrown by the pro-German King Constantine. Nevertheless, Allied troops landed at Salonika. The landings came too late to save Serbia. Nevertheless, the 600,000-strong Anglo-French army remained in the malaria-ridden swamps of Macedonia, failing to break through the mountainous terrain. Salonika became, in effect, a huge Allied prisoner-of-war camp until 1918.

## The Western Front: September–October 1915

By August 1915, there were 28 British divisions on the Western Front – some 900,000 men. The few survivors from 1914 had been supplemented by the arrival of Territorial units, troops from the dominions and the first of Kitchener's New Armies. Given the inexperience of most of the men, the British government would have preferred to remain on the defensive until the full force of the New Armies could take the field in 1916. But Kitchener and the French were keen to launch an offensive to help Russia. Consequently, British troops, led by Haig (see page 159), attacked at Loos (25 September). Thousands of men were mown down by enemy machine guns. Units that managed to break through into enemy trenches failed to make further advances, partly because French mishandled the disposition of his tactical reserves. The operation spluttered on until mid-October, by which time the Germans had clawed back most of the territory they had earlier lost. Britain suffered 50,000 casualties, the Germans 20,000.

## The naval war

In February 1915, the Germans announced the start of unrestricted submarine warfare, whereby any ship in British waters was liable to be torpedoed. Given that merchant seamen were conventionally thought of as non-combatants, Britain denounced the practice as barbarous. Fortunately for Britain, Germany's 37 U-boats were not sufficient to starve the country into surrender. Moreover, the U-boat campaign had serious consequences for Germany. Inevitably, it resulted in the sinking of neutral ships and the loss of innocent lives. The USA – Britain's greatest trading partner– protested. In May, the liner *Lusitania* was sunk by a U-boat, resulting in the loss of over 1000 lives, including 128 Americans.

Sinking of the
*Lusitania*: May 1915

Key date

This led US President Woodrow Wilson to issue an ultimatum to Germany. Rather than risk war with the USA, Germany agreed to abandon unrestricted submarine warfare around Britain. While Britain had won the first round of the submarine war, the Royal Navy had no real answer to the U-boat threat. Moreover, Germany continued building U-boats with the aim of conducting a more concerted campaign in the future.

### Air war

**Zeppelin**
A type of large airship, designed by Ferdinand von Zeppelin.

A new kind of 'barbarous' war was unleashed on Britain over the winter of 1914–15: **zeppelin** bombing raids. When zeppelins proved vulnerable to ground fire, aeroplanes were used instead (from 1917). The effects were trivial by Second World War standards: 1117 British civilians and 296 combatants lost their lives as a result of aerial bombing in the entire war. But the raids caused much dislocation. Lighting restrictions were imposed and factories stopped work when a single raider was sighted.

### Sir William Robertson

In November 1915, Sir William Robertson, a dour Yorkshireman and an avowed 'westerner' (see page 150), became Chief of the Imperial General Staff (CIGS). Henceforth the CIGS alone, not the War Secretary, would determine strategy, advise the government and issue orders to commanders in the field. Kitchener's functions, in his own words, were 'curtailed to the feeding and clothing of the army'. Largely disregarded by his colleagues, he remained only as a patriotic symbol: 'the great poster', as Margot Asquith said.

### Haig replaces French

**Key question**
How good a commander was Haig?

In the wake of Loos, recriminations broke out between French and Haig about the responsibility for the misuse of the reserves. Haig, highly regarded by the royal family, told the king on his visit to the Front in October that French was 'a source of great weakness to the army, and no one had confidence in him any more'. In December 1915, French was prevailed upon to resign and Haig took his place. Strategy thus passed into the hands of the Robertson–Haig partnership, where it remained for the next two years.

Haig remains a controversial character (see page 159). His critics claim he was a typical product of the pre-war army, a cavalryman, a stickler for military etiquette, and lacking in imagination. However, Haig had advanced in the army by virtue of hard work and by taking his profession seriously. He was a stabler character than French: resolute in command, certain of ultimate victory and unruffled by defeat. He thought that his role was to set strategy and then let his army and corps commanders get on with the job with minimal interference. Given the nature of his command, it was inevitable that his GHQ was located many miles behind the front, distancing him from battlefield events physically and mentally. Stern and unapproachable, few people (let alone his staff or army commanders) dared to confront or even approach him for open discussion on critical matters.

## Summary diagram: The war in 1915

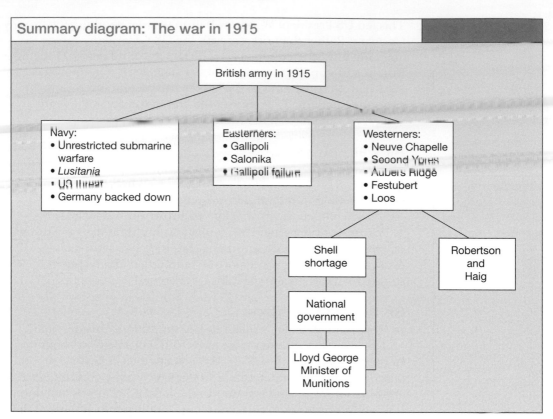

## 5 | The War in 1916

In early 1916, Kitchener's New Armies poured into France. By June 1916, there were 57 British divisions on the Western Front (compared with 95 French and 117 German divisions). Britain now had a continental-sized army on the continent. It was needed because in 1916 the German high command refocused its attention on the west.

## Recruitment problems

In mid-1915, depite an intensive government recruiting campaign, the number of men enlisting in the army began to decline. A national register, taken in August, revealed that five million men of military age were still not in the forces. Conservatives began to demand conscription, insisting that all citizens had a duty to serve the nation in its hour of peril. Lloyd George thought the same. But Asquith held back:

**Key question**
Why was conscription introduced?

- The Labour movement opposed conscription. Its introduction might imperil the industrial truce (see page 205) essential to Britain's war effort.
- Many Liberals opposed conscription on the ground that it would undermine traditional British liberties. Some, like Reginald McKenna at the Treasury and Walter Runciman, President of the Board of Trade, were not convinced that Britain needed a 70-division army and feared that conscription would harm the country's manufacturing ability.

In September, Asquith placed Lord Derby in charge of a scheme whereby men (aged 18–41) not yet in the armed forces were invited to 'attest' their willingness to serve if called on to do so, on the understanding that bachelors would be co-opted before married men. Liberal and Labour MPs hoped that this would avoid the need for conscription, Conservatives hoped that it was the preliminary to it. This initiative, apart from stimulating a rash of weddings, was disappointing. When the returns from the Derby scheme were analysed in December it was found that only about half the available single men and 40 per cent of married men had been prepared to attest. This situation helped to remove the final objections to conscription.

## Conscription

On 29 December, faced with the threat of Lloyd George's resignation if compulsory recruitment was not adopted, Asquith persuaded the cabinet to accept conscription for unmarried men and widowers aged 18–41. A Military Service Bill followed. The measure exempted the unfit, conscientious objectors, sole supporters of dependants and men engaged on essential war work. The Commons voted through the bill by 403 votes to 105, the minority consisting of 60 Irish Nationalists, 11 Labour and 34 Liberal MPs. The Military Service Act became law in January 1916.

Following the call-up in March 1916 of married men who had attested under the Derby scheme, pressure grew for equality of sacrifice. Thus, in May a second Military Service Act extended liability for military service to all men, single or married, aged 18–41. Voluntary recruiting was retained in Ireland, since it would have been hazardous to impose compulsion there in the wake of the Easter Rising (see page 197).

Compulsory service did not achieve its purpose of providing more men for the army. Instead of unearthing 650,000 'slackers', conscription produced 748,587 new claims to exemption, most of them valid, on top of 1.5 million already granted immunity by the Ministry of Munitions. In the first six months of conscription, the average monthly enlistment was not much above 40,000 – less than the rate under the voluntary system. The competing needs of the military and of war industries remained a contentious issue until November 1918.

## The need for British action

**Key question**
Why did Britain attack on the Somme?

**Key date**
Battle of Verdun: February–August 1916

It was apparent that Britain's New Armies would have to shoulder a major role:

- Russia had suffered huge losses of life and territory in 1915.
- In February 1916, Germany launched a massive assault on Verdun, a symbolically important French fortress. Gambling on French determination to defend the place, Falkenhayn planned to bleed the French army 'white'. French troops clung on to Verdun, just as Falkenhayn had hoped. However, as more German troops were sucked into the fighting, they too suffered heavy casualties. It thus became important for the Germans to capture Verdun to justify the sacrifice of so many men.

In an effort to take pressure off the beleaguered French, Haig was authorised to concert an offensive with Joffre. While Haig would have preferred an attack in Flanders, he and Robertson accepted Joffre's plan for a combined Anglo-French operation on the River Somme. Robertson believed that an offensive would lead to a drain of manpower, favourable to the Allied cause. Haig thought there was a real chance of achieving a decisive breakthrough. He believed that previous attacks had failed from lack of weight. Following a hurricane artillery bombardment, he envisaged his infantry clearing up the wreckage and his cavalry charging into open country. (Hundreds of thousands of horses were kept in France throughout the war for this opportunity.)

Battle of the Somme: July–November 1916

Key date

**Helmet**: the steel helmet was introduced in 1915. It was soon apparent that sunlight glistening off the helmet aided German marksmen. Thus most soldiers created makeshift covers from hessian sacking.

**Bayonet**: a 17 in. sword blade

**Rifle**: the mark III Short Magazine Lee Enfield Rifle, introduced in 1903, had a magazine of 10 rounds. Its bullet could penetrate 18 in. of oak at 200 yards.

**Uniform**: khaki green tunic, worn over long johns, vest and heavy flannel shirt. The woollen uniform soaked up the damp.

**Equipment**: soldiers carried two ammunition packets (each holding 75 rounds), an entrenching tool, a water bottle, a small haversack, a large pack and a mess tin. Inside the pack and haversack, men carried great coat, cutlery, sewing kit, washing and shaving equipment, and food rations.

**Gas mask**: the Small Box Respirator (1916), held in a canvas bag strapped to the chest, was the best gas mask of the war. Its filter box, made of charcoal, gauze and neutralising chemicals, was attached to the rubberised canvas mask by a flexible tube.

**Boots**: black leather boots with hard hob-nailed soles and steel toecaps. Woollen puttees were worn above the boot.

A British soldier, France 1916.

## Profile: Douglas Haig 1861–1928

| | |
|---|---|
| 1861 | – Born in Edinburgh: his father was head of the family's whisky distillery |
| 1880–3 | – Attended Oxford University |
| 1883–4 | – Attended the Royal Military College at Sandhurst |
| 1885 | – Commissioned into the 7th Hussars |
| 1898 | – Saw active service in Kitchener's Omdurman campaign |
| 1899 | – Served in the Boer War; mentioned in despatches four times |
| 1906 | – Appointed Director of Military Training |
| 1909 | – Appointed Chief of the Indian General Staff |
| 1914 | – Became Commander of I Corps of the BEF |
| 1915 | – Replaced French as Commander-in-Chief of the BEF |
| 1916 | – Directed the Battle of the Somme |
| 1917 | – Became Field Marshal; directed the Passchendaele campaign |
| 1918 | – Led the Hundred Days Offensive |
| 1921 | – Helped to create and presided over the Royal British Legion |
| 1928 | – Died: his funeral was a huge state occasion |

Many, at the time and since, have criticised Haig's leadership. Lloyd George never rated him. (He is said to have described him as 'brilliant – to the top of his boots'.) Churchill accused Haig of blocking enemy machine gun fire with 'the breasts of brave men'. More recently Haig's critics have included Gerard De Groot, Paul Fussell and Alan Clark (whose book *The Donkeys* led to the popularisation of the phrase 'lions led by donkeys' used to describe British generalship). Haig is blamed for being unimaginative, for his rigid command style, and for being self-obsessed, petty-minded, devious and disloyal. Today he is often portrayed in popular media as an inept commander who exhibited callous disregard for his men's lives.

However, Haig had and has his defenders. He was praised by US General Pershing as 'the man who won the war'. Military historian John Terraine portrayed him as one of Britain's greatest ever commanders, claiming that he pursued the only possible strategy given the military situation in 1916–18. His attrition tactics wore down the German army and finally delivered the knock-out blow in 1918. Gary Sheffield has called the Hundred Days Offensive (see page 177) 'by far the greatest military victory in British history'. Popular opinion has still failed to grasp that under Haig the BEF adopted a style of war in 1918 that was very different from 1916–17.

## The artillery bombardment

The Somme battle commenced in late June with a week-long bombardment. Some 2200 British guns fired 1.7 million shells. Unfortunately, the artillery did not have the expertise, enough heavy guns or the right type of shells to do the job it had been given.

The bombardment failed to cut German barbed wire, left deep dug outs largely untouched and failed to destroy enough enemy guns. Many shells detonated in no man's land, making the ground even more difficult to cross. Up to a third of shells, hastily produced by the Ministry of Munitions, did not explode at all.

## The first day of the Somme

The 1st of July began with an Allied artillery barrage of 600,000 shells, fired by 1500 guns. Then, at 7.30a.m., 14 British and three French divisions advanced. General Rawlinson, who led the 4th Army which undertook the offensive, allowed his divisional commanders freedom to decide how they would cross no-man's land. Most accepted his suggestion that the men attack in slow, methodical waves, walking at intervals of two or three paces. (Rawlinson believed that if men were close together this would give them added confidence.)

The troops were loaded with shovels, sandbags, **Mills bombs** and 200 rounds of ammunition in anticipation of the consolidation and German counterattack phase of the operation. This proved to be wildly optimistic. The artillery barrage was too far ahead of the advancing troops, lifting over the front-line enemy trenches some minutes before the British infantry could reach them. The race for the parapets was thus won by the Germans, leaving them able to man their machine guns. The result was that British troops advanced into a hail of fire. Half of the first wave of attackers became casualties within 30 minutes. During the course of the day Britain suffered 57,470 casualties including 19,000 deaths, the greatest loss in one day in the British army's history. German losses were about a tenth of this.

**Mills bomb**
A type of hand grenade.

Key term

## The Somme continues

Piecemeal attacks on the Somme followed throughout the summer and as the Germans counterattacked, the body count no longer told so heavily in their favour. In September, the British used 36 tanks for the first time in the war. (Virtually all of them broke down.)

Haig continued to pound away, to little purpose, until 19 November when the Somme offensive was finally called off. It seems likely that Britain incurred 420,000 casualties, France 194,000 and the Germans 465,000. After more than four months of fighting, the Allies had advanced no further than seven miles.

**Key question**
What, if anything, did the Somme achieve?

What had the Somme offensive achieved?

- It had some attritional effect. The Germans, with fewer men, could less afford the losses their forces sustained.
- It may have helped to relieve pressure on Verdun.
- It did not relieve the pressure on Russia (whatever Haig boasted).

**Key question**
Why did warfare (1914–18) favour the defender?

## Blame?

It is all too easy to blame Haig for the débâcle on the Somme. But the critics, then and later, were unwilling to recognise the dilemma he faced. Doing nothing was not an option, not least because it would have sown doubts in French minds about the seriousness of Britain's commitment.

Lloyd George observed that the French thought 'that they are making all the sacrifices and we are endeavouring to preserve our trade and carry on as usual'. Haig had to attack. And the technology of war continued to operate against attacking forces. Machine guns, positioned in trenches protected by barbed wire, gave defenders a massive advantage. Heavy artillery bombardment was needed if the attackers were to have any chance of a breakthrough – but such a bombardment warned the enemy of a coming attack. Nor had any army yet found a foolproof way of co-ordinating artillery and infantry. If the infantry, under cover of an artillery barrage, made initial progress, this merely took it beyond the support of its own gunners, who feared to go on firing since they might hit their own troops. Moreover, if attackers broke through the first defence line, there was a second line. If they broke through the second line, defending generals could move in reserves and plug gaps more quickly than the attacking side could advance.

There were also problems of battlefield command. If troops advanced in close order they were mown down. If they advanced in open order, officers lost control of them. As historian John Keegan recognised: 'communications consistently lagged behind weaponry'. According to Keegan, 'Generals were like men without eyes, without ears and without voices, unable to watch the operations they set in progress, unable to hear reports of their development and unable to speak to those whom they had originally given orders once action was joined'.

**Key question**
To what extent was Haig responsible for the Somme failure?

## Lloyd George's influence

In June, Kitchener drowned when the *HMS Hampshire*, on which he was on his way to Russia, hit a mine. Northcliffe believed his death a godsend. But by 1916 Kitchener's powers were limited, first by the encroachments of Lloyd George and then by those of Robertson. In July, Lloyd George became War Secretary. He had little power over events on the Somme. He grumbled that he was merely a butcher boy, rounding up men for the abbatoir. The Somme destroyed his confidence in the military high command. In September, he visited the front and expressed views critical of

GHQ. Haig, belying his pose as a bluff, apolitical soldier, was adept at keeping in touch with sympathetic pressmen (like Northcliffe) and prompted them to warn against government interference in military matters.

## The Eastern Front

In June, the Russian commander, Brusilov, launched an offensive against Austria-Hungary. His forces went forward in strength at several points, making it hard for the enemy to shift resources. Over one-third of the Austrian army was captured or killed. Romania now joined the war on the Allied side, hoping to gain Transylvania. But German forces hit back, halting the Brusilov offensive and defeating Romania's forces. The fall of Bucharest in December marked the end of Romania's war effort.

## Mesopotamia

In Mesopotamia, British military leaders repeated the mistakes of Gallipoli, underestimating the Turks and setting objectives beyond the capacity of the army. General Townshend's army, advancing on Baghdad, was not strong enough to break through Turkish defences and was besieged in Kut. A relief force lost 23,000 men in an effort to save the 12,500 men in Kut. In April 1916, Townshend was forced to surrender.

## The naval situation

Germany had difficulty in using its High Seas Fleet on which it had lavished so much money. In material terms, Britain retained the whip-hand. In April 1916, the ratio stood at 31:18 in modern battleships, 10:5 in battlecruisers. Once it entered the North Sea, the German High Seas Fleet came under the surveillance of the Royal Navy at Rosyth and Scapa Flow. Unbeknown to the Germans, Britain had the additional advantage of having captured the German naval code books. Intercepted German radio signals were decoded and analysed in a newly created department within the Admiralty Old Building, Room 40.

**Key question**
Was Jutland a British victory or a British defeat?

**Key date**
Battle of Jutland: May 1916

## The Battle of Jutland

Soon after midnight on 31 May, the High Seas Fleet left port. Commanded by Admiral Scheer, it hoped to lure a detachment of the Grand Fleet into battle. Given that Room 40 had radio intelligence of Scheer's plans, Britain had it within its power to catch the Germans in their own trap. Jellicoe left Scapa Flow with the Grand Fleet while Beatty's 5th Battle Squadron sailed from the Forth. The German fleet seemed to be steaming towards annihilation. But a breakdown of communications at the Admiralty, where staff officers mistrusted the intelligence from Room 40, let Scheer off the hook. Thinking that the High Seas Fleet was still in harbour, Jellicoe sailed south slowly to conserve fuel. Consequently, his ships were too far from the enemy at the very moment when Beatty's force was perilously close.

Early in the afternoon Beatty spotted enemy battlecruisers. A running engagement followed, the German commander luring

Beatty towards the main High Seas Fleet. Beatty followed, his squadron soon coming under heavy fire. Two British battlecruisers were blown up. The appearance of the main body of the German fleet forced Beatty to flee northwards towards Jellicoe's ships. Soon after 6.00p.m. there took place the only battle between two great modern fleets ever fought in European waters: 250 ships were present and 100,000 men. Jellicoe commanded 28 battleships, nine battlecruisers, 34 cruisers and 80 destroyers; Scheer 16 battleships, six pre-Dreadnoughts, five battlecruisers, 11 cruisers and 63 destroyers. Realising the danger, Scheer turned away. Jellicoe, fearing mines and U-boats, and aware that the cost of a British naval defeat far exceeded the benefits that would follow a crushing victory, did not pursue. Scheer thus escaped back to port. The Battle of Jutland lasted less than an hour. The Royal Navy lost three battlecruisers, four armoured cruisers and eight destroyers with 6000 dead. The Germans lost one battleship, one battlecruiser, four light cruisers and five destroyers with 2500 dead. It seemed that the High Seas Fleet had won a victory.

But appearances were deceptive. The High Seas Fleet had fled. It only left harbour again three times in the course of war and then to no purpose. Scheer's 'outing' has been described by Keegan as 'an assault on the gaoler, followed by a return to gaol'. But if Jutland

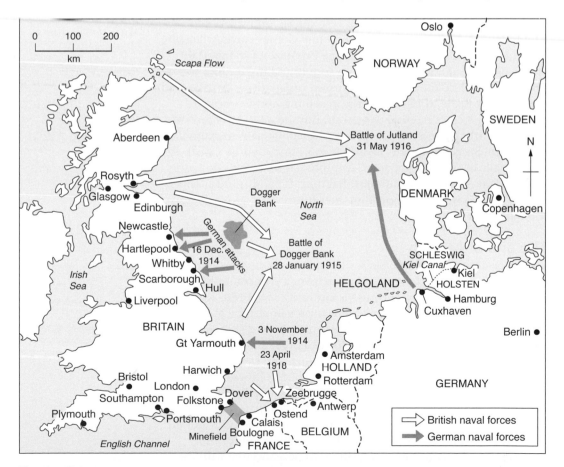

The war at sea.

was a British victory, it was also a disappointment to most Britons. Confidence in the Admiralty declined. In November, First Sea Lord Admiral Jackson was replaced by Jellicoe. Beatty replaced Jellicoe as commander of the Grand Fleet. He pursued a similar cautious strategy.

## The 1916 December crisis

By late 1916, Britons were losing confidence in Asquith. Everywhere the war seemed to be going badly. Within the government there was growing pessimism. There were tensions among leading Liberals. While Lloyd George and Edwin Montagu, Minister of Munitions, favoured the adoption of industrial conscription, Runciman and McKenna opposed further extension of state controls. Conservative MPs, critical not just of Asquith but also of Bonar Law, demanded a more energetic conduct of the war. On 25 November, Bonar Law met Lloyd George and **Sir Edward Carson**, who chaired the influential Unionist War Committee. They agreed on a scheme for streamlining the machinery of government by creating a small inner war council, under Lloyd George's chairmanship, which would run the war. Asquith turned down this proposal, insisting that he himself must preside over the council and that it must be subordinate to the cabinet.

On 2 December, Lloyd George sent Bonar Law a letter saying 'the life of the country depends on resolute action by you now'. The following day Bonar Law and his chief Conservative colleagues, the 'three Cs' – Lord Curzon (see page 7), **Austen Chamberlain** and **Robert Cecil** – signed a letter to Asquith calling on him to resign. Meanwhile they offered their own resignations. An alarmed Asquith now wrote to Lloyd George accepting his war council proposal. The crisis seemed to be over. But the next day *The Times* carried an article, describing the war council in terms disparaging to Asquith. Suspecting that the article was Lloyd George's work (it was actually inspired by Carson), Asquith determined to do battle with his War Secretary. Confident that most Liberals (and many Conservatives) would support him, he withdrew his agreement to the war council.

## The end of Asquith

On 5 December, Lloyd George resigned. Asquith also resigned, defying Bonar Law or Lloyd George to form a government. This manoeuvre, aimed at reasserting his authority, backfired. King George V initially asked Bonar Law to form a ministry. He would only do so if Asquith agreed to join. Asquith refused. Bonar Law then advised the king to send for Lloyd George. On 7 December, assured of Conservative and Labour support, and (according to his ally Christopher Addison) the support of 136 Liberal MPs (the reality was more like 40–50), Lloyd George became Prime Minister. Leading Conservatives agreed to join his government. Lord Derby was appointed War Secretary. All the prominent Liberals followed Asquith's lead and stayed out. Only Liberal politicians of the second rank, like Addison, were willing to be associated with the new government.

**Key question**
Why did Lloyd George replace Asquith as Prime Minister?

**Key figures**

**Sir Edward Carson**
The leader of the Ulster Unionists.

**Austen Chamberlain**
Son of Joseph Chamberlain and brother of future Prime Minister Neville Chamberlain.

**Robert Cecil**
Son of Lord Salisbury, he was a leading figure in the Conservative Party.

**Key question**
What were Lloyd George's main qualities?

**Key date**

Lloyd George became Prime Minister: December 1916

**Key term**

Privy council
A committee of advisers to the monarch, comprising past and present members of the cabinet and other eminent people.

## Lloyd George

Lloyd George's accession to power was more than a change of government. It was, in A.J.P. Taylor's view, 'a revolution, British-style'. Newspaper proprietors and backbench MPs (defying party leaders and whips) had combined to ensure that Lloyd George became Prime Minister, the first man of humble origin to reach that position. Thereafter, in Taylor's view, he was the nearest thing Britain has known to a Napoleon, a supreme ruler maintaining himself by individual achievement. Almeric Fitzroy, clerk to the privy council, wrote in 1918, 'The effects of the change in direction two years ago may be compared to the substitution of dynamite for a damp squib'.

Lloyd George's advent to power – with new departments of state, new men, new methods of control, and a new form of cabinet government – gave a boost to morale. Nevertheless, his position was not strong. He did not lead a party. Many Liberals, socialists and Irish Nationalists regarded the new ministry with suspicion, while many Conservatives mistrusted Lloyd George. The forces that had carried him to power might just as easily turn against him.

### Lloyd George's war cabinet

Lloyd George ran the war through a new war cabinet. Initially it had only five members (later six and for a few months seven) chosen, in theory, for their ability, not because of the offices they held or to satisfy the balance of the parties. Only the Chancellor of the Exchequer, Bonar Law, had departmental duties. Henderson spoke for Labour. Curzon and Milner – experienced bureaucrats – were popular with Conservatives, the army and Northcliffe. Where the old cabinet rarely met more than once a week and kept no record of its proceedings, the war cabinet met practically every day (300 times in 1917) and Sir Maurice Hankey organised an efficient secretariat, preparing agenda, keeping minutes and ensuring that particular departments carried out decisions made, thus ending some of the muddles that characterised Asquith's regime.

Fearing the collapse of national morale, Lloyd George was anxious to reduce the loss of life of soldiers who he thought Haig and Robertson were squandering. He hoped that the war cabinet's creation would help him to establish mastery over the service departments. This did not happen. The service ministers, no longer in the war cabinet, became more independent than before. Carson, at the Admiralty, fiercely championed his professional advisers, while Lord Derby supported Robertson. The latter, who regarded the war cabinet as 'the enemy' and Lloyd George as 'a real bad 'un', provided the government with little military information.

## Summary diagram: The war in 1916

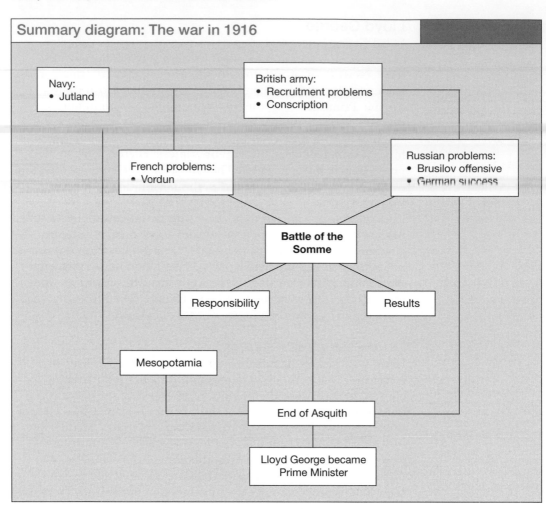

## 6 | The War in 1917

Arguably the best way to prevent more slaughter would have been to accept President Wilson's attempt at mediation, launched in December 1916. But Lloyd George's administration had been formed with a view to winning the war, not negotiating peace. Ministers, therefore, were relieved when Germany refused to agree even to consider Belgian independence, thereby sabotaging any chance of peace. In Germany, Generals Hindenburg and Ludendorff replaced Falkenhayn. They became effectively (if not particularly effective) military dictators. Hoping for success in the east, they planned to remain on the defensive on the Western Front in 1917.

### The U-boat threat

On 1 February 1917, Germany renewed unrestricted submarine warfare. Aware that this might well bring the USA into the war, German leaders gambled that U-boats would starve Britain into surrender before significant US military aid could reach Europe. The hope was realistic. Germany now had over 100 U-boats. In

Germany renewed unrestricted submarine warfare: February 1917

Key date

April they sank over a quarter of all ships leaving British ports. British wheat stocks dwindled to six weeks' supply.

## The USA enters the war

**Key question**
Why was the USA's entry into the war so important?

**Key date**
USA entered the war: April 1917

The reintroduction of unrestricted submarine warfare led to Wilson severing diplomatic links with Germany. Some American politicians and newspapers urged a declaration of war. Wilson hesitated. While his sympathies had always been with the Allies, he was still anxious to avoid war. However, in March, a telegram from German Foreign Secretary, Zimmermann, to the German minister in Mexico promising that Mexico would receive Texas, New Mexico and Arizona if it declared war on the USA, was intercepted by British intelligence, passed on to Wilson and published in the USA. The Zimmerman telegram caused a wave of anti-German sentiment in the USA. The March Revolution in Russia (see below) removed a further obstacle to US entry into the war, a war which now did seem like a struggle between autocracy and democracy. Late in March, three American ships were torpedoed. On 6 April, the USA declared war on Germany. The USA entered the war as an 'associated power', not as an ally of Britain and France. This reflected Wilson's determination to distance the USA from the ambitions of the European powers. In Wilson's view the war was a crusade for democracy and freedom, not a sordid struggle for land and colonies.

American entry into the war gave the Allies a tremendous boost. However, it would take many months before the USA was able to mobilise its forces. In the meantime, Britain had to deal with the U-boat threat.

## The convoy system

**Key question**
Why was the convoy system successful?

Britain laid mines to try and keep U-boats in their bases but struggled to find a more effective measure of defence. While some experts suggested introducing the convoy system (which was already operating successfully on selected routes, for example, troopships to France), the Admiralty was sceptical, arguing that:

- merchant captains could not keep station
- convoys would offer a larger target to U-boats
- 2500 ships entered and left British ports each week – too many to convoy.

In late April, Lloyd George went in person to the Admiralty, forcing it to produce a convoy scheme. It was one of his most decisive achievements. By December 1917, over half of Britain's overseas trade was being conducted under convoy, at a loss rate of under one per cent. The official naval history stated: 'the chief objections against the system before it was tried had one and all proved to be unfounded'. Destroyers and new classes of patrol craft, as well as airships and seaplane patrols, which sometimes accompanied convoys, managed to contain the U-boat menace. Success against the U-boat engendered a new mood of confidence at the Admiralty. This received a further boost, first in July 1917 when Eric Geddes replaced Carson as First Lord, and then in December when Geddes sacked Jellicoe, replacing him with Admiral Wemyss. Wemyss commanded a huge force: 420,301 men in late 1917.

## The British army in 1917

- Conscripted men were recruited for general service and posted to units as required, not raised as a body of distinct formations. This tended to remove or blur many of the differences between the regular, Territorial and New Armies As the highly localised character of the pals regiments evaporated, the army increasingly became a 'nationalised' force.
- By 1917, the engineers, tank corps and flying corps were growing in importance.
- Given the growth of the army and the heavy casualties, there was a need for more officers. (In total, 229,000 had been commissioned by 1918.) While many 'temporary gentlemen' were ex-public schoolboys, there was a noticeable increase in lower middle-class officers by 1917. The change in social tone was particularly marked in the army's technological branches, for example, the tank corps.

**Key question**
How was the British army in 1917 different from that in 1914?

## Gambling on Nivelle

Lloyd George thought that victory was most likely to be achieved if the Allies acted as one. In January 1917, he attended the first general conference of the Allies in Rome. He wanted a combined offensive on the Italian front (Italy had joined the war on the Allied side in 1915) but Italy refused the doubtful honour. The best hope thus seemed to lie with French General Nivelle, who had replaced Joffre as generalissimo. Nivelle claimed he knew how to win the war with fewer casualties. Oddly, Lloyd George had faith in the French general (while having none in his own). In February, to Haig's and Robertson's horror, he placed Nivelle in supreme command over British forces for the coming offensive. That offensive, if it was to have any chance of success, depended on swift action. Instead, there were delays. The Germans forestalled the attack by withdrawing to the **Hindenburg line**.

**Hindenburg line**
A fortified German defence system, prepared over the winter of 1916–17.

**Combined arms tactics**
Fighting the enemy by blending together the different branches of the army (for example, artillery, infantry and tanks).

Key terms

## The Battle of Arras

A preliminary and diversionary offensive, the Battle of Arras (9–14 April), started well with British forces advancing three and a half miles on the first day and Canadian forces capturing Vimy Ridge. Allied troops approached the narrow front through tunnels and an element of surprise was achieved by shortening the length of the opening bombardment. The artillery now had the equipment and the expertise to fight the sort of battle to which it had aspired on the Somme. The battle was fought as series of limited attacks, leap-frogging each other, with pauses to consolidate. Arras showed that **combined arms tactics** and careful preparation could break the enemy line. But the great problem remained unsolved. Cavalry were unable to cross broken ground while infantry could not easily advance beyond the range of artillery support. New defensive positions were improvised more quickly than attackers could plod forward. Nevertheless, the Arras

**Key question**
What lessons had British commanders learned by 1917?

attack achieved its purpose. The Germans doubled their strength in the sector, diverting men from the River Aisne where Nivelle intended to attack.

## Nivelle's failure

Nivelle's offensive, delayed until mid-April, was a disaster. It cost 29,000 French dead for no gain. After the attack, a large part of the French army mutinied. The Germans, largely unaware of what was happening, failed to exploit the situation and order was restored by Pétain, the hero of Verdun. He promised no more bloody offensives. Nivelle's failure vindicated Haig and Robertson in their opposition to Lloyd George's project of a supreme command. Moreover, by supporting Nivelle, the Prime Minister had undermined his authority with regard to strategic matters.

Haig renewed the Arras offensive on 23 April but failed to break the German lines. When the fighting ended in June the enemy had incurred over 100,000 casualties but the British had suffered 150,000.

## The imperial contribution

In March 1917, the prime ministers of the dominions gathered for a meeting of the Imperial War Cabinet in London. Botha of South Africa was represented by Smuts, his Minister of Defence. Lloyd George hoped that the Imperial War Cabinet would be an **executive** for the Empire. The dominion prime ministers, however, insisted that they were responsible to their own governments. The Empire thus remained an association of sovereign states while the Imperial War Cabinet was essentially a diplomatic conference of friends. Smuts was persuaded to remain as a member of the British war cabinet, one of the few cabinet ministers of modern times to have no connection with either house of parliament.

**Key term**

**Executive**
The body with the power and authority to devise policy and put laws into effect.

## The war against the Turks

After the humiliation at Kut (see page 162), Britain strengthened its army in Mesopotamia. With increased artillery, new leadership and improved transport systems, a British expedition took Kut and then Baghdad.

In 1916, Sir Archibald Murray captured the Sinai. In March 1917, British forces captured Gaza but then withdrew after an order was mistakenly interpreted. When Murray tried to repeat the attack, he was repulsed. Murray was replaced by General Allenby. Heavily reinforced, Allenby captured Beersheba, Gaza and then (in December) Jerusalem.

In the Hejaz desert, Lieutenant Colonel T.E. Lawrence became a national hero, fomenting an Arab revolt against Turkish rule and capturing Aqaba in July 1917. Other exploits by Lawrence of Arabia (as he became known) followed but his military role, while important, was not critical to the Middle East campaign.

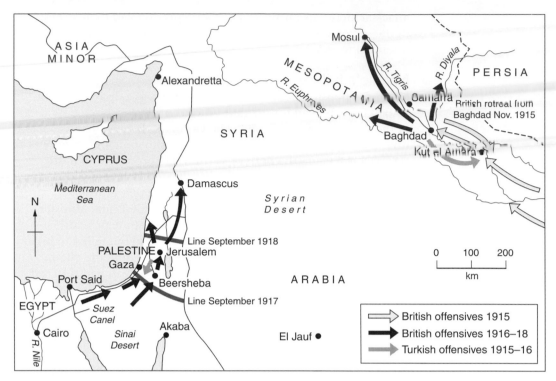

The war against Turkey.

## Haig's 'show'

By mid-1917, the BEF had replaced the French army as the main force on the Western Front. Haig, confident that 'the German was now nearly at his last resources', was eager to take up an idea which he had long cherished: a great offensive in Flanders. Here, he believed, he could win the war. British forces would break out of the Ypres salient, reach the Belgium coast and roll up the entire German front. By June, an almost unstoppable momentum had built up behind Haig's project. Even the Admiralty supported a Flanders offensive, hoping that it would result in the capture of U-boat bases in Belgium. Robertson was also supportive. While doubting whether Haig's 'show' would result in a major breakthrough, he thought:

- There was a military advantage to be gained if the Germans could be driven from the heights overlooking the Ypres salient.
- This was terrain which Germany dare not abandon for fear of losing control of the vital railway link between Menin and Ostende.
- The fact that the Germans were likely to stand and fight was a powerful recommendation to Robertson, who favoured an attritional strategy.

### Lloyd George's position

Lloyd George, fearing another bloodbath, remained sceptical. He preferred prioritising Italy and waiting for the Americans. Moreover, he had little confidence in Haig's capacity. However:

- British success at Messines Ridge (7 June), following the detonation of a million pounds of high explosives under German trenches, was a cause for confidence.
- The situation in Russia was dire (see below).
- Fearing that a pro-peace government might come to power in France, Lloyd George accepted that British action somewhere was essential.

The new War Policy Committee (essentially the war cabinet, minus Henderson and with the addition of Smuts) examined Haig between 10 and 21 June. He radiated confidence. Despite Lloyd George's hesitancy, the committee gave the go-ahead for Haig's Flanders offensive, agreeing with Robertson that the aim should be not the breaking of the German line, but 'wearing down and exhausting the enemy's resistance'.

## Passchendaele

On 31 July, Haig launched the third Battle of Ypres, popularly known as Passchendaele. The battle began with a massive artillery barrage: 2299 guns, one to every five yards, employing four times as many shells as were fired off before the Somme. British batteries eliminated around half of the German guns. But the fortnight-long bombardment cratered the ground and destroyed the Flanders' drainage system, turning the countryside into a quagmire. The attack which followed the bombardment was geared to a **creeping barrage**. Unfortunately, the Germans were ready. They had built concrete pillboxes and bunkers. They had also divided their troops into two separate formations: a trench garrison and counterattack troops in the rearward battle zone. This new defence-in-depth scheme halted the attack on the right, limited it in the centre, and prevented a gain of more than two miles on the left. Tactically, the British attack showed more imagination than that on the Somme. Initial losses were thus smaller: 35,000 casualties before 3 August. Then it rained for a fortnight. After a series of costly pushes later in August, Haig turned over the offensive from General Gough to General Plumer.

Haig persevered through a dry September and a wet October, perhaps misled by John Charteris, his Intelligence Chief, who insisted that the Germans were 'used up'. A series of battles – Menin Road Ridge (20–7 September), Polgon Wood (26 September to 3 October), Broodseinde (4 October) – was costly in British lives. Haig justified the continuation of fighting by invoking the French mutinies, the situation in Russia and the setbacks in Italy. Lloyd George was appalled by events: 'Haig does not care how many men he loses', the Prime Minister said in private. 'He just squanders the lives of these boys'. Lloyd George contemplated making a personal intervention to stop the carnage but was persuaded by Milner not to do so on the grounds that Haig would have the support of the Conservatives and the press.

The Canadian capture of the village of Passchendaele on 6 November marked the effective end of the campaign. Haig's forces had advanced no more than 10,000 yards, failing to reach all

**Key question**
Was Haig unlucky at Third Ypres?

**Key date**
Third Battle of Ypres: July–November 1917

**Key term**
**Creeping barrage**
An artillery bombardment where the shells are meant to keep falling just ahead of the attacking troops.

The battle of the mud. A stretcher party carrying a wounded soldier duirng the battle at Passchendaele in 1917.

the objectives that had been set for the first day. The advance had simply made the Ypres salient more precarious.

## Passchendaele: conclusion

Third Ypres – more a succession of distinct battles than a single operation – suffered from strategic incoherence, with Haig and (initially) Gough harbouring ambitions of a breakthrough, while Plumer and Rawlinson set greater store by **'bite and hold'**. For this confusion, Haig must bear ultimate responsibility. He had also chosen a battlefield where German defences were strong and where the water-logged terrain made it impossible to use the tank corps effectively.

Unreliable casualty statistics make it hard to know whether the battle was a success in attritional terms. Most authorities agree that some 70,000 British troops were killed and over 170,000 wounded – perhaps 275,000 casualties in all if the Messines operation is included. The Germans probably suffered some 220,000 casualties. 'No doubt the morale of the German army was shaken by Passchendaele', wrote A.J.P. Taylor. 'It is unlikely that the morale of the British army was much improved.'

## Cambrai

In November, Haig authorised another attack, this time at Cambrai. Some lessons had been learned. A short preliminary but very accurate artillery bombardment concentrated on eliminating previously spotted German guns. The attack, when it came on 20 November, took the enemy by surprise. Smokescreens and dummy smokescreens aided the infantry assault. So did 324 tanks which crushed the enemy barbed wire. British troops advanced

**'Bite and hold'**
A term used to describe the tactic of capturing part of the enemy trench line and then defending it when the Germans counterattacked.

Key term

over three miles, neutralising two German divisions for the relatively low loss of 5000 men. Bells to celebrate a victory were rung in London for the only time during the entire war. The rejoicing was premature. There were insufficient infantry reserves to consolidate the opening and German counterattacks quickly recovered all the ground previously lost. When the fighting ended on 7 December Britain had lost two-thirds of its tanks and suffered another 45,000 casualties, the same number as the Germans.

Cambrai seemed to give the lie to Haig's claim that the BEF had broken the spirit of the German army during Third Ypres. For the first time, newspapers started to voice criticisms of Haig. Lloyd George considered making a clean sweep of the military high command but drew back because Derby threatened resignation and Conservative MPs were certain to resist any civil encroachment into military affairs. Instead, Lloyd George looked towards Allied co-operation as a way of reducing Haig and Roberton's influence. In November, at Lloyd George's prompting, a Supreme War Council, composed of the Allied prime ministers and their military advisers, was set up at Versailles. The council was supposed to provide a co-ordinated direction of the war. To some extent it did. But in the military field it could only discuss and advise. Robertson, for the most part, refused to work with it.

### The air force

In 1917, German planes bombed civilian targets in Britain. Many Britons demanded reprisal attacks on German towns. But aerial experts opposed this idea. They held that planes were best used in co-operation with the army. Smuts (see page 169), given the task of judging air power by the war cabinet, claimed that, given enough planes, Germany could be bombed into submission. Lloyd George, whose mind was always open to innovation, liked the idea. An independent air ministry was set up under Rothermere, younger brother of Northcliffe. Trenchard, head of the Royal Flying Corps, was made chief of staff to the **RAF**.

**Key term**

**RAF**
Royal Air Force.

### The Eastern Front

From an Allied perspective, developments on the Eastern Front were disastrous:

- In March, Tsar Nicholas II's government was overthrown.
- Hope that the new provisional government would give fresh impetus to the Russian war effort quickly died.
- In November, the Bolsheviks, led by Lenin, seized power in Russia.
- In December, Lenin signed an armistice with Germany. The Eastern Front had ceased to exist.

### Italy

In October, German and Austrian forces trounced the Italians at Caporetto, forcing the Italians into a 50-mile retreat. Against Robertson's wishes, tens of thousands of British troops were sent to Italy to bolster Italian resistance.

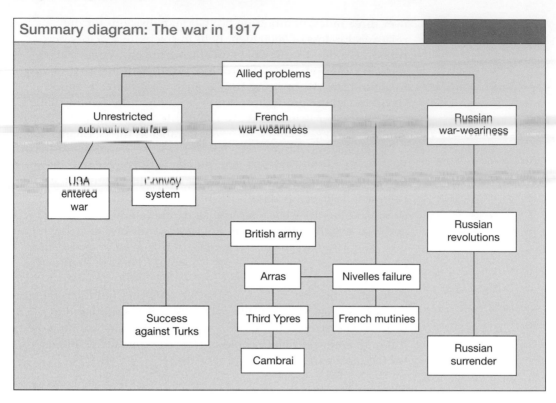

Summary diagram: The war in 1917

## 7 | 1918: The End of the War

Key question
Why did the war end in 1918?

Few observers predicted the end of the war in 1918. The fact that Russia had pulled out of the war meant that Germany was able to transfer large numbers of men to the west. By the Treaty of Brest-Litovsk Russia surrendered its Polish territories, the Ukraine, Finland and the Baltic States, an area three times the size of Germany. However, Germany faced serious problems. Its allies seemed on the verge of defeat and surrender. There was also the prospect of having to fight huge numbers of American troops. The outcome of the war was thus delicately balanced.

### The British army in 1918

Key question
How well prepared was the British army in 1918?

With a 'wastage' level of some 76,000 men a month on the Western Front in 1917 – double the rate of enlistments – the army faced a manpower crisis. The army was low on the government's December 1917 list of priorities, which put the navy and air force first, followed by the merchant navy, shipbuilding and coalmining, then the manufacture of tanks and aeroplanes, followed by food and timber production. Instead of the 600,000 men that Haig demanded, he was promised only 100,000.

The balance between different branches of the army was changing. Infantry, which had made up 64 per cent of the BEF in 1914, made up under 52 per cent in 1918. By 1918, cavalry comprised only one per cent of the BEF compared to eight per cent in 1914. A growing number of men served in non-combatant branches of the army.

Under Churchill, Minister of Munitions from June 1917, the volume and variety of weaponry pouring out of factories gave Allied armies the means to defeat Germany.

Given the manpower shortage, Britain planned to stay largely on the defensive in 1918, awaiting the arrival of US troops.

## The end of Robertson

In February, the Supreme War Council, with Lloyd George's support, resolved to create a general reserve of British and French divisions under control of its own military advisers. Under this scheme, grand strategy would be determined in Versailles, not by CIGS in London. Robertson resisted. On 16 February, Lloyd George offered Robertson the option of either going to Versailles as Britain's military representative or staying on as CIGS with much reduced powers. Robertson refused both offers. Although Robertson had the support of the king and many Conservatives, Lloyd George and Bonar Law determined to get rid of him. He was replaced by Sir Henry Wilson.

Haig survived. Smuts, after touring the Western Front, reported that there was no one better. Some historians have claimed that Australian Sir John Monash, a civil engineer by profession, would have been a good replacement for Haig. But his appointment would have led to an uproar that would probably have been counterproductive.

## The German Spring Offensive

**Key question**
Why did the German Spring Offensive initially succeed?

**Key date**
Ludendorff Spring Offensive: March–July 1918

Ludendorff, with 192 German divisions in the west facing 178 Allied divisions, determined to strike before the Americans arrived in overwhelming numbers. His attack, codenamed Operation Michael, began on 21 March, on the Somme at the join between the British and French armies. It was successful for several reasons:

- The attack, expected in Flanders, took the British by surprise.
- Gough's 5th Army, which bore the brunt of enemy attack, was below strength.
- The Germans adopted a new style of attack. There was no warning bombardment beforehand. Specially trained troops (stormtroopers) broke through weak spots in the Allied line. Instead of consolidating, they pressed forward, leaving pockets of resistance to be dealt with later.
- A heavy fog helped the German attack.

The British line was blown wide open. Gough lost one-third of his force. While some units fought bravely, others surrendered *en masse*. In a single day the Germans captured over 98 square miles, to a depth of four and half miles, virtually the same area that had been captured by the BEF during the entire Somme offensive. Over the next week, British troops fell back over 40 miles. The German advance threatened the vital railway junction at Amiens.

## Allied co-operation

The crisis drove the Allies into co-operating more effectively. On 3 April, French Marshal Foch was appointed Allied Commander-in-Chief, with the task of co-ordinating the operations of the Allied armies. Foch shaped the military situation to some extent by his control of the reserves. However, without a staff and with ambiguous powers, his appointment had a limited impact. In Britain, Lloyd George strengthened his grip, replacing Derby with Milner.

## German problems

Fortunately for the Allies, the German offensive began to lose momentum, partly due to stiffening resistance but largely because of Ludendorff's pursuit of short-term tactical advantage at the expense of an overall strategic plan. By switching his attack on 28 March to Arras, which was successfully defended by the British 3rd Army, Ludendorff blurred the focus of operations. His advance was also slowed down by:

- heavy German losses, especially of élite troops
- ill-discipline of some troops who gorged themselves on captured supplies
- the fact that the Germans were far ahead of their supply lines while the British were falling back on theirs.

On 4–5 April, a last German attempt to capture Amiens failed.

## Operation George

On 9 April, Ludendorff launched Operation George, an attack in Flanders. Again the initial German assault was successful, threatening the Channel ports. On 11 April, Haig issued his 'Backs to the Wall' order, declaring British troops must fight to the end. The BEF held out. On 25 April, Operation George was aborted. Meanwhile the Allied armies grew stronger:

> **Key question**
> Why did the German Spring Offensive fail?

- The BEF was strengthened by 500,000 troops recalled from Britain, Palestine and Italy.
- US troops were arriving in France at the rate of 250,000 a month.

## The 1918 Military Service Act

In April, the government rushed through a new Military Service Act which:

- raised the age of compulsory military service from 41 to 50 and reduced the minimum age to 17 and a half
- curtailed rights to exemption from vital industries
- extended compulsion to Ireland, with the assurance that it would be applied only when Ireland received Home Rule.

Fierce opposition ensured that the Act was not enforced in Ireland (see page 197). Attempts to impose conscription on Ireland would have tied down more British soldiers than it would have raised.

### The Maurice debate

In April, the *Morning Post* accused Lloyd George of putting the BEF at risk by starving it of men in the course of his vendetta against GHQ. In response, he declared in the Commons that the British army had been stronger in January 1918 than it had been in January 1917. On 7 May, Sir Frederick Maurice, the recently retired Director of Military Intelligence, wrote to *The Times* accusing Lloyd George of lying about the BEF's strength in January 1918. Asquith's supporters demanded a select committee to inquire into the truth of Maurice's allegations. In the so-called Maurice debate (8 May) Lloyd George defended himself by showing that the figures he had announced had actually been given to him by Maurice's department. Asquith did not withdraw his motion, which was effectively one of no confidence in the government. Lloyd George survived the challenge by 293 votes to 106.

### German failure

In late May the Germans struck against the French, advancing to within 40 miles of Paris. US troops and five British divisions, which had been brought south to recuperate, helped to staunch the German advance. On 15 July, Ludendorff launched his last offensive against the French. It failed.

### The Hundred Days Offensive

**Key question**
Why was the Hundred Days Offensive so successful?

**Key date**

Hundred Days Offensive: July–November 1918

By late July, the Germans had shot their bolt. Foch was keen to attack. But all he could do was suggest. His role was more that of a cheerleader than a commander. Haig continued to behave as though he was independent, probably deferring less to Foch than he had once done to Joffre. But well supplied with traditional arms and ammunition and with new weapons (for example, Mark V tanks, mustard-gas shells and rifle grenades), Haig was ready to attack.

Haig now showed considerable skills in generalship. His most impressive victory was at Amiens on 8 August (dubbed by Ludendorff as 'the black day of the German army'). The BEF attack, spearheaded by Australian and Canadian troops, gained eight miles, captured 400 guns and inflicted 27,000 enemy casualties. (The British incurred 8000 casualties.) British firepower – 2000 guns, 450 tanks and 1900 planes – overwhelmed the Germans. Learning from previous experience, Haig stopped the attack after a couple of days. Instead of creating an unwieldy salient, he started a second attack at another point where the Germans had depleted their reserves in order to stem the first advance. A succession of short jabs forced the enemy to withdraw back towards the Hindenburg line.

### The importance of aircraft

**Key question**
How important were aircraft in 1918?

Aircraft made an important contribution to Haig's success. Technology in this area changed rapidly, with the result that advantage during the war had swung from one side to the other. But by 1918 the Allies had a huge advantage. Aerial combat in 1914

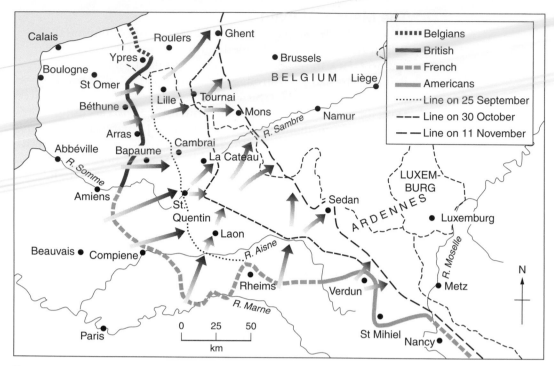

The Hundred Days Offensive 1918.

had been largely an individual affair. By 1918, it was a matter of attacks by massed aircraft, sustained as much by the capacity of the industrial base as by the skills and courage of the pilots.

In 1918, the Allies produced over 11,000 planes a month, the Germans under 2000. Control of the skies allowed the Allies to reconnoitre battlefields with impunity. Aircraft could also provide tactical support for infantry and launch raids on enemy supply lines, communication centres and reserves. By late 1918, Trenchard, father of the RAF, was planning to launch bombing raids deep into Germany, hoping to bomb the country into submission.

## Allied advance

The BEF, with an overwhelming superiority in artillery, continued to push home its advantage:

- On 29 August, the 3rd Army entered Bapaume.
- On 2 September, Monash's Australians took Peronne.
- On 29 September, British troops crossed the Canal du Nord, a seemingly impregnable part of the Hindenburg line. The attack followed a 56-hour artillery bombardment, using 1637 guns on a 10,000-yard front. A record 945,052 shells were fired in the last 24 hours.

German frontline troops continued to fight but in the rear areas, there were problems of desertion and disobedience.

## Armistice talks

On 29 September, Ludendorff told the German government it must seek an armistice. Believing they would get better terms from the USA than from Britain or France, the Germans appealed to Wilson for the opening of peace negotiations. For three weeks Wilson and the Germans negotiated alone, to Lloyd George's consternation.

## The military situation in autumn 1918

The Hundred Days Offensive rolled on. Nevertheless, the German line was never broken for more than a few hours. The BEF incurred 264,383 casualties from 21 August to 11 November – a daily loss of 3645 men – higher than that sustained on the Somme or Third Ypres. One-third of all officers and men of the tank corps became casualties during the last 96 days of the war. By late October, given deteriorating weather, the offensive seemed set to slow down. German troops still controlled most of Belgium and large parts of France. American troops would not be ready to fight in large numbers until 1919. However, the enemy faced even greater problems.

## The defeat of Germany's allies

- On 15 September, Allied forces in Salonika (see page 154) at last broke out, forcing the Bulgarians to surrender a fortnight later.
- On 19 September, Allenby defeated the Turks at Megiddo and went on to capture Damascus. On 30 October, the Ottoman government signed an armistice with Britain.
- On 23–4 October, the Italians defeated the Austrian army at Vittorio Veneto. On 3 November, Austria-Hungary concluded an armistice with Italy.

## Armistice

On 23 October, Germany accepted Wilson's **14 Points** as the basis of peace negotiations. Amid mounting chaos, a new German government dismissed Hindenburg and Ludendorff (26 October). Admiral Scheer now planned to break the Allied blockade by a 'do or die' assault on the Grand Fleet on 30 October. He was defied by mutinous sailors who joined workers and set up soviets on the Russian model. A wave of strikes made continuation of the war almost impossible. On 9 November, Wilhelm II abdicated and fled to Holland. The German government accepted the armistice terms and agreed that the war would end at 11.00a.m. on 11 November.

The armistice terms were designed to remove Germany's ability to fight:

- German troops had to withdraw beyond the River Rhine.
- Germany had to hand over large quantities of war *matériel*.
- The blockade of Germany would continue until peace terms had been drawn up and accepted.

British leaders were happy to accept the armistice. The country was desperately short of manpower, for both economic and

**Key question**
Why did Germany seek to end the war in 1918?

**Key date**

Armistice agreed: November 1918

**Key term**

**14 Points**
These were Wilson's peace aims, first outlined in January 1918. Wilson supported the principles of self-determination, reduction in armaments, and the establishment of a 'general association of nations' to preserve peace in future.

military purposes. (In the opinion of historian J.M. Bourne, from Britain's point of view the war ended 'not a day too soon.') 'We have won a great victory', said Lloyd George on 11 November, 'and we are entitled to do a bit of shouting'. Work ceased in factories, shops and offices as jubilant crowds spilled out into the streets to celebrate.

The armistice did not end all the fighting. In 1918, British forces had been sent to Russia to guard Allied supplies at Archangel and Murmansk. As Russia degenerated into civil war, British troops aided anti-Bolshevik forces. Fighting continued into 1919.

## The peace-making process

In January 1919, Allied leaders assembled in Paris to make peace. The main decisions were taken by the Big Three: Wilson, Lloyd George and Clemenceau (the French leader). Clemenceau wanted German power permanently reduced so that never again would it be able to threaten France. Wilson, by contrast, was primarily concerned with establishing a just and lasting system of international relations. During the December 1918 election campaign (see page 195), Lloyd George had given the impression that he favoured a harsh peace. However, he was not as anti-German as the British electorate expected. Realising the danger of leaving an embittered Germany, he was inclined to leniency. Thus, while he 'talked hard' for home consumption, on most key issues he stood with Wilson against Clemenceau.

## The Treaty of Versailles

By the terms of the Versailles Treaty (28 June 1919):

- Germany lost all its colonies.
- Alsace-Lorraine was returned to France.
- The Rhineland was to be demilitarised.
- Germany lost land to Poland.
- The German army was limited to 100,000 men.
- Germany's armed forces were not allowed tanks, planes, battleships or submarines.
- Germany was to pay reparations for the war. (In 1921 the sum was fixed at £6600 million.)

Arguably, Versailles was the worst of all worlds: too severe to be acceptable to most Germans and too lenient to constrain Germany. The Versailles Treaty and the wider Versailles settlement, encompassing the Treaties of St German (with Austria), Trianon (with Hungary), Neuilly (with Bulgaria) and Sèvres (with the Ottoman Empire), left many countries, not just Germany, with grievances. The peacemakers were not unaware of the settlement's deficiencies. This was why the League of Nations was created. Lloyd George said that it would 'be there as a Court of Appeal to readjust crudities, irregularities, injustices'. This was perhaps putting too much faith in an organisation that lacked enforcement powers and also lacked the USA. The US Senate refused to ratify the Versailles Treaty, and thus the USA did not become a member of the League.

Treaty of Versailles: 1919

**Key date**

## Military losses

Ten million men died in the Great War. Twenty million were seriously wounded. Britain lost 750,000 (1.5 per cent of the pre-war population) and another 200,000 from the Empire. International comparisons suggest that demographically Britain escaped relatively lightly. Of British males in the age range 15–49 some 6.3 per cent were killed. (The Scots suffered a 10.9 per cent mortality rate.) Serbia lost 22.7 per cent, France 13.3 per cent, Germany 12.5 per cent, Austria-Hungary nine per cent and Turkey 14.8 per cent.

Unlike earlier wars, most of the deaths were due to battle, not disease. (Deaths from battle outnumbered deaths from disease in a ratio of 1:15.) British soldiers benefited from the use of antiseptics and from a mass inoculation programme. Although **trench foot** and venereal disease immobilised large numbers, various sanitary precautions limited the damage. Improved anaesthetic and X-ray techniques and the impressive work of the Medical Service Corps all contributed to a high recovery rate from wounds. Blood transfusion developments, especially the ability to preserve and therefore store blood, also did much to save lives in 1917–18.

## The military experience

During the war 5.7 million men passed through the British army's ranks, over a fifth of the male population. Roughly half were volunteers, the other half conscripts. There was no 'universality of experience':

- Not all men served on the Western Front.
- The experience of officers was different from that of privates, the experience of the artillery different from that of the cavalry or infantry.
- The experience of those who served in 1914 was different from that of those who served in 1918.
- Many soldiers never experienced **going over the top**. Over a third of a million men in the BEF in 1918 were involved in supply and support work.

### Key terms

**Trench foot**
As a result of prolonged exposure to water, soldiers' feet swelled, blistered and rotted. This could result in amputation.

**Going over the top**
Attacking the enemy across no-man's land.

### Key question
Did British soldiers share a common experience?

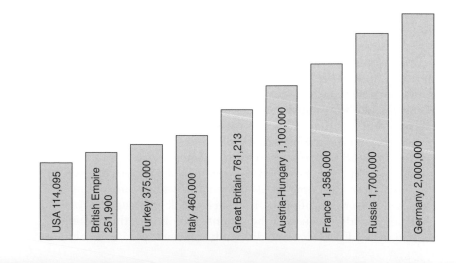

Military losses.

USA 114,095 | British Empire 251,900 | Turkey 375,000 | Italy 460,000 | Great Britain 761,213 | Austria-Hungary 1,100,000 | France 1,358,000 | Russia 1,700,000 | Germany 2,000,000

Nevertheless, over half of all combatant troops were infantry and most infantrymen fought on the Western Front. Over one in four was wounded, one in eight killed. Whatever romantic expectations and images soldiers may have had about war quickly dissipated. About two-fifths of an infantryman's time was spent in the front line but participation in major battles was infrequent. Tedium and discomfort, punctuated by moments of sheer terror, formed the lot of most infantrymen. The trench experience varied considerably, depending on soil and geography. But for many **Tommies** the principal fight was one waged against the weather, rats and lice. Inclement weather caused frostbite and trench foot. Rats carried disease and spoiled food. The blood-sucking louse was even more irksome (95 per cent of soldiers coming out of the line were infested). At the front, the men's main concerns were food, alcohol, clean water and cigarettes. When they did go over the top, many experienced panic but others felt exhilaration and (if they got the opportunity) killed the enemy with relish, avenging the deaths of former pals. Surviving letters, diaries and memoirs show a vast array of attitudes on this as on other subjects. It is a gross simplification to see the soldiers as mere sacrificial victims. Expressions of enthusiastic patriotism often crop up in correspondence even in 1917–18. Some men enjoyed the adventure and camaraderie of war. Among NCOs and privates the predominant stance seems to have been one of stoicism, tinged with black humour.

**Tommies**
The nickname for British soldiers in the First World War.

*Key term*

Discipline in the BEF never broke down. Most men, even in appalling circumstances, performed their duty more or less uncomplainingly. Nor, except when the 5th Army's positions were overrun in the spring of 1918, did British soldiers surrender in droves. Most soldiers seem to have been determined not to let down their 'mates', a sentiment naturally strong in the pals battalions. Censors in early 1918 made a careful examination of the letters that troops were sending home. They found a great deal of grumbling about food but no sign of serious disaffection with the war effort. The relationship between officers and men was generally harmonious. While soldiers sometimes voiced complaints about incompetent and bullying officers, most seem to have borne no general grudge against the officer class as a whole, reserving their hatred for the staff. The staff were also unpopular with junior officers: this was a functional, not a class dispute.

British military authorities operated a strict disciplinary regime. Between August 1914 and March 1920 over 300,000 soldiers were court-martialled, mostly for trivial offences, especially drunkenness. Some 270,927 were convicted and 3080 were sentenced to death but only 346 had their sentences carried out. Those who faced the firing squad were, in most cases, guilty of desertion while on active service. Only 18 were executed for cowardice in the face of the enemy. Half of those executed had committed a serious offence for at least a second time. It is, however, likely that some of the executed men were suffering from shell shock (see page 223).

Britain's soldiers retained their identification with the existing civilian order. Ex-servicemen did not become a separate, let alone a violent, political group as they did in some countries. The army experience had a lasting impact on some men, who felt estranged when returning to civilian life, but apparently little effect on others.

## The naval experience

While 84 per cent of all servicemen were troops, over 500,000 men served in the Royal Navy. The navy lost one in 16 of its officers and men, 43,244 in all. While naval engagements came few and far between, stress was a constant companion of the blockade enforcers who spent long spells at sea in conditions of acute discomfort. Boredom was a problem for those at Scapa Flow. One officer claimed that sailors at the remote base passed through three stages: first they talked to themselves, then they talked to the sheep and lastly they thought the sheep talked to them.

## Airmen's experience

Initially airmen seemed to be participating in an older kind of war, one marked by individual heroism and gallantry. Lloyd George called them 'the knighthood of the war, without fear and without reproach'. But fatalities among aircrew were exceptionally high, at 14,166 (8000 of these died in training accidents). Most faced the prospect of death by burning, a fate which pilots shared with tank crews.

## The female experience

Fighting remained an almost entirely male activity. It was with reluctance that the service ministries sanctioned the use of female personnel. Nevertheless, in 1917 volunteer bodies were consolidated into the Women's Auxiliary Army Corp (WAAC), followed by the Women's Royal Naval Service (WRNS) and later the Women's Royal Air Force (WRAF); in total over 100,000 women. Serving as typists, drivers, telephonists, clerks and cooks, they released more men for combatant duty. Some 40,000 women worked as nurses or female orderlies in Britain and in field hospitals in France.

| Key question |
| Was the First World War a purposeless conflict? |

## The purpose of the war

For later generations the dominant image of the Great War is one of futile carnage, an image heavily dependent on:

- a few poets such as Wilfred Owen (many of whose poems were not anti-war) and Siegfried Sassoon
- a number of novels critical of the war which began to appear in 1929. They included Robert Graves's *Good-Bye To All That* and E.M. Remarque's *All Quiet On The Western Front*
- the view of the political left, who sought to condemn the conflict as a capitalist struggle.

Recent books, plays and films have continued to fix the war in the minds of posterity as futile and purposeless.

This was not the way it was viewed by most contemporaries. The war inspired a huge literary outpouring, particularly of poetry, with 2225 poets, whose works were published between 1914 and

1918 having been identified. Very few expressed sentiments similar to those of Owen and Sassoon. John Oxenham, the war's most popular poet, celebrated heroism and sacrifice. So did most of the war novels which appeared between 1918 and 1939. Most combatants continued to believe the war had a purpose: saving Britain from German domination. The Victory Medal, issued to all those who had served, put it simply: 'For Civilisation'.

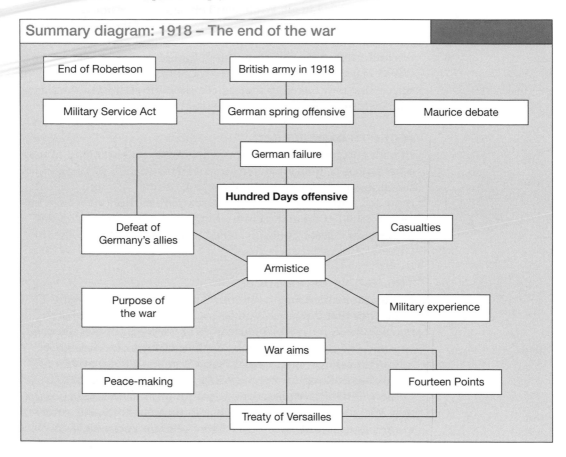

Summary diagram: 1918 – The end of the war

## 8 | Key Debate

What was Britain's contribution to Allied victory?

## The Royal Navy's role
- It ensured Britain's safety from invasion.
- It transported men and supplies to France.
- It maintained links with the Empire.
- Its blockade gradually throttled the German economy, contributing to deprivation which helped to destroy civilian morale.

## The BEF's role
The BEF played a vital role. Its 1918 offensive won the war. By 1918:

- British artillery had become a very effective force, with huge destructive power, neutralising enemy guns and defences long enough for the infantry to advance. Enormous strides had been made in the use of the creeping barrage (see page 171) and in survey techniques.

- There was sophisticated co-ordination, helped by wireless telegraphy, of the various military branches: artillery, infantry, machine guns, tanks, gas and aircraft.
- The BEF was the most highly mechanised army the world had ever seen, an army, says Bourne, reliant on 'a vast force of specialists and technicians closer in spirit to the world of mass production'.
- Tactical lessons had been learned. Rather than aiming to capture pre-set objectives, the 1918 offensives took place across a wide front with the centre of attack repeatedly switched from one area to another, preventing German resistance solidifying. The new tactics entailed a departure from earlier centralised battle-plans, masterminded from GHQ. Army commanders now had to show greater initiative and flexibility. They in turn relied even more on corps and divisional leadership as the war became more mobile and technical.

## Britain's economic role
By 1918, the German army was outgunned by the BEF in nearly all areas of munitions. British industry delivered the materials that made victory possible.

## Britain's technological role
Churchill viewed the war as an 'engineers' war' in which Allied technology and ingenuity in weapons design were decisive factors. The Royal Naval Air Service proved to be particularly innovative: its engineers and inventors can claim to have originated tanks and aircraft carriers. Tanks were certainly a useful weapon in 1918, the most striking evidence of Britain's ability to integrate science, technology and tactics with greater success than the Germans. However, technological inventiveness, by itself, could not guarantee victory. The tank is a case in point. While tanks were put to good use in August 1918 at Amiens, subsequently only once (on 29 September) was Britain able to place 100 or more tanks in the field, so prone were the machines to breaking down and so high was mortality among their crews.

## British leadership
- Lloyd George was a magnificent war leader. As Minister of Munitions, he ensured that Britain began to produce the materials that eventually won the war. As Prime Minister he kept Britain united and committed to victory.
- Debate continues on the effectiveness of Haig's leadership (see page 159). He undoubtedly made mistakes in 1916–17, but arguably he learned from these mistakes and helped to bring about victory in 1918.

## British morale

British morale, among both soldiers and civilians, remained high. Unlike all the other European armies, British troop morale never crumbled.

## The contribution of the British Empire

Dominion troops, as well as mopping up German colonies in their vicinity, fought at Gallipoli and on the Western Front. In 1916, New Zealand adopted conscription, as did Canada in 1918. Although the Australian electorate rejected conscription, 413,000 Australians enlisted – 90 per cent of all eligible males. This was a higher contribution than that made by Canada (27 per cent) but smaller than New Zealand (40 per cent). In total, the dominions provided some 1.3 million men to the Allied cause. Haig thought the dominion troops his finest and in 1917–18 used them for the BEF's most difficult operations. For this, they paid a high price. Canadians sustained 42,000 casualties in the final four months of the war while Australians and New Zealanders incurred a heavier death rate than Britons.

There were 827,000 Indian troops mobilised during the war. Many fought in the Middle East and in Africa. African troops from Sierra Leone, the Gold Coast and Gambia helped to capture Togoland. Some 56,000 African troops also took part in fighting in East Africa, a campaign which continued until 1918. By 1918, many Africans were participating on the Western Front as members of the labour corps (as well as Indians, West Indians and Chinese).

Nor was the Empire's contribution to the war confined to raising troops. All parts of the Empire helped the war effort by placing their resources at Britain's disposal. In economic terms, the greatest assistance was rendered by Canada. One-third of the BEF's munitions in 1917–18 were made in Canada.

---

**Some key books in the debate**

I.F.W. Beckett, *The Great War, 1914–1918* (Longman, 2000).
J.M. Bourne, *Britain and the Great War 1914–1918* (Arnold, 1989).
P. Hart, *1918 – A Very British Victory* (Weidenfeld & Nicolson, 2008).
G. Sheffield, *Forgotten Victory: The First World War, Myth and Realities* (Headline, 2001).
H. Strachan, *The First World War* (Simon & Schuster, 2003).

---

## Study Guide

### In the style of Edexcel

Do you agree with the view that Haig's handling of the Battle of the Somme was successful? Explain your answer using Sources 1, 2 and 3 and your own knowledge.                                            (40 marks)

### Source 1

*From: Andrew Marr,* The Making of Modern Britain, *published in 2009.*

The military historians argue persuasively that, although awful blood sacrifices were made, the generals cannot be blamed as easily as they once were. This was a new kind of fighting, which nobody was properly prepared for, including the Germans. The trench system could not have been broken by some other unexplained but somehow cleverer strategy. Realise just what Haig's dilemma was, how scanty his intelligence, how pressing his need to relieve the French, being hammered to pieces at Verdun. Dispose of some of the myths about men being made to advance slowly out of military stupidity. After all that, one is still left with the trembling lieutenants putting their whistles to their lips and leading their men straight to almost certain death.

### Source 2

*From: an account of a Somme attack on 14 July 1916, written a week later by Second Lieutenant Norton Hughes-Hallett.*

Everything was perfect. Not a sound was made and the Bosche showed no sign of having seen us, even when we were 100 yards from his line. We had to wait some time there. At 3.20 our barrage was going to be put on to their first line, and was to last exactly till 3.25; then the barrage was to lift to their second line and behind it. As the barrage lifted we were to go forward, the first waves crossing the front line and going forward to the second line. We had aeroplane photographs correct to July 13th showing he had no line beyond his second.

3.25 the line went forward. Immediately rifles and machine guns started spitting fire at us. We reached the wire, but found it absolutely uncut and far too thick ever to get through. For about two minutes we hacked at it, the men falling by scores the while.

### Source 3

*From: Gary Sheffield,* Forgotten Victory: The First World War – Myths and Realities, *published in 2002.*

Haig's initial attempt to achieve a breakthrough on 1 July [1916] was a failure. The battle that developed was nonetheless a success for the British army. In February and March 1917, the Germans abandoned their positions on the old Somme. This was in part an acknowledgment of British success on the Somme; the German army was not prepared to endure another such defensive battle on that ground.

*Exam tips*

*The cross-references are intended to take you straight to the material that will help you to answer the question.*

The sources here address the debate outlined for you in the profile of Field Marshal Douglas Haig and the additional material in Chapter 6 (page 161). Sources 1 and 2 provide evidence of failure: the loss of life and the difficulties of combat in the first months, given the defensive strengths of the German forces. However, they also provide evidence in mitigation:

- Source 1 shows that Haig appeared to have little alternative.
- Source 2 provides evidence of careful planning.

Keegan's views given in Chapter 6 (page 161) emphasise too the problems of communication which hampered changes of plan in the light of circumstances. These points might be used to counter charges of military stupidity, but they do not amount to evidence of success.

On the other hand, Source 3 acknowledges the failure in the short term of the Somme offensive, but argues explicitly for its eventual success, allowing you to argue for this if a longer term view is taken. This can be developed using the views of John Terraine and also Gary Sheffield's view of the Hundred Days Offensive on page 159.

Your answer should attempt to balance arguments for and against the stated claim. This is an issue over which historians disagree, and gives you the opportunity to come to a conclusion by giving weight to the criteria you apply to measure success or failure.

# 7 The Impact of the First World War on Britain

**POINTS TO CONSIDER**

The First World War broke the empires of Germany, Russia, Austria-Hungary and Turkey, triggered the Russian Revolution, forced the USA onto the world stage, sowed the seeds for conflict in the Middle East and paved the way for the Second World War. The Great War thus shaped the twentieth-century world. It also helped to shape Britain's political, economic and social future. This chapter will consider the war's impact on Britain by examining the following themes:

- The political impact
- The impact of the media and propaganda
- Opposition to the war
- The economic impact of the war
- The social impact of the war
- The defence of Britain 1918–29

**Key dates**

| | | |
|---|---|---|
| 1914 | | Defence of the Realm Act |
| 1915 | March | Treasury Agreement |
| | May | Lloyd George became Minister of Munitions |
| | July | Munitions of War Act |
| | September | McKenna war budget |
| 1916 | | Lloyd George became Prime Minister |
| 1917 | May | Strikes |
| 1918 | March | Fisher Education Act |
| | July | Representation of the People Act |
| | December | Coupon election |
| 1919 | | Addison's Housing Act |
| 1921 | | Irish independence granted |
| 1922 | | Washington Naval Agreement |

## 1 | The Political Impact

**Key question**
What were the main political results of the war?

Asquith's Liberal government took Britain into war. In the December 1918 election, a (predominantly Conservative) coalition, led by Lloyd George, won a resounding victory. Labour became the second largest party. Asquith's Liberals finished a poor third. How had this happened?

## The Defence of the Realm Act (DORA)

In August 1914, parliament enacted the Defence of the Realm Act (DORA). This gave the government sweeping power to rule by decree. Initially designed to safeguard ports and railways from sabotage, its provisions were progressively extended to cover press censorship, direction of the munitions industry, control of the sale of alcohol and food regulations. Year by year, the state acquired the right to intervene in most aspects of life. Many Liberals had an ideological aversion to government intervention, especially in economic matters. As the war wore on, they had constantly to choose between betraying their principles and damaging the war effort.

## Asquith's failings

Asquith, a competent peacetime premier, was a far less successful war leader. He is sometimes attacked for doing too little. However, far from being a doctrinaire liberal, he was Prime Minister when most of Britain's traditional liberal 'freedoms' were suspended. Perhaps his main failings were:

- He believed that it was the Army's job to run the war and was reluctant to interfere, even when it was clear that many military leaders were incompetent.
- At a time when decisive leadership was required, he failed to instil a sense of urgency in many departments of government.

**Key question**
Why was DORA judged to be necessary?

Defence of the Realm Act 1914

Key date

Herbert Asquith (1852–1928) being saluted by a policeman as he leaves the War Office in 1915. Historian A.J.P. Taylor described Asquith as being 'as solid as a rock but like a rock, incapable of movement'. Is this fair?

## Profile: David Lloyd George 1863–1945

| | | |
|---|---|---|
| 1863 | – | Born in Manchester |
| 1864 | – | Moved to Llanystumdwy in Wales |
| 1890 | – | Elected as Liberal MP |
| 1899–1902 | – | Gained fame by his opposition to the Boer War |
| 1905 | – | President of the Board of Trade |
| 1908 | – | Chancellor of the Exchequer: responsible for introducing old-age pensions, the people's budget and National Insurance |
| 1915 | – | Minister of Munitions |
| 1916 June | – | Secretary of State for War |
| 1916 Dec. | – | Became Prime Minister |
| 1918 | – | Won the December election |
| 1919 | – | Attended the Paris Peace Conference |
| 1922 | – | Resigned as Prime Minister |
| 1926 | – | Became Liberal Party leader |
| 1931 | – | Resigned as Liberal leader |
| 1945 | – | Died |

Lloyd George had and has many critics. The economist J.M. Keynes portrayed him as a political chameleon, 'rooted in nothing'. He is often depicted as being devious, unscrupulous and delighting in improvisation, so much so that for him the means justified themselves almost irrespective of the ends. He cared little for conventional rules, neither those economic rules of free enterprise to which his Liberal colleagues attached so much importance nor rules of personal behaviour. He left office flagrantly richer than he entered it and, as Prime Minister, lived openly with his mistress. His reputation as a womaniser led to his being nicknamed 'the Goat'.

However, Lloyd George also had and has his supporters. Some regard him as the most inspired and creative British statesman of the twentieth century. Historian A.J.P. Taylor thought of him as 'the greatest ruler of Britain since Oliver Cromwell'.

In his *War Memoirs*, Lloyd George compared himself to Asquith:

> There are certain indispensable qualities essential to the Chief Minister of the Crown in a great war … Such a minister must have courage, composure and judgement. All this Mr Asquith possessed in a superlative degree … But a war minister must also have vision, imagination and initiative – he must show untiring assiduity, must exercise constant oversight and supervision of every sphere of war activity, must possess driving force to energise this activity, must be in continuous consultation with experts, official and unofficial, as to the best means of utilising the resources of the country in conjunction with the Allies for the achievement of victory. If to this can be added a flair for conducting a great fight, then you have an ideal War Minister.'

Lloyd George believed he had these qualities. Many historians agree. If Lloyd George had not replaced Asquith as Prime Minister, it is conceivable that Britain might have lost the war.

In May 1915, Asquith tried to counter growing criticism by bringing leading Conservatives – Bonar Law, Lansdowne, Balfour, Carson and Curzon – together with the Labour leader Henderson, into the cabinet. His most important move, however, was the appointment of Lloyd George as Minister of Munitions (see page 153). Lloyd George's vigour and ability to get things done (as well as to promote his own achievements) contrasted sharply with Asquith's apparent lethargy and detachment.

## Lloyd George as Prime Minister

In December 1916, Lloyd George replaced Asquith as Prime Minister (see page 164). According to historian K.O. Morgan, 'Lloyd George's war premiership was almost without parallel in British history. No previous Prime Minister had ever exercised power in so sweeping and dominating a manner'. His ministry was dominated by Conservatives, few of whom trusted him. But most recognised his talent. From the start he was a more dynamic and unconventional leader than Asquith:

**Key question**
How good a war leader was Lloyd George?

Lloyd George became Prime Minister: 1916

- He set up a small war cabinet which took all the main decisions (see page 165).
- He realised that the twin pressures of war and coalition government had made party largely redundant.
- He had his own private secretariat and advisers. This was known as the Garden Suburb because it met at first in huts in the garden behind No. 10 Downing Street. He soon came to resemble a US president, often relying more on unofficial advisers than on members of his cabinet.
- He appointed men from outside parliament to head important ministries.
- More government controls than ever were introduced (see pages 209–13). Most of the organisations he created were replicated at the start of the Second World War. As **Lord Beaverbrook** observed: 'There were no signposts to guide Lloyd George.'

Lloyd George's leadership was far from perfect:

- He was a poor administrator and delegator. While he brought a new dynamism to the work of government, dynamism, as historian Gerard DeGroot has said, is not the same thing as method.
- It is easy to exaggerate the changes brought about by his government.
- By no means all his new ministries operated effectively.

**Lord Beaverbrook** Max Aitken, a Canadian, became Lord Beaverbrook in 1917. A successful newspaper proprietor, he acquired the *Daily Express* in 1916 and turned it into Britain's most widely read newspaper.

## Political destabilisation

War and coalition government led to the destabilisation of party politics. There were cross-party alliances on many issues. While the destabilisation of party loyalties weakened Asquith and created difficulties for Bonar Law, Lloyd George relished the freedom that this gave him. Most of his acts sprang from no particular doctrine:

they were the response to the challenge of events. He has been blamed for the decline of the Liberal Party. In his defence, his paramount aim was to win the war, not to preserve the Liberal Party.

## Liberal decline

Key question
Why did the Liberal Party decline?

Arguably the Liberal Party was in serious trouble before 1914:

- It was divided. The radical wing favoured state action to bring about social reform; the traditional wing wanted to keep government intervention to a minimum.
- The Liberals did not do particularly well in the 1910 election. They were only able to remain in office with Irish Nationalist and Labour support.
- Long-term social changes were causing large sections of the working class to look towards Labour.
- The growing trade union movement (its membership increased from 2.47 million to 4.13 million between 1909 and 1913) preferred to fund Labour rather than the Liberal Party.
- The Liberals failed to deal effectively with serious problems before 1914 – potential civil war in Ireland, the suffragette campaign and industrial unrest – leaving Britain (according to historian George Dangerfield) on the verge of anarchy.

However, none of this proves that the Liberal Party was in terminal decline. Arguably there was plenty of life left in the party in 1914.

- The party had adapted to the social changes taking place and its policies attracted support from workers. Historian Peter Clarke showed that in Lancashire Labour was losing ground to the Liberals after 1910.
- The Labour party was seriously divided pre-1914. It did not do well in the 1910 general election and had no by-election success between 1910 and 1914.
- Dangerfield's claims are not generally accepted.

## Liberal problems

The First World War seriously harmed the Liberals. Historian Trevor Wilson compared the war to a 'rampant omnibus' which first knocked down and then ran over the Liberal Party. Its prestige was damaged by its (perceived) fumbling conduct of the first years of the war. Then came the split between Lloyd George and Asquith. Asquith, who continued to be Liberal leader, was unable to forgive Lloyd George for his 'betrayal'. After 1916, while claiming to be giving the government his general support, Asquith (and his supporters, the 'Squiffites') hoped to turn Lloyd George out. The seriousness of the Liberal divisions was demonstrated in May 1918 during the Maurice debate (see page 177). Lloyd George won but 98 Liberals voted against the government, 71 for. Eighty-five Liberal MPs, shrinking from the unpleasant necessity of choosing between a Liberal leader and a Liberal Prime Minister, did not vote.

## The rise of Labour

During the war the Labour Party extended its influence. The war gave some of its members cabinet experience and at local level working-class representatives were co-opted onto a variety of public bodies. Although deeply divided over the war, common grievances and shared ideals held the Labour movement together. This enabled Sidney Webb to produce a set of policies behind which Labour supporters could rally. His manifesto, *Labour and the New Social Order*, included support for:

- nationalisation of mines, iron, steel, railways, canals, armaments, shipping, gas, electricity and land
- a statutory basic wage for men and women
- full employment and unemployment insurance
- the development of health services.

Trade union expansion (see page 209) swelled Labour's coffers, making possible an extension of its organisation at constituency level. More middle-class intellectuals, including ex-Liberals like Haldane, joined the party, making it look less working class. Labour did well in a series of by-elections in 1917–18. The extension of the franchise (see below) seemed certain to further help Labour's cause.

## The Representation of the People Act

In 1914, Britain was far from being a democracy. It had the most restrictive franchise of any European state (except Hungary). Only 60 per cent of adult males could vote in parliamentary elections. MPs were soon concerned at several franchise anomalies:

- War service meant that most servicemen lost their **residential qualifications for voting**.
- Many working-class men, who were making an indispensable contribution to the war effort, did not have the vote.
- Most Britons believed that women should have the vote.

In 1916 Asquith referred the franchise question to an all-party conference. Most of the conference's recommendations were incorporated in the Representation of the People Act (July 1918):

- The vote was given to all males at the age of 21.
- Women householders were given the vote at the age of 30. (MPs feared that if women had electoral equality, female voters would outnumber male.)
- All voting in general elections was to take place on the same day instead of being spread over several weeks as previously.

The act added more voters to the voting register than all previous parliamentary reform acts put together. The war thus smoothed the way for democracy, 'one of the few things to be said in its favour', thought A.J.P Taylor.

**Key question**
Why did the Labour Party increase its strength in the war?

**Key question**
How democratic was Britain (a) in 1914 and (b) in 1918?

**Key date**

Representation of the People Act: July 1918

**Key term**

**Residential qualifications for voting**
Men had to live in a constituency for a year before an election to be entitled to vote.

**Key question**
Why did Lloyd George's coalition win the coupon election?

Key date

Coupon election: December 1918

## The December 1918 election

On 14 December 1918, the first general election since 1910 took place. The case for an election was overwhelming:

- Parliament had outlived its statutory term by three years because of the war.
- The electorate had been more than doubled by the extension of the franchise.
- The government needed popular endorsement before it negotiated a peace settlement.

Many voters – six million women and two million extra men – were voting for the first time. They faced a complicated situation. Lloyd George determined to continue the wartime coalition. This meant that in many constituencies there were two Liberal candidates: a Lloyd George coalition Liberal and an Asquith Liberal. The election became known as the 'coupon election' because Lloyd George and Bonar Law issued coupons (signed letters) to their candidates, so that the electors would know who were the genuine coalition candidates. The Conservative Party did not put forward candidates in some 150 constituencies where coalition Liberals were standing. Labour entered the election united and better prepared than the Liberals. It put forward 388 candidates, as opposed to only 72 in 1910.

Despite the Labour challenge, the coalition won easily, mainly because of Lloyd George's popularity as the man who had led Britain to victory. His promises to create a 'fit country for heroes to live in' and to make Germany pay 'the whole cost of the war' were also popular. His coalition won 478 seats, made up of 335 Conservatives, 133 coalition Liberals and 10 coalition Labour and other supporters. The main opposition consisted of 63 Labour MPs, 28 Asquith Liberals and 48 Conservatives who refused to support the coalition. Seventy-three Sinn Féin MPs did not take their seats at Westminster.

## The importance of the 1918 election

The election result was a disaster for the Liberals. Asquith and nearly all his closest colleagues lost their seats. Labour became the main opposition party. Although it had only a few more seats than it had pre-1918, Labour secured 2.4 million votes – over a fifth of the vote. But the overwhelming victor in 1918 was the Conservative Party. Intent on restoring, in large measure, the pre-war economic and social order (albeit also prepared to introduce moderate social reform), the Conservatives dominated government during the inter-war period. Between 1918 and 1939, there were only three years (1924 and 1929–31) when the Conservatives were not in government.

## Lloyd George's premiership 1919–22

The war had brought major changes in the organisation of government. This was not maintained. Most of the wartime ministries disappeared. The war cabinet continued for a few months but by October 1919 Lloyd George had restored the old peacetime cabinet of some 20 members. Given that the Conservatives had a majority of seats in the Commons, Lloyd George had to rely on his own personal achievements to remain securely in office. He did not change his dictatorial style. Treating his colleagues, except Bonar Law, as subordinates, he tended to disregard the cabinet and settled affairs with a few cronies or by means of the Garden Suburb. In 1922, Conservatives discovered that Lloyd George had been selling knighthoods and peerages for money, his intention being to use the funds to create a new party comprising Liberals and Conservatives. Criticism of his handling of the **Chanak crisis** in October 1922 led to most Conservatives abandoning the coalition. A general election followed.

**Chanak crisis**
An international crisis which almost resulted in a war between Britain and Turkey in 1922.

Key term

## The 1922 and 1923 elections

In 1922, still divided between the Lloyd George and Asquith factions, Liberals won fewer seats than Labour (142 Labour to 116 Liberal) for the first time. While the Liberals succeeded in reuniting under Asquith's leadership for the general election of December 1923, Asquith was now over 70 and out of touch with most of the electorate while Lloyd George had lost much of his popularity. If the party's leaders were not impressive, neither were its policies. All the things the Liberals had stood for were ceasing – or had ceased – to be major issues (for example, free trade and Irish Home Rule). Even so, the Liberals were not far behind Labour, polling 4.31 million votes to Labour's 4.43 million. This gave Labour 191 seats to the Liberals 159. (The Conservatives won 258 seats.) Arguably, even at this stage, all was not lost. With dynamic leadership and some creative policies, the Liberals might have muscled Labour into third place. But after 1923 the party found neither leader nor policies and its support dwindled. Somewhat ironically, the Liberals would have fared better if proportional representation had been introduced, as it might have been in 1918 if either Asquith or Lloyd George had thrown his weight behind it.

## Ireland and the First World War

In 1914, Ireland seemed on the verge of civil war. There were two private armies: the Ulster Volunteers, formed to resist the Third Irish Home Rule Bill; and the Nationalist Volunteers, formed to defend it. In August 1914, Home Rule was postponed until the end of the war. Most Irish people accepted this and Irish Nationalist leader Redmond placed his men at the disposal of the government. (The Ulster Volunteers were even more willing to join the British army.) Not all Irish nationalists were happy about Redmond's action and southern Irish enthusiasm for the war soon dissipated. The British government, anxious not to arouse unrest, ensured that the Military Service Acts of 1916 did not apply to Ireland (see page 157).

**Key question**
How did the First World War lead to Irish independence?

## The Easter Rising 1916

Extreme Irish nationalists saw Britain's preoccupation with the war as a chance to win independence. Hopeful of German support, they made plans for a rebellion to take place on Easter Sunday 1916. When no German help materialised, some leaders tried to call off the rebellion. But others went ahead. On Easter Monday they proclaimed an Irish Republic and seized key points in Dublin, including the General Post Office, hoping that the rest of the country would rise in sympathy. No such rising took place. After five days of sporadic fighting, which resulted in the loss of 100 British soldiers and 450 Irish, the surviving rebels surrendered. The execution of 16 rebel leaders caused a great outburst of anti-British feeling. More Irish now demanded not just Home Rule but complete independence.

## Home Rule efforts

Both Asquith and Lloyd George favoured Home Rule. In 1916, Lloyd George secured an agreement between Carson, the Ulster Unionist leader, and Redmond: immediate Home Rule for 26 counties; the six counties of Ulster to remain part of the United Kingdom until after the war, when an imperial conference would review the issue. Aware of Conservative opposition, Asquith reduced the concessions made to Redmond. Ulster's exclusion from Home Rule was to be permanent and Irish representation at Westminster was to be cut to 43 MPs. Redmond refused these conditions. Further attempts at compromise in 1917 failed. Many southern Irish now turned away from the Irish Nationalists, supporting instead the more extreme Sinn Féin Party, which won four by-elections in 1917.

Support for republican nationalism reduced the flow of southern Irish volunteers to a trickle: 19,000 in 1916, 14,000 in 1917. Many Britons fumed at the privileges accorded to Irish 'slackers'. Accordingly, the 1918 Military Service Act extended conscription to Ireland but with the assurance that it would be applied only when Ireland received Home Rule. Lloyd George hoped this would ensure that the Unionists would accept Home Rule while the Irish accepted conscription. His manoeuvre failed. The Irish Catholic Church denounced conscription and congregations pledged themselves to resist it.

On 23 April, the Irish TUC called a general strike which affected all Ireland (except Belfast) for 24 hours. In the face of these protests, the government made no effort to enforce conscription. Instead, it invented a German plot and arrested Sinn Féin leaders, a move which merely enhanced their popularity. By 1918, much of Ireland had effectively seceded from the UK. The war, which had initially seemed to promise a more amicable relationship between Ireland and the rest of Britain, instead had driven the two apart.

## Irish independence

The Irish problem reached its most severe phase after 1918. In theory, British authorities continued to rule from Dublin castle. In reality, the **Dáil,** set up by Sinn Féin, acted as though an independent Irish republic already existed. The Irish Republican Army (IRA) waged war against the British authorities. The British sent 50,000 troops to Ireland, including the brutal **Black and Tans**. Meanwhile political negotiations continued. Ironically, a truce was signed in July 1921, just as the IRA was about to admit defeat. Months of further bargaining followed. On 21 December 1921, the British parliament approved a treaty granting southern Ireland independence with dominion status. Ulster was to remain within the United Kingdom. Most Unionists resented the manner in which Lloyd George had ended the Union with Ireland. Most Irish nationalists resented the loss of Ulster.

**Key date**

Irish independence granted: 1921

**Key terms**

**Dáil**
The Irish parliament.

**Black and Tans**
Armed, auxiliary policemen, most of whom were ex-servicemen.

## Summary diagram: The political impact

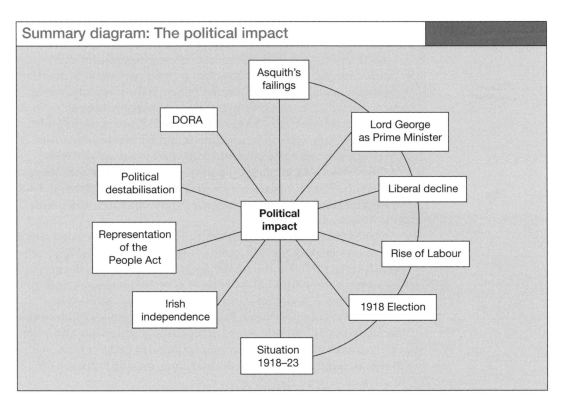

# 2 | The Impact of the Media and Propaganda

From the start of the war, the government was concerned about military secrecy, using DORA to censor all cables and foreign correspondence. As well as regulating the flow of information, it was also involved in a range of attempts to shape opinion and maintain commitment. Regulation 27 of DORA prohibited reports or statements 'by word of mouth or in writing or in any newspaper periodical … or other printed publication' which were 'intended or likely to undermine loyalty to the King, recruitment or confidence in the currency'.

**Key question**
To what extent did the government control the press?

## Newspaper censorship

The press reached perhaps its highest point of influence in the First World War. (Radio was still in the future.) In 1914, the government was concerned that newspapers might divulge information which might be of use to the enemy. Thus:

- Any paper publishing unauthorised news, or speculating about future strategy, ran the risk of prosecution.
- No war correspondent followed the army to France in 1914. In 1915, six correspondents were invited to GHQ 'for a limited period'. They remained in this privileged position for the rest of the war.
- A press bureau was established. This distributed statements from GHQ and from government departments, provided advice about the publication of other news, and could recommend prosecutions if it thought that DORA regulations had been infringed.

**Key term**
**D-Notice system** Instructions sent by the government to newspapers, asking them not to publish certain information. (D is short for defence.)

In practice the press largely censored itself. Northcliffe, proprietor of the *Daily Mail* (the largest selling newspaper) and *The Times* (which claimed to be the national voice), for example, did not allow his papers to criticise the Gallipoli campaign, however much he fumed in private. Northcliffe's papers, like the press generally, took a patriotic line. For this reason, the **D-Notice system**, which was introduced to warn newspapers off 'sensitive' topics, was rarely employed. While a few papers were prosecuted for breaches of security, no papers were prosecuted for expressing unwelcome opinions. Despite the limitations on their freedom, newspapers performed a vital function, providing more in the way of opinion than most MPs.

**Key question**
How effective was government propaganda?

## Propaganda

Some left-wing critics have ascribed British patriotism to the manipulation of gullible masses by government agencies. It is certainly true that the Parliamentary Recruiting Committee (PRC), which drew together MPs from all parties, worked tirelessly to get across its message, sending out 50 million posters and other publications as well as hosting countless rallies. This must have had some effect. But given that the first dramatic surge in recruiting took place before the PRC was established, it is likely that it was preaching to the converted.

The government's first direct initiative on the propaganda front was taken in September 1914, when it established a bureau at Wellington House in London. But this agency directed its propaganda almost entirely at opinion in neutral countries, especially the USA. Essentially it employed famous literary figures such as Arthur Conan Doyle and Thomas Hardy, who were expected to put a high-minded gloss on Britain's war activities.

**Key figure**
**John Buchan** A popular author of adventure novels.

In February 1917, a Department of Information under **John Buchan** was set up. It became a full ministry, under Beaverbrook, proprietor of the *Daily Express*, a year later. The department/ministry made use of a wide variety of populist devices, including pamphlets, posters and film. But it was concerned more with international than home opinion. One department, under Rudyard Kipling, focused on American and Allied opinion. A second focused on neutrals. In February 1918, Northcliffe finally consented to serve the government as Director of Propaganda in Enemy Countries. Delighting in ingenious methods, he used balloons to deluge Germany with news of Allied successes and the German lines with certificates promising good treatment for those who surrendered. His efforts probably did little to shake enemy morale.

Worried by what it saw as flagging commitment, the government established a National War Aims Committee in mid-1917. This body issued propaganda literature, printed a stream of posters (on such issues as the need for food economy) and organised speakers to address public meetings.

## The effectiveness of government propaganda

It is a moot point how effective official propaganda was in generating support for the war. In some respects it may have been a self-defeating activity. Many saw it as being somehow un-British. Arguably, German behaviour constituted the most effective propaganda agency of all. The invasion of Belgium, the savage treatment of some of its people and the naval bombardment of east coast towns created intense British anger in 1914. Thereafter, whenever it seemed enthusiasm for the war was flagging, the German army or government did something sufficiently barbarous to confirm Britons in the belief that they were engaged in a righteous cause, for example, the use of gas at first Ypres, the sinking of the *Lusitania* and zeppelin raids on civilian targets.

## Non-government propaganda

Much of the wartime propaganda was generated by private individuals, firms and agencies rather than by the government:

- Journalists, academics, writers, poets and ordinary people churned out anti-German material.
- Business manufactured propaganda materials, illustrated by the production of toys and comics for children. Toy tanks, for example, were available for sale in Britain within six months of their being used in battle.
- A variety of groups and associations (for example, The Victory League) campaigned for British victory.
- British film-makers produced some 250 pro-British war films between 1915 and 1918. Few of these were directly inspired by government departments.

## Anti-German hysteria

Those of German descent or those with German-sounding names were early victims of wartime hysteria. (During the war, the royal family changed its name from Saxe-Coburg-Gotha to Windsor.) The sinking of the *Lusitania* in 1915 led to serious anti-German rioting in many towns. While there were no further disturbances on this scale, when tempers became frayed all foreigners were liable to be

> **Key question**
> Why did the war generate hysteria and rabble-rousing?

attacked. Flickering lights, particularly near the coast, were thought to be signals to the enemy. The press and best-selling novels (like John Buchan's *The Thirty-Nine Steps*) gave the impression that Britain was awash with German spies. This was not the case. In 1914, British intelligence agencies swiftly rounded up 22 German agents. Another 201 people were eventually detained on suspicion of being in contact with the enemy. To deal with such problems MI5 was formed in 1916 out of earlier intelligence bodies.

## Rabble-rousers

Rabble-rousing, anti-German speakers often attracted huge audiences. The most famous was Horatio Bottomley. So successful was he as a speaker that in 1915 he managed to call off a major Clyde shipwrights' strike (see page 208). In his journal, *John Bull*, he declared a 'blood feud' against the Germans, arguing that 'you cannot naturalise an unnatural beast – a human abortion – a hellish freak. But you can exterminate it'. He campaigned for Germans in Britain to be forced to wear special badges and to be deported. So popular was Bottomley that it seemed he might be given a cabinet position in 1918. Lloyd George wisely held back. (Bottomley was later found guilty of fraud and sentenced to seven years' imprisonment.)

While from a government perspective Bottomley had his uses, the same could not be said of Noel Pemberton Billing. By linking his 'Germany Must Be Destroyed' message to a number of genuine grievances (for example, profiteering), he became an increasing nuisance to the authorities, especially after his election as an independent MP in 1916. His supporters, who called themselves the 'Vigilantes', searched for the enemy within: pro-Germans, aliens, Jews, and those who were allegedly sabotaging the war effort. Vigilante candidates secured over 30 per cent of the vote in two by-elections in 1917 and 1918. Billing's popularity was shown in a libel trial in 1918, following his allegation that Asquith, his wife and his closest friends featured among the names of 40,000 'sex perverts' contained within a German 'Black Book'. This book was supposedly being used to blackmail them into sabotaging the British war effort. In defiance of every principle of justice, the jury acquitted Billing.

**Emmeline** and **Christabel Pankhurst** swelled the chorus of hatred. In 1915, they renamed their paper *Britannia* and then in 1917 founded the 'Women's Party', an organisation which had little to say about women but a great deal to say about the evils of Germans and Liberals who were thought to be soft on Germany. *Britannia* on one occasion called Asquith 'the flunky and toady and tool of the Kaiser'.

## Alien restriction

The 75,000 enemy aliens who resided in Britain came under close surveillance. The Aliens Restriction Act of 5 August 1914 stipulated that those of military age should be interned and 32,000 duly were. This measure did not satisfy the Pankhursts, who called for the repatriation of all Germans. In August 1918, a petition bearing

**Key figures**

**Emmeline** and **Christabel Pankhurst**
Mother Emmeline and daughter Christabel had led the campaign for votes for women before 1914.

1.25 million signatures calling for stronger action against aliens was presented to Lloyd George. Bowing before the storm, the government gave itself the powers to revoke British naturalisation previously granted to Germans. Meanwhile the process of repatriation continued. By 1919, there were only 22,254 German residents in Britain. Most German-owned properties had been confiscated.

## Patriotism

Some self-appointed publicists – poets, journalists and churchmen – invested the defeat of Germany with deep spiritual significance, regarding the war as a great crusade, a just war to save Europe and mankind from the 'Hun'. Such views were not necessarily typical. But most Britons were solidly patriotic and committed to victory. The war probably strengthened the sense of national unity. 'God Save the King' started to be sung regularly at public entertainments and events during the war and continued for decades thereafter.

**Hun**
The derogatory name for Germans in the First World War. Historically, the Huns were a barbarian tribe who had overrun much of Europe in the fifth century.

Key term

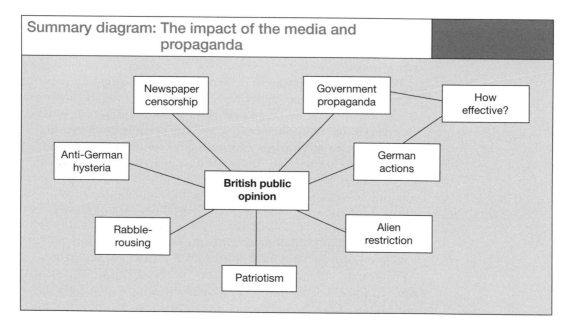

Summary diagram: The impact of the media and propaganda

- Newspaper censorship
- Government propaganda
- How effective?
- Anti-German hysteria
- **British public opinion**
- German actions
- Rabble-rousing
- Alien restriction
- Patriotism

## 3 | Opposition to the War

There were a number of organisations that opposed the war and campaigned for peace. However, the 'pacifists' – a word used for the first time – were small in number and far from united.

**Key question**
Why did some British people oppose the war?

## Socialist opposition

In 1914, the British Socialist Party was the only political party to call for an immediate end to hostilities. However, a number of other socialist groups, for example the ILP, had members (like Keir Hardie) who opposed the war, mainly because they thought it was being fought by the ruling classes in pursuit of imperialist or capitalist interest. Socialist opposition was small in scale (the British

Socialist Party had only 6435 members in 1917) and socialist 'Stop-the-War' candidates in by-elections performed poorly, attracting far fewer voters than maverick jingoists. Socialist anti-war papers saw their circulations drop during the war.

## Other anti-war groups

- Most Quakers opposed the war, often providing support to peace organisations.
- The Union of Democratic Control supported the securing of peace by negotiation. Its leader, E.D. Morel, a former Liberal candidate, was imprisoned in 1917 for violating DORA, his offence being the posting of two publications to someone in neutral Switzerland.
- The No-Conscription Fellowship, founded in 1914, was pledged to resist all war service. Drawing support from the ILP, the Quakers and radical intelligentsia (like the philosopher Bertrand Russell), it never had more than 5500 members. Russell was imprisoned for six months in 1918 for publishing 'seditious' material.

## Conscientious objectors

**Key question**
Why have the conscientious objectors had a better press since 1918 than they had in the war?

Britain and the USA were the only combatant nations that recognised the existence of conscientious objectors during the war. Lloyd George had little sympathy for objectors: 'I will make their path as hard as I can', he declared. Those who objected to military service (amounting to only 0.33 per cent of the men in the armed forces) were allowed to state their case before tribunals. Over 80 per cent were given some form of exemption. Ninety per cent of those whose claims for exemption were rejected accepted an alternative form of national service. Of these, 7000 agreed to perform non-combatant service, usually in ambulance work; another 3000 were put to work in labour camps. Finally, there were 1300 'absolutists', men who refused all compulsory service from religious or political conviction. These men were drafted into military units and sentenced to imprisonment by court martial when they refused to obey an officer's order. They received harsh treatment: 10 died as a result of the experience.

The absolutists' suffering has obscured the fact of their atypicality. The largest single bloc of conscientious objectors were the **Christadelphians**, who rested their case on a literal reading of the Bible. Provided they were not forced to fight, they were prepared to do other kinds of war-related work. The courage of the objectors has been more honoured by posterity than it was at the time. The 'conchies', as they were derisively called, were stigmatised under the terms of the 1918 Representation of the People Act by being denied the vote for five years.

**Christadelphians**
Members of a small religious sect.

Key term

## The threat of class war

'Troublemakers' within the industrial working class were more a government concern than pacifists. An industrial truce whereby the unions agreed not to strike was established in 1914 and worked reasonably effectively. However, there were signs in 1917–18 that the truce was breaking down. Left-wing activism, led by militant **shop stewards**, was growing stronger. In the event of strike action, the government had the problem of distinguishing between 'justifiable unrest' and 'deliberate agitation' – no easy task, since they were usually interconnected. In 1917, it did seem that working men's economic grievances might become political. The situation in Russia, where workers had overthrown the Tsar, revived faith in the notion of an international brotherhood of the working class. In June 1917, 1100 socialists, meeting in Leeds, called for the establishment of workers' and soldiers' councils (as in Russia). There was fear in some quarters that the spirit of revolution might even reach the armed forces.

But industrial unrest did not translate into serious political action:

- Industrial unrest often arose as a result of war-accelerated changes which threatened the privileged position of skilled workers. The latter thus found it hard to unite with semi-skilled and unskilled workers.
- Disgruntled workers and restless troops had little in common. Indeed, most Tommies were angry because they believed that there was a vast army of 'shirkers' in Britain.
- There was a strong jingoist element within the organised Labour movement.

Only in Glasgow was revolutionary defeatism (which led to Russia's collapse in 1917 and Germany's defeat in 1918) a major threat. Even here, militant shop stewards suspended industrial action during the 1918 German Spring Offensive, an offensive which led to an upsurge of patriotism at a time of national peril (see page 175). Industrial disputes died down and productivity soared as people, sacrificing their Easter holidays, worked flat out to replace lost *matériel*.

## Calls for a negotiated peace

Opponents of the war divided the Commons three times during 1917, calling for a negotiated peace:

- 32 MPs voted in favour of a Russian peace programme (a peace without annexations and indemnities) in May.
- 19 MPs voted in favour of a *Reichstag* **peace resolution** in July.
- 18 MPs voted in support of the conference of all socialist parties (allied, neutral and enemy) which met at Stockholm in August, hoping to bring about peace.

While the majority of MPs who sought peace were on the left, there were some on the right who wished to end the war. In November 1917, Lord Lansdowne had a letter published in the *Daily*

**Key question**
To what extent was Britain threatened by militant left-wing activism?

**Shop stewards**
Men who represent groups of workers.

***Reichstag* peace resolution**
The German parliament (*Reichstag*) passed a resolution in 1917 in favour of peace without annexations or indemnities.

Key terms

*Telegraph* which made the case for a negotiated settlement on both economic and humanitarian grounds. But it was clear that neither Lansdowne (who wanted peace to conserve the old order) nor the extreme left (who wanted peace in order to change it) had much support. Between October 1916 and April 1918, the five 'Peace by Negotiation' by-election candidates secured only 16 per cent of the total vote.

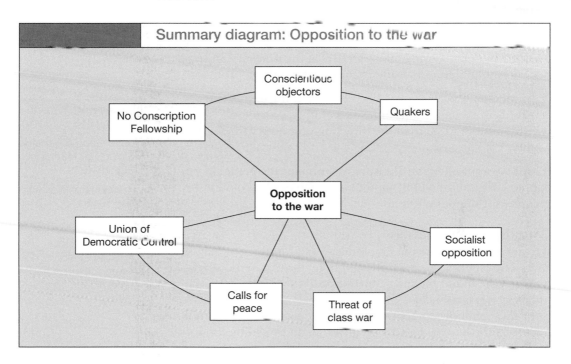

Summary diagram: Opposition to the war

## 4 | The Economic Impact of the War

**Key question**
What were the main economic effects of the war?

The war demonstrated the strength and flexibility of Britain's economy. In spite of millions of men being mobilised for the armed forces, industrial output increased and factories churned out weapons. Germany's economy, by contrast, contracted.

### The immediate economic effects
In August 1914, the government, although still imbued with the philosophy of *laissez-faire*, took some important economic actions:

- Trading with the enemy was prohibited.
- Merchant ships were requisitioned for the transport of armed forces.
- Railways were taken over by the government. (This made little difference in practice. Railway managers ran the railways for the Board of Trade.)

On 24 August, trade unions declared an industrial truce for the duration of the war. Despite the government's slogan, 'Business as Usual', the war brought a substantial degree of economic dislocation. While some industries boomed, others saw a sharp increase in unemployment.

The surge of men into the army and the demand for military supplies led to an improvement in job prospects generally in late 1914.

## The Treasury Agreement

The most urgent problem in munitions factories was 'dilution'. Unskilled workers and women had to be brought in if output was to expand. However, skilled workers refused to relax their traditional standards. The government, fearing industrial strife, was reluctant to use its compulsory powers under DORA. In March 1915, Lloyd George met engineering union leaders at the Treasury. In return for accepting 'dilution', trade unions received three promises:

- Traditional practices would be restored at the end of the war.
- Profits in the munitions industry would be restricted.
- Unions were to share in the direction of industry through local joint committees.

Lloyd George called the Treasury Agreement 'the great charter for labour'. It established his claim to be the man who could enlist 'the people' for the war effort.

**Key dates**

Treasury Agreement: March 1915

Lloyd George became Minister of Munitions: May 1915

Munitions of War Act: July 1915

## Munitions production

Lloyd George became the first Minister of Munitions in May 1915. When he entered the requisitioned hotel that housed his new ministry, he found too many mirrors and no staff. By 1918, the ministry was employing a headquarters staff of 25,000 and had over three million workers under its direction. In 1915, munitions were in short supply. Lloyd George set about providing them (see page 153).

**Key question**
Why did Lloyd George support and trade unions oppose 'dilution'?

The Munitions of War Act (July 1915) gave the Ministry of Munitions the power to declare any essential plant a 'controlled establishment' where 'dilution' of jobs could be introduced and where restrictive practices were suspended, strikes banned, fines could be levied for absenteeism and workers could move jobs only if they received 'leaving certificates' from their employers. While most trade unions were unhappy with the regulations, Lloyd George won them over by guaranteeing reasonable minimum wages and by favouring firms that used union labour.

Lloyd George contracted out work so that firms could, with appropriate guidance, adapt their plant to munitions production. There were soon 20,000 'controlled establishments' and a host of new state-owned munitions enterprises.

The Ministry of Munitions was, as Lloyd George recognised, 'from first to last a businessmen's organisation'. Staffed by businessmen ('men of push and go', according to Lloyd George), it handled other businessmen – who ran the munitions effort at a local level – gently. Manufacturers were glad to accept the system of 'costing' which gave them the costs of production plus 'a reasonable profit'. Usually the costs were those of the least efficient firm. Thus, many well-run businesses were well rewarded.

In desperate haste to boost production, Lloyd George took some dangerous short-cuts. Nor was he noted for his administrative

The war of munitions.
A woman checking
shell primers in 1917.

efficiency. It needed his successors Montagu, Addison and
Churchill to impose method on the Ministry's chaotic operations.
But under Lloyd George's inspiration, the Ministry of Munitions
ensured the massive production of weaponry that eventually helped
to win the war.

## Women's economic role

**Key question**
How significant was
women's war work?

In 1914, Suffragette groups suspended their campaign for women's
right to vote, demanding instead that they be allowed to serve the
country by undertaking work that would release men for military
duty. Trade union opposition initially made this difficult. (Unions
feared that female labour would reduce wages for men.) But as
the labour shortage intensified and the principle of dilution was
accepted, women began to find work. The number of females
employed in munitions production (where women had long been
engaged in shell-filling) rose from 82,859 in July 1914 to 947,000
by November 1918. Some 200,000 women entered government
departments and 500,000 took over clerical work in private offices
while the number of females in the transport sector rose from
18,200 to 117,200.

It would be wrong to overstate the extent of the changes in
women's role:

- The total number of women doing waged work did not increase
  dramatically. In 1914, 5.9 million women were employed; by 1918
  7.3 million – a 22.5 per cent rise. Many of those taking up work
  in munitions transferred from other employment, perhaps a
  quarter coming from domestic service. (Munitions work offered
  more freedom and better remuneration.) Germany made better
  use of female labour than Britain.
- In 1918, five-sixths of women were still doing what was
  considered to be 'women's work'. While the number of domestic

servants declined by 400,000, most women were still employed as domestic servants.

- The increase in women's employment was not securely built. By 1917, one woman in every three in employment had replaced a male worker. Under industrial agreements, these jobs would revert to men once the war was over. Work in munitions industries would also end when the war ended.
- Women still earned substantially less than men doing the same work.
- Male attitudes to women workers were often negative. To unskilled men, women were an immediate and long-term threat. While the war lasted, women's ability to do men's work meant that more men were likely to be conscripted. In the longer term, women threatened wages.

Trade union views reflected contrasting attitudes of different sections of the male workforce. Some, for example the General and Municipal Workers' Union, had always recruited women members and continued to do so. Some, for example, the National Union of Railwaymen, recruited women for the first time. Others, for example, those representing Lancashire cotton spinners, refused to admit women as members. Nevertheless, the numbers of female trade unionists rose from 437,000 in 1914 to 1,342,000 in 1920.

Labour demands during the war brought about an improvement in women's pay (as it did for other traditionally low-paid groups). Women in munitions work earned over £2 a week by 1918. (This compared to an industrial average of 11s. 7d. a week in 1914.) However, outside munitions, women's wages barely kept pace with the increase in the cost of living (see page 222).

## Industrial unrest 1915–16

The Treasury Agreement and the Munitions of War Act did not end industrial action.

Many workers believed that trade union leaders had caved in too easily to patriotic blackmail. Local shop stewards took up their grievances, leading resistance to:

- the infringements of customary trade union rights
- employers' high profits which were not shared with workers
- the employment of female workers.

In 1915, the main flashpoint was Clydeside, where there was unrest throughout the year. In 1916, militant shop stewards feared that conscription would be extended to industrial life or even used as an instrument of industrial discipline. (Men who went on strike might be conscripted into the army.) These fears seemed to be confirmed when skilled engineers who thought that they had been guaranteed exemption from military service found themselves called up. Strikes in Sheffield and Barrow followed. The government capitulated, accepting the Trade Cards Agreement which allowed the main engineering union to decide which of its members could be exempted from military service.

Key question
How successfully did the government deal with trade unions?

**Key date**

May strikes: 1917

## The May strikes

In early 1917, there was a wave of strikes. Workers were angry at the government's decision to extend 'dilution' to many more businesses and at its repudiation of the Trade Cards Agreement. By May, trouble had spread to 48 towns and the loss of 1.5 million working days. The government was conciliatory:

- It fixed the price of certain essential foodstuffs.
- It offered skilled men in the industrial workforce a 12.5 per cent war bonus, later extended to semi-skilled and unskilled workers.
- It set up a Commission on Industrial Unrest, which uncovered a wide range of discontents within working-class communities.
- Leaving certificates came to an end in August 1917.

In July 1917, Lloyd George made a significant gesture towards removing workers' discontents by turning the Reconstruction Committee into a fully fledged ministry, holding out to workers the prospect of extensive social reforms as a reward for wartime co-operation. The protests petered out.

## Lloyd George and the unions

Generally Lloyd George handled workers well. ('Boys', he told the workers of Clydeside, 'I'm as keen a Socialist as any of you'.)

- On forming his government, he created two new ministries – Labour and Pensions – filling each with a trade union stalwart.
- He found a place in the war cabinet for Labour leader Henderson and then for George Barnes.
- He listened to workers' demands.

**Key question**
In what ways did the war benefit the trade union movement?

**Key term**

**National bargaining**
The situation when wages and conditions of workers in a particular occupation are settled at national rather than at local level, ensuring all receive the same wages and work to the same conditions.

## The war and the unions

The war had a positive effect on the trade union movement:
- The number of workers affiliated to the TUC grew from 4.1 million in 1914 to 7.8 million by 1918.
- The needs of war led to a rise in **national bargaining** along with an increase in the numbers and status of shop stewards at plant level.
- Trade unions were seen as necessary partners in the war effort.
- The creation of the Ministry of Labour, along with promises of social reform, were concessions to the power of organised workers.
- Unions may have enhanced their reputation with their responsible attitude. The number of working days lost in strikes during the war averaged a quarter of those lost before the war and only a tenth of those lost immediately after it. Nevertheless, 27 million days were lost due to strike action in Britain during the war; by comparison, Germany lost only 5.3 million days.

**Key question**
What was war socialism?

## War socialism

In 1916 there were demands for greater government control of the economy. For those Liberals who continued to put their faith in free enterprise, the implications were alarming. Lloyd George had no such qualms. After coming to power, he created 12 new ministries: Blockade, Reconstruction, Information, Munitions, Shipping, Food Control, National Service, Labour, Pensions, Air, Health and Transport. The new ministries were headed by new men, mostly businessmen with no political background. They enlisted the co-operation of producers and owners, who largely ran what some called **war socialism**.

Perhaps Lloyd George has been given too much praise for his role in expanding the wartime government:

- Several of the new state agencies were in the pipeline prior to the change of premiership.
- The multiplication of ministries, running side by side with old departments, sometimes created more confusion than they resolved.
- The new ministries (or ministers) were not always successful (see below).
- War socialism was an improvised and not a specifically planned programme.

**War socialism**
The government's wartime control of many aspects of economic and social life.

**Requisitioning**
Government action forcing firms to supply materials for the war effort.

## The allocation of manpower

A scheme launched in 1917 by the newly created Department of National Service, under Neville Chamberlain, failed to give the government full powers to regulate the allocation of manpower. Lacking statutory powers, it relied on voluntary enrolment for 'work of national importance', and failed. In August 1917, General Auckland Geddes replaced Chamberlain at the head of the department which was upgraded to ministerial status. Geddes had a clear mandate and enhanced powers. At long last, the properly co-ordinated use of mobilised manpower began, a fact underlined by the transfer of control of recruiting from the War Office to the new ministry in November 1917. From this point on, the army's manpower demands were accorded a lower priority than those of shipbuilding, tank and aircraft production (see page 174). However, not until mid-1918 did Geddes receive powers to allocate labour and to monitor its distribution. Only at the end of the war, therefore, did the government have a coherent manpower policy.

## Merchant shipping

**Requisitioning** for naval and military purposes took nearly a quarter of British shipping out of ordinary service in 1915. Shipyards could not build enough ships to fill the gap. Given the competing demands on men and materials from the Admiralty and the Ministry of Munitions, merchant shipbuilding sank to a third of the pre-war figure. Until 1916, the government essentially left things to market forces, relying on the impact of higher freightage rates to reduce imports. The flaw in this free-market approach was that there was no guarantee that enough necessities would be imported. The situation became even more serious with unrestricted submarine warfare.

**Key question**
Why was merchant shipping so vital for Britain?

Under Lloyd George, the government took a firmer grip. The Ministry of Shipping, led by Glaswegian shipowner Joseph Maclay:

- extended requisitioning to cover all ocean-going mercantile ships; the owners became virtually agents of the state, working at a limited rate of profit and on fixed freight charges
- reorganised the ports, cutting delays in unloading and reloading cargo
- began a vast shipbuilding programme which required many skilled workers to be brought back from the front. After March 1917, the gross tonnage of ships launched each month doubled. By June 1917, new ships overtook the tonnage lost to U-boat attack.

The government supplemented these efforts by taking responsibility for Britain's entire imports. In 1918, it managed to reduce the volume of imports by five million tons, thanks largely to Milner, whose Priority Committee adjudicated between claims on materials being made by the armed services and by key civilian industries, and grading imported goods according to their national importance.

## The food situation

**Key question**
How successfully did the government tackle the food problem?

Shipping and food were related problems. In 1914, 60 per cent of food consumed in Britain was imported. In 1914–15, there were no real shortages but food prices rose. By mid-1916, they were on average 59 per cent above the level of July 1914, a fact resented by many working-class families and widely blamed on profiteers. In late 1916, supplies of food began to dwindle and long queues formed outside shops. Some areas introduced local rationing schemes and there were calls for national rationing.

In December 1916, Lloyd George set up a Food Agency, with Lord Lee as its director. This began the process whereby food production became subject to national planning:

- Landowners were directed to use their land more efficiently. If not, they could be dispossessed and their land worked by others.
- In July 1917, skilled agricultural labourers were exempted from conscription.
- The Corn Production Act (August 1917) was designed to make Britain more self-sufficient in agricultural products. Under state direction three million acres of pasture and parkland were converted to cereal production. The act also imposed controls on agricultural rents.

By 1918 (despite a shortage of fertilisers), the wheat crop was 65 per cent higher than the pre-war average, while allotments became a useful source of vegetables.

The government also took responsibility for the distribution of foodstuffs. The first Food Controller, Lord Devonport, became something of a laughing-stock with his attempts to introduce a scheme of voluntary rationing. In 1917, he was replaced by Lord Rhondda. Rhondda was far more prescriptive and successful, issuing 500 orders during his time in office – one for each working day.

## The introduction of rationing

In early 1918, there was a sudden panic about food distribution, even though the situation was much better than in 1917. (The U-boat menace was no longer so serious and the 1917 wheat harvest was the best of the century.) To allay alarm, the Food Control Ministry introduced rationing. Individuals who registered with a particular shop received coupons for particular foodstuffs. The system, geared to human needs rather than capacity to pay, was designed to help the poor. While there was no rationing of wheat, the price of bread was kept stable by government subsidy. By the end of the war, 85 per cent of all food consumed by the civilian population was being bought and sold through government agencies that fixed prices and profit margins for each stage of the distribution. This eliminated shortages and discontent. In 1917–18, the calorific content of the average diet dropped by three per cent, a limited fall compared with the experience of most Europeans.

## Control of alcohol

Given the view that drunkenness was a major cause of absenteeism and, as such, an impediment to the war effort, a government campaign against excessive drinking was launched. King George V was persuaded to take the King's Pledge of total abstention of alcohol for the duration of war. Few followed his example, certainly not Lloyd George or Asquith.

In 1915, under the authority of DORA, the government set up the Central Liquor Control Board, which:

- restricted drinking by reducing opening hours (usually from noon to 2.30p.m. and from 6.30p.m. to 9.30p.m.)
- took steps to weaken beer and placed curbs on the distillation of spirits
- took responsibility for drinking habits in the area around the great munitions centre at Gretna, acquiring 119 licensed premises and buying up breweries.

These measures, while probably having little effect on industrial production, had some success:

- Beer consumption had halved by 1918.
- Consumption of spirits, mainly as a result of heavy increases in duty, declined from 35 million gallons in 1915 to 15 million in 1918.
- England and Wales averaged 3388 convictions a week for drunkenness in 1914; in 1918 just 449.
- The nation's health was improved.

## Other government initiatives

- The government fixed the prices of many commodities (not just food) in an attempt to prevent speculation and profiteering and to stabilise the cost of living.
- Coalmines were **nationalised** in 1917. This did not result in an improvement in productivity or any attempt to modernise the pits.

**Key question**
Why did the government seek to control alcohol consumption?

**Nationalised**
Taken over and run by the government.

Key term

- The Ministry of Munitions pioneered a range of reforms, aimed at improving working conditions and thereby increasing workers' productivity.
- Cocoa magnate Seebohm Rowntree (see page 119), who headed the Health of Munitions Workers Committee, demonstrated that the reduction of excessive factory hours actually increased output (by up to 25 per cent) mainly through cutting down absenteeism and accidents.
- Model housing was provided for workers in areas like Gretna.
- Workers' canteens proliferated.
- The ministry subsidised the creation of crèches in factories.

## Socialism or free enterprise?

While there was far more state control in 1917–18 it was not quite socialism. Although Lloyd George presented himself as someone who had broken with old-fashioned *laissez-faire* economics, he accepted the need to work through the business community. Most industry was left in private ownership. Those who had run things pre-1914 generally continued to do so. For example, Maclay, having requisitioned all British merchant ships, then employed the owners as managers. The county committees which directed agriculture were composed of local landowners. Food rationing was really a voluntary system, operated by shopkeepers.

## Scientific and technical advances

For two decades before 1914, efforts had been made to improve scientific research at British universities and make its results more widely available to industry. This became even more vital after 1914. In 1916, the government created the Department of Scientific and Industrial Research. Scientists and engineers were recruited in large numbers by the service departments and the Ministry of Munitions, where they assumed responsibility for a host of projects, rendering invaluable service.

The war gave an enormous boost to the automobile and aeronautical industries and to wireless telegraphy while technological advances created what were, in effect, a range of new industries geared to the production of such commodities as scientific instruments and ball bearings.

## Demobilisation

The Ministry of Labour devised an elaborate scheme for demobilisation in 1918–19, aiming to release first the men most required by industry. However, these were often the last to have been called up. Servicemen who had served longer were indignant and there were mutinies in camps at Calais and Folkestone. Churchill settled the trouble by scrapping the existing scheme and substituting the principle first in, first out. By mid-1919, 80 per cent of soldiers had been discharged. Nearly all the demobilised men were absorbed into industry with surprising ease, many women handing over their jobs. There was a (short-lived) economic boom in 1919–20.

## Financing the war

Initially, Chancellor of the Exchequer Lloyd George was not interested in balancing the budget; he hoped to pay for the war by borrowing. Reginald McKenna, who took charge of the Treasury in May 1915, began by continuing Lloyd George's reliance on borrowing. But the loan, issued in June 1915, brought in only half of the £1000 million that McKenna had hoped to raise. To meet the war's spiralling costs, he introduced a war budget in September 1915 which greatly increased taxes:

**Key question**
How did Britain pay for the war?

McKenna war budget: September 1915

Key date

- Income tax went up from 1s. 2d. to 3s. 6d. in the pound and the exemption limit was lowered, meaning that people on lower incomes would have to pay.
- Supertax rates went up.
- An Excess Profits Duty (EPD) of 50 per cent was imposed on any increase in pre-war profits on all war-related industries.
- McKenna imposed duties at 33.3 per cent on some 'luxury' articles, for example, cars and watches.

Nevertheless, McKenna still faced a huge deficit. This meant that he and his successors had to keep on increasing taxation. In 1916, the standard rate of income tax went up again, this time to 5s. in the pound and ultimately to 6s. in 1918. The sugar duty was increased and new duties were slapped on a range of products. EPD rose to 60 per cent and 80 per cent in 1917. (This tax provided a quarter of the total tax revenue in the war period.) Direct taxes were the easiest to increase. Reliance on them was also a matter of social policy: it appeased the working classes by 'soaking the rich' and it did not push up the cost of living as the increase of indirect taxation did.

In 1915–16, only 20 per cent of the national expenditure was being met from taxation. Later improvements raised it to only 30 per cent. Thus most war expenditure was met from public borrowing. Treasury officials were not greatly disturbed by this. The budget was artificially divided into a normal peacetime budget which was balanced in the ordinary way, and wartime expenses which were left to look after themselves. McKenna laid down the doctrine that there need be no limit on government borrowing so long as taxation was enough to cover the payment of interest on the national debt. This rose during the war from £625 million to £7809 million.

## International finance

Government financial policies (which resulted in the printing of a great deal of extra money), coupled with the fact that there were fewer goods available, inevitably led to inflation. By 1919, the pound brought only a third of what it had done in 1914. Britain was able to pay for the (rising) costs of its imports because exports, though much reduced in volume, brought in as much sterling as before the war, thanks to the rise in their prices. Britain's **balance of payments** remained favourable until 1918: positive balances of £200 million in 1915 and £101 million in 1916, an equal balance

**Balance of payments**
The difference between a nation's total receipts (in all forms) from foreign countries and its total payment to foreign countries.

Key term

in 1917 and a negative balance of £107 million in 1918. Britain was wealthy enough to provide loans to its allies. Russia received £585 million, France £434 million, Italy £412 million – a total, including money given to lesser countries and the dominions, of £1825 million.

Britain's main financial problem was with the USA. The war increased Britain's need for supplies from the USA without increasing British exports to the USA. There was thus a dollar shortage. This was met partly by raising loans on the American market, partly by sales of American **securities** held by British citizens. Several politicians – Liberals Runciman and McKenna, and Tory Lord Lansdowne – feared that Britain was becoming dependent on US credit and might end up bankrupting itself. (Most ministers agreed with Bonar Law that bankruptcy was preferable to defeat.) US entry into the war in 1917 meant that Britain no longer had any difficulty raising loans in the USA. By late 1918, Britain had amassed debts to the USA of about £1000 million.

**Key term**

**Securities**
Bonds or certificates which provide evidence of holdings of property or money owed (by, for example, a government).

## Summary diagram: The economic impact of the war

- Borrowing:
  - US loans
- Financing the war
- Increased taxes
- Treasury Agreement
- Industrial unrest:
  - 1915–16
  - May strikes
- Trade unions
- **Economic impact**
- Immediate economic effects
- Women's role
- Munitions production
- War socialism
  - Control of alcohol
  - Allocation of manpower
  - Merchant shipping
  - Food control/rationing
  - Demobilisation

## 5 | The Social Impact of the War

Key question
What impact did the war have on social development?

Historians continue to debate the war's impact on social developments. Derek Fraser claims: 'The war quite simply swept away a whole world and created a new one and the Edwardian epoch became a vision of the distant past.' Martin Pugh is more cautious: 'On investigation, many of the trends and innovations attributed to the great war turn out to be not so much the direct product of war as the outcome of long-term developments whose origins lie in the pre-1914 period.'

### State involvement in life

By 1918, the state was involved in all aspects of life in a way it had not been in 1914. Civilian life became more regimented and controlled the longer the war went on. Examples are conscription, rationing, working conditions and news censorship. During the course of the war, the notion spread that working-class people deserved some rewards for their sacrifices. By 1917, it was taken for granted that the state would play a large role in this process. In response to the May strikes (see page 209), Lloyd George created a Ministry of Reconstruction, headed by Addison (see page 209). It soon sprouted dozens of committees, which surveyed practically every aspect of British life. Reconstruction, claimed its spokesmen, would not only be a culmination of the earlier quest for national efficiency (see pages 117–18); it would, in Addison's words, 'mould a better world out of the social and economic conditions which have come into being during the war'. Lloyd George and Addison thus raised expectations of a brave new post-war world, expectations that would prove difficult to meet.

### Unemployment insurance

The demobilisation of millions of servicemen and the conversion of industry from war to peace production looked certain to cause massive, if temporary, unemployment in 1918–19. Only a third of workers were covered by the government's 1911 unemployment insurance scheme. Lloyd George's government acted quickly, establishing principles that shaped unemployment relief through the inter-war years:

- In November 1918, ex-servicemen were given free unemployment insurance for a limited period.
- In 1920, insurance against unemployment, financed from contributions by employers and employees, was extended to virtually the entire workforce (except domestic servants, agricultural labourers and civil servants).

### Women's role in society

Key question
Did the war have a major impact on women's role in society?

Arguably, the war led to a revolution in women's position in society:

- During the war women undertook a variety of jobs previously done by men (see pages 207–8). Some historians claim that this increased women's self-confidence. It certainly gave some women more economic independence and a legitimate excuse for escaping from the confines of domesticity.

- The horizons of many young women opened out after 1914. They were able to smoke, spend money on entertainments and come and go without the protection of chaperones. Such females ('flappers' as they came to be known) tended to wear short skirts and lipstick and to shorten their hair. These developments caused widespread dismay, especially among older women.
- By 1918, some women were allowed to vote in parliamentary elections and could also stand as MPs,

However, it is possible to claim that the war's positive effects on women's status have been exaggerated:

- Women rarely did skilled work and were usually paid much less than men. This only 'increased antagonism between the sexes', says DeGroot, 'and, needless to say, did nothing for gender equality'.
- Most women were forced to leave their wartime jobs once the war ended.
- The notion that the war revolutionised men's minds about the sort of work of which women were capable may well be a deception. Traditional views of women's role remained strong.
- If most men continued to think women's place was at home, many women agreed. Indeed, the war may have strengthened the ideology of domesticity. Motherhood was increasingly presented as an honourable state service, akin to soldiering. Several women's organisations developed this line of argument in support of family allowances and state subsidies for child-bearing mothers – money that would encourage women to stay at home.
- Arguably, women would have received the vote by 1918 even if there had been no war. The war simply created the circumstances in which votes for women could be granted with minimum political disturbance since the existence of the wartime coalition government meant that the suffrage issue was no longer intertwined with party rivalries. Moreover, given that the Suffragette movement had ended its disruptive campaign in 1914, male MPs could give women the vote without being reproached for giving way to violence. The argument that women deserved the vote because of their wartime service was something of a myth. Those who had really helped the national cause – women under 30 who worked in munitions factories – did not get the vote.
- Few women stood as prospective MPs – just 17 in 1918. Only Countess Markievicz of Sinn Féin won a seat in 1918 and she refused to take it. (The first woman to appear in the Commons was a Conservative, Lady Astor, returned in 1919.)

## Heartache and gender imbalance

For many women, the war brought heartache and loneliness rather than a great release. Constant anxiety over the fate of loved ones often culminated in the agony of bereavement. In the longer term, women had to endure another of the war's legacies: a worsening of the gender imbalance. Among those aged 20–34, the female surplus rose from 463,000 in 1914 to 773,300 in 1921. Thanks to the war one woman in six could look forward to a lifelong spinsterhood.

## Greater sexual freedom

The war may have led to freer sexual relationships. Perhaps some young women were tempted to have a last fling with boyfriends before they set off to the front. Some were convinced that this encouraged a rise in the illegitimacy rate (from 4.3 per cent in 1913 to 6.3 per cent in 1918). There were press outcries at the numbers of single women expecting 'war babies' in areas where large numbers of troops were stationed. But the rise in illegitimacy may have been simply a reflection of the obstacles presented by the war to the common practice whereby men agreed to marry women (with whom they had slept) if they became pregnant.

More worrying than the rise in illegitimacy was the increase in venereal disease, which affected something like one soldier in five. French co-operation in organising brothels, with some rudimentary medical control, was not enlisted until 1916. Protective sheaths were not issued to the troops until 1917. Through wider distribution of sheaths more married couples probably became familiar with contraception during and immediately after the war. But Marie Stopes's book *Married Love* (1918), which popularised birth-control techniques, suggested in its title that it was concerned with marriage enrichment, not sexual pleasure for its own sake. Women perhaps came to benefit from the growing use of contraception: it rescued some wives from a non-stop succession of pregnancies. But otherwise the war did not much advance the cause of sexual liberation.

> **Key question**
> Did the war lead to sexual liberation?

## Housing

The shortage of working-class housing was a problem in 1914. It became more of a problem thereafter. Lack of materials and labour meant that house building came virtually to a halt. Given the house shortage, rents in some areas soared. This led to a rent strike at Clydeside in 1915, involving 20,000 tenants. The government responded by passing the Rent Restriction Act, fixing rents on working-class houses at pre-war levels. But this initiative had a downside. Landlords lost the incentive, and sometimes the means, to finance repairs.

The need to house workers forced the Ministry of Munitions into house building and led to government subsidies to local authorities and private firms. Government housing schemes, such as those around Gretna, provided high standards of accommodation. Even so, many munitions workers were forced to live in hostels.

By 1917, aware that housing shortage was causing industrial unrest, the government gave a commitment to support post-war housing. Committees within the Ministry of Reconstruction drew up plans for securing sites, labour and building materials. Lloyd

> **Key question**
> How successful was Addison's Act?

**Key date**

Addison's Housing
Act: 1919

George, who had talked of providing 'homes fit for heroes' in
1918, supported the Addison Housing Act (1919). This provided
government money for local authorities to clear slums and to build
working-class houses with sensible rent levels. The aim was to build
500,000 houses in three years. In some respects the Act failed:

- By the end of 1922, only 213,000 houses had been built.
- Addison's scheme, which proved very expensive, was abandoned
  in 1922 as part of the government's economy drive.

Nevertheless:

- The fact that 213,000 good working-class houses had been built
  was a considerable achievement.
- Addison's Act established the basic principles of local
  government obligation and central government subsidy which
  underpinned subsequent housing policy.

**Key question**
How did the war
affect Britain's health?

## Health

The war drew attention to the nation's health-care needs while
disrupting the existing provision. By mid-1915, a quarter of the
medical profession had joined the armed forces. In January 1918,
there was one doctor for 367 soldiers but only one doctor for 3000
civilians. Despite the lack of doctors, the overall impact of the war
on civilian health was benign:

- Full employment and higher real wages for the poorest section
  of society promoted physical well-being.
- Controls on alcohol (see page 212) had a positive impact on
  health.
- Life expectancy for men (aged 45 and over) rose between 1911
  and 1921 from 49 to 56 years and for women from 53 to 60.

Not everything was positive, however:

- Measles and whooping cough, although not war related, took a
  heavy toll of babies and young children.
- Venereal disease was a major problem (see page 218).
- Some 150,000 Britons died of influenza in the winter of 1918–19.
  (This epidemic, which killed some 20 million people worldwide,
  was not war related.)

### Support for expectant mothers and children

Partly in response to the falling birth rate, but more generally
because the saving of infant lives seemed necessary to replace those
who had died in battle, great efforts were made by government
and private agencies to provide support for expectant mothers
and children. In 1914, there were 400 Infant Welfare Centres
and Schools for Mothers. By 1918, there were more than 1000.
The Local Government Board gave financial incentives to local
authorities to improve midwifery, health visiting and other welfare
services. The 1918 Maternity and Child Welfare Act consolidated
and extended many of the wartime measures.

## A Ministry of Health

Wartime consciousness of health issues gave impetus to the move to establish a Ministry of Health which would co-ordinate the health services provided by the Board of Education, the Poor Law, the insurance commission, public health authorities and voluntary agencies. As a result of opposition from several powerful vested interests, the ministry was not set up until after the armistice. Moreover, important areas of health provision remained outside its control.

## Wartime innovations

The immediate care and long-term needs of badly wounded servicemen influenced emerging medical specialisms as well as existing technologies. Nevertheless, wartime innovations did not necessarily transfer to civilian life. For example, although blood banks had been set up on the Western Front in 1917–18, centralised civilian blood banks did not appear until the late 1930s.

# Education

Asquith's government intended to bring forward an education bill in late 1914. While the outbreak of war prevented this, it served to emphasise the importance of the issues demanding attention: the physical condition of children, the shortage of teachers and of secondary school places, and the need to make the most of the nation's physical and mental resources. The efficiency of German schools, described by Lloyd George as the most formidable institution Britain had to fight, underlined the deficiencies of British education, deficiencies made worse by the war:

- Many male teachers were lost to the forces.
- Large numbers of children left school early, lured by opportunities in munitions factories.

By 1917, all the major political parties were committed to education reform. Lloyd George's appointment of H.A.L. Fisher as President of the Board of Education and his support of Fisher's costly proposals indicate the priority accorded to action in this area. Fisher sought to 'repair the intellectual and physical wastage which had been caused by the war'. By the terms of the 1918 Education Act, the school-leaving age was raised from 13 to 14, more free places at secondary schools were made available for bright children from poor backgrounds, and Local Education Authorities had the power to raise the school-leaving age to 15. Fisher also proposed continuation classes for employees aged 14–18 and encouraged the development of nursery schools, physical education and extensions in school medical services. Separate measures to raise teachers' salaries and pensions aimed to improve the standing of the profession.

While some employers supported and introduced continuation classes, there was opposition from other employers and from unions in industries such as cotton and coalmining where child labour was widely used. Ultimately Fisher had to compromise on continuation classes, restricting them to those aged 14–16.

**Key question**
How successful was Fisher's Education Act?

Fisher Education Act: March 1918

Key date

## Life on the home front

Those on active service were often dismayed, when on leave, to discover life at home apparently going on much as usual. While music halls may have lost custom, their place was taken by cinemas – part of the growing Americanisation of popular culture. But many civilians had a drab time. Clothing, shoes and furniture were scarce and often of poor quality. Food and coal sometimes ran short.

Civilian status no longer conferred safety:

- 14,287 merchant seamen and fishermen died as a result of U-boat attacks.
- Civilians in coastal towns faced German naval bombardment.
- Bombing raids, by zeppelins and by planes, killed over 1000 people.
- The workforce employed in the munitions industry ran the risk of injury and death. Some 300 **munitionettes** died from **TNT** poisoning or explosions.

**Key terms**

**Munitionettes**
The name given to women who worked in the munitions industries.

**TNT**
A high explosive.

**Key question**
Which class was hit hardest by the war?

## War and class

People of different social class contributed to the war effort – and were affected by the war – in different ways.

### The upper class

Imbued with a strong sense of patriotic duty, public school boys rushed to enlist in 1914. (All but eight of the 5439 boys who left Winchester school between 1909 and 1915 volunteered.) Virtually all received commissions. They paid a price for this. In the armed services 13.6 per cent of all serving officers were killed compared with 11.7 per cent of other ranks.

Some landed families were hit hard economically, particularly when the death of the head of the household was followed by death in battle of his heir. The estate was then saddled with two sets of death duties. Like all propertied people, landowners also faced greatly increased taxation. While there was a temporary rise in agricultural prices, landlords were prevented by the Corn Production Act from raising rents. Finding themselves in straitened circumstances, many landowners sold parts of their estates after 1918, to such an extent that almost a quarter of Britain's land changed hands.

The war may have accelerated the tendency for landowners to change their traditional way of life for a business career. Businessmen generally did well out of the war. By 1916, average profits in coal, iron, engineering and shipbuilding were a third higher than in 1914. While profits were heavily taxed (see page 214), most businessmen involved in munitions work made money.

### The middle class

Middle-class men were more likely to end up in uniform than working-class men. They were more likely to volunteer and more likely to be conscripted. For example, in London only 45 per cent of the former manufacturing workforce served in the armed forces compared with 63 per cent of men in finance and commerce. Many middle-class entrants into the army received commissions. Thus, middle-class status carried with it increasing risks of becoming a casualty. Sixteen per cent of London's pre-war banking employees died during the war (compared with only four per cent of its pre-war manufacturing workforce).

As a result of high inflation, middle-class citizens living on fixed incomes were among the war's greatest economic losers. Those on salaries also fared badly. Given that they had to pay higher taxes, many middle-class families saw the value of their savings decline.

## The working classes

As with the middle class, there were great variations among working-class families and their experiences of the war varied considerably. Some occupational groups showed greater patriotic zeal than others. While miners registered some of the highest enlistment rates, textile workers were proportionately under-represented in the army. After 1916, many skilled workers were exempt from conscription, while a third of the urban poor were deemed unfit for military combat. To generalise broadly, a working man's chances of surviving the war were least promising if he was unskilled and possessed good health. But he still stood a better chance than a man with a middle-class occupation.

While many working-class households were hard hit by the rise in prices of food, fuel, clothing, alcohol and tobacco, several factors helped to protect the living standards of the bulk of the population:

- The war resulted in the virtual disappearance of unemployment.
- By 1917, real wages had caught up with prices and ran slightly ahead by 1918.
- On average, workers did 10 hours of overtime a week. This enabled some workers to accumulate substantial savings.
- The expansion of female employment meant that many households drew a double income.
- The poorest, in particular, experienced a rise in living standards. The payment of flat-rate bonuses meant a flattening of wage differentials. Thus, a skilled man's wages rose by less than those of the semi-skilled and unskilled.

## The 'lost generation'

During the war some 750,000 British servicemen were killed. A further 1.6 million were seriously ill or wounded, many so severely that they could never work again. Of males aged between 19 and 22 in 1914, over one in three did not survive the war. After 1918, people talked about the 'lost generation'. Some imagined a cohort of extra-gifted young men who, if they had lived, would somehow have averted the errors made by inter-war governments. Eugenists (see page 122) feared that Britain had lost the cream of its youth (before they had chance to procreate) while the physically and mentally unfit had survived. However, despite the horrendous

**Key question**
To what extent was there a 'lost generation'?

fatalities, the telling fact is that 86 per cent of British men of military age in 1914 survived the war. The 1921 census revealed a 2.4 per cent increase in population since 1914. The reason for this was that the war greatly reduced emigration. Between 1910 and 1914, 300,000 people a year, mainly young men, emigrated to the dominions or the USA. Thus, the net result of the war was to make the loss of men less than it would have been if emigration had continued at its old rate. The lost lives (and the decline in births during the war) were partly compensated by the baby boom of 1920, when the birth rate rose to 25.5 per thousand, just above its pre-war level, before resuming its long-term downward path.

Such statistics offered scant consolation to wives who found themselves widowed and children left fatherless. Something was done to ease material suffering through the payment of war pensions. By 1921, 239,000 allowances were being paid to soldiers' wives and 395,000 to soldiers' children. But for many the loss of loved ones had a life-long impact. Some women turned to spiritualism, whose growth in popularity during and after the war provides testimony to a deep-seated urge to deny the finality of death.

While the war was in progress, the process of grieving was eased by the establishment of street shrines which sprang up in all British cities in 1915. Civic war memorials and church monuments later played an important part in the rituals of remembrance, as did the war graves in France and Belgium. The war was not forgotten. Even to this day Armistice Day is observed by a national two-minute silence.

## Wounded men

**Key question**
Were wounded men well treated?

Coming to terms with injury generated a different kind of anguish:

- Some 40,000 men were left blind or partially blind by the war.
- In 1922, some 50,000 men received war pensions on mental health grounds. Most had suffered from a newly designated condition called 'shell shock' – a mental collapse due as much to the stress and horror of trench warfare as to intense artillery bombardment. (Today the condition is known as post-traumatic stress disorder.) Soldiers exhibited a range of symptoms, the most severe being hysteria, delusion, limb paralysis and loss of speech. Special hospital units were established for shell-shock patients, perhaps the most famous being that at Craiglockhart hospital where war poets Wilfred Owen and Siegfried Sassoon were treated. Treatment regimes were based around gently talking through the symptoms.
- Over 40,000 men lost as least one limb. Providing sufficient artificial limbs was a major problem during the war's early stages. However, by 1918 limb quality had improved and generous post-war government grants ensured that research and development continued.
- Some men suffered terrible facial injuries. Often unrecognisable to friends and family, their return to civilian life was traumatic. The Queen's Hospital at Sidcup, opened in 1917, specialised

in facial wounds. Despite advances, especially the use of skin grafts, there were limits to what could be achieved. While the basic elements of a face might be partially restored, for most the disfigurement remained profound and permanent.

While injuries were initially badges of courage, this heroic status gradually diminished as the war wounded became subsumed into the general disabled population.

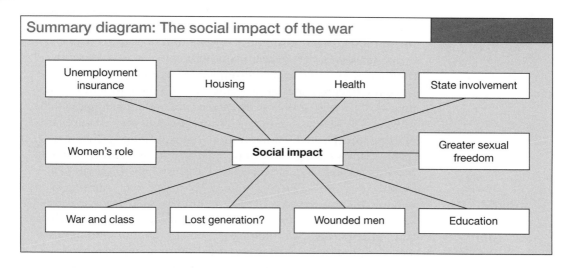

Summary diagram: The social impact of the war

- Unemployment insurance
- Housing
- Health
- State involvement
- Women's role
- **Social impact**
- Greater sexual freedom
- War and class
- Lost generation?
- Wounded men
- Education

## 6 | The Defence of Britain 1918–29

After 1919, members of the League of Nations agreed to disarm to 'the lowest point consistent with national safety'. Most British governments in the 1920s favoured disarmament for economic reasons.

Key question
How strong were Britain's armed forces in the 1920s?

### Britain's military position in 1918

Britain emerged from the First World War as a great power. In November 1918, it had:

- an army of 3.5 million men
- a Royal Navy with 58 battleships
- an RAF with over 20,000 planes.

Britain's strong position was enhanced by the weakness of its rivals. Germany was defeated: its army was no longer a major force and its fleet scuttled itself at Scapa Flow in 1919. Russia, a rival for much of the nineteenth century, was in chaos. Moreover, Britain seemed to have little to fear from the other victorious powers:

- France had been hard hit by the conflict.
- Common ties of language, culture and tradition meant that there was already talk of a 'special relationship' between Britain and the USA.
- Japan and Britain had been on good terms since 1902.

### The Ten-Year Rule

In 1919, Lloyd George's government decided, and the armed forces planned on the assumption, that 'the British Empire will not be involved in any large war over the next 10 years'. This Ten-Year Rule, which was used to justify keeping defence spending as low as possible, continued until 1932. (In 1913, 30 per cent of Britain's government expenditure had been on defence; by 1933, this had fallen to 10 per cent.) Given that there was no major threat to world peace in the 1920s, this made some sense. However, savage defence cuts meant that Britain's arms industry virtually disappeared. There was thus no guarantee that the country would have the capability to rearm if a serious threat appeared.

### The British army

After 1918, the army reverted to its pre-war roles of imperial police force and home security. Always short of men, it was increasingly dependent on obsolete weapons and equipment. The CIGS on more than one occasion stated officially that the army was 'completely out of date' and unfitted to respond to any contingency in Europe. Given the slow promotion system, many progressive-minded officers left the service. Nevertheless, a band of middle-ranking officers in the 1920s were zealous and innovative. Basil Liddell Hart and J.F.C. Fuller, for example, established international reputations with a spate of publications critical of the conduct of the recent war and advocating a variety of reforms. Fuller was an out-and-out advocate of mechanised warfare. The underfunded army continued its pioneering efforts on tanks and mechanisation through to the early 1930s.

### The Royal Navy

**Key date**

Washington Naval
Agreement: 1922

In 1922, the main naval powers accepted the Washington Naval Agreement under which capital ships allowed to the countries concerned would be in the following ratios: USA 5; Britain 5; Japan 3; Italy 1.75; and France 1.75. No new capital ships were to be constructed for 10 years. Some Britons opposed the agreement:

- Britain no longer had naval superiority.
- The size of Britain's fleet would now be determined by the treaty, not by an assessment of its strategic needs.

However, the agreement did avoid a wasteful naval race with the USA and Japan.

### The RAF

After 1919, many experts thought that planes (particularly bombers) were the cheapest way of preventing aggression (by deterrence) or of winning a war if one came. Nevertheless, the RAF, while preserving its separate identity, remained small in size.

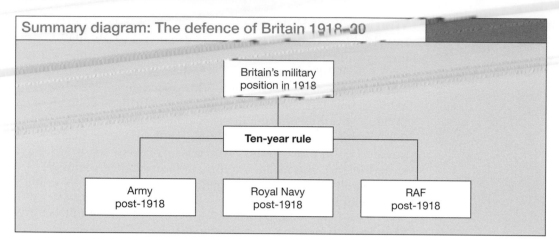

Summary diagram: The defence of Britain 1918–20

Britain's military position in 1918

Ten-year rule

Army post-1918 | Royal Navy post-1918 | RAF post-1918

## 7 | Key Debate

To what extent did the First World War have major political, economic and social consequences for Britain?

## Political consequences
### Major consequences?
- The war led to radical changes in the electoral system, with the electorate increasing from eight million to 21 million. Women could now vote and stand for parliament.
- The war assisted the rise of the Labour Party (see page 194).
- It resulted in the decline of the Liberal Party (see page 193).
- It ensured Conservative dominance for a generation after 1918.
- It led to a shift in the location of political power from the landed classes to businessmen.
- It led to Irish independence. Britain thus lost 22 per cent of its national territory, relatively more than Germany lost by the terms of the Treaty of Versailles.

### Minor consequences?
- Opponents of female franchise, like Asquith, had been ready to concede defeat in 1914.
- While the war probably speeded, it did not cause Labour's political advance. Much of the base on which Labour was to build was in place before 1914.
- The Liberal Party was possibly in decline pre-1914 (see page 193).
- The Conservative Party was always likely to regain its dominance.
- The declining influence of the landed class was evident before 1914.
- Irish Home Rule was on the verge of being granted in 1914.

## Economic and financial consequences
### Major consequences?
- The financial costs of the war had left Britain with a huge national debt, 14 times greater than in 1914. Its service took nearly half the yield from taxation in the 1920s, against 14 per cent before the war.

- In 1914, income tax had been a burden on a rich minority. By 1918, the number of income tax payers had more than trebled.
- Britain owed huge sums of money to the USA, a situation made worse by the fact that the Bolshevik government reneged on Russia's debts to Britain.
- Britain had been forced to sell off many of its overseas investments. This had a damaging effect on the country's balance of payments.
- During the war *laissez-faire* policies were abandoned in favour of state intervention.
- Serious labour shortages possibly accelerated the development of production-line processes, creating increased opportunities for semi-skilled and unskilled workers.
- The war helped the process of income equalisation (see page 222).
- In the years immediately after 1918, Britain saw first inflation and then unemployment rise to levels not seen for more than a century.
- Trade unions had advanced their political and economic bargaining positions (see page 209). Their right of access to government or to representation on committees or commissions continued to be acknowledged post-1918.
- In some respects, the war had damaged Britain's industrial capacity. In many industries replacement and improvement of plant and machinery had been postponed as Britain concentrated on producing munitions. However, while some industries were in desperate need of capital investment, others, for example shipbuilding and steel, had seen considerable investment. Moreover, the war helped to promote several industries, not least the automobile industry.
- Britain lost lucrative markets, especially in Latin America and the Far East, to the USA and Japan.
- The war helped women to escape from domestic service and accentuated the trend towards female employment in offices and shops.

## Minor consequences?
- In itself, the national debt did not do much to damage the British economy.
- So healthy was Britain's economy that it was able to pay for the war largely out of its own resources. Its balance of payments remained in the black for the war years as a whole. Its foreign investments went up during the war by £250 million and the country was able to loan vast sums of money to other governments. Although Britain owed money to the USA in 1918, most of this debt had been contracted on behalf of its allies, who owed Britain more money than it owed the USA.
- Most politicians, businessmen and many trade unionists regarded the state's wartime controls as evils which should be got rid of as soon as possible. This happened. By 1921, practically all wartime economic regulations had disappeared. Direct government

involvement in economic matters remained limited throughout the inter-war years.

- Trade union power had been growing before 1914. Unions' attempts to flex their muscles in the early 1920s were not successful, evidenced by the failure of the general strike in 1926.
- Market forces quickly reasserted themselves after 1918. It is likely that 'new' industries (for example, automobiles) would have done well and 'old' industries (for example, textiles) badly, with or without a war.
- Although Britain lost some markets to American and Japanese firms, it gained others at Germany's expense.
- Most ex-servicemen returned to their old jobs. By 1920, two-thirds of women had withdrawn from their wartime jobs. By mid-1921, the proportion of women in waged work was lower than in 1911. Thus the aftermath of the war saw only a minimal expansion in the range of work open to women.
- Given the increased use of new household gadgets, domestic service would have shrunk naturally.

## Social consequences
### Major consequences?

- After 1914, Britons became used to the idea of state intervention in most aspects of life, especially welfare. By 1919, the state provided security against sickness, unemployment and old age and accepted responsibility for circumstances resulting from the war: the payment of disability, widows' and orphans' benefits.
- The war encouraged the redistribution of wealth. The high rates of income tax, supertax and death duties introduced during the war were little reduced afterwards. A rich man paid eight per cent of his income in tax before the war, one third after it. This helped to fund improvements in welfare.
- The war forced a new independence and enterprise on women. Many got used to having more responsibility within the home. The challenge to the myth of male work skills, resulting from women's war work, may have served to undermine masculine assumptions of authority generally.
- After 1918, there was a marked decline in church attendance.
- After 1918, the opening hours of pubs continued to be tightly limited (until the 1990s). Britain became a more sober society.

### Minor consequences?

- By 1914, there had already been an increase in state activity. While state intervention increased during the war, it greatly reduced after 1918. Most welfare reform grew out of measures introduced by pre-war governments.
- There were huge income differentials in the inter-war years.
- Women's role did not change a great deal as a result of the war. Management within the home had always been a female prerogative. And home was where most married women stayed. Outside the home, women remained second-class citizens. In almost every occupation, women were paid less than men for doing the same work. General attitudes towards married women

**Key term**

**Marriage bar**
Married women were not allowed to work in many professions.

working had altered little. In many professions a **marriage bar** operated in the 1920s.

- In the inter-war period, there were never more than 20 women MPs, no women directors of large companies, no women judges and virtually no women professors at universities. Women did not get the vote on the same terms as men until 1928
- By valorising combat, the war perhaps reinforced older notions of what it meant to be a man or a woman.
- Church attendance was declining pre-1914.
- Opening hours of pubs were restricted pre-1914.

---

**Some key books in the debate**
G. DeGroot, *Blighty: British Society in the Era of The Great War* (Longman, 1996).
A. Marwick, *The Deluge: British Society and the First World War* (Macmillan, 1991).
M. Pugh, *The Making of Modern British Politics, 1867–1939* (Blackwell, 1982).
G.R. Searle, *A New England? Peace and War 1886–1918* (Oxford, 2004).
J.M. Winter, *The Great War and the British People* (Palgrave Macmillan, 2003).

---

## Study Guide

### In the style of Edexcel

How far do these sources suggest that the First World War had the effect of changing attitudes to women's work? Explain your answer using the evidence of Sources 1, 2 and 3.               (20 marks)

### Source 1

*From: a letter sent by Cecil Walton to the* Bulletin *newspaper, 3 September 1917. He was replying to the newspaper's criticisms of women munitions workers.*

To one who is proud to control many thousands of girl munitions workers, the leading article published in last Monday's *Bulletin*, comes somewhat as a shock.

I have stated on many occasions that the women of Great Britain have saved the Country. During the past two years I have been responsible for placing thousands of women. Almost without exception they have not only done magnificent work, but have set an example to the country of steadiness under stress. The vast majority are not the 'pampered crowd' they are made out to be, but have taken their places in the war with a solid determination to provide the means to carry on the war in the absence of skilled and unskilled men.

## Source 2

*From: an advertisement for Glaxo baby food which was published in* The Woman Worker *magazine in 1918.*

*Munitions and Motherhood*

Not even a woman can eat her cake and have it, not even she can make the munitions to save the present and tend the children who are to be the future. But the present day requires that women shall leave their homes where the future should be made, and should take the place of men in the factories …

If women are to make munitions, or serve their country in any capacity, it is necessary for our nation's future that special steps are taken to guard the children who are the natural, sacred and supreme care of womanhood.

## Source 3

*From: the report of the war cabinet committee on women in industry, 1919.*

The conditions under which women were employed before the war did not enable them to develop full health and vigour. Low wages and unsatisfactory diet resulted in physical inefficiency and caused both men and women to place too low a value upon the woman's strength and capacity. The results of employment of women under wartime conditions have proved they can be employed upon more occupations than has been considered desirable in the past, even when these involve considerable activity, physical strain, exposure to weather, etc.

---

### Exam tips

This example of an (a) question asks you to test a claim against the evidence of the three sources given to you. You should expect to find evidence that points to change and also evidence that suggests attitudes had not altered significantly. Your answer will be stronger if, rather than dealing with each source separately, you group together points that suggest change and those that suggest continuity.

Sources 1 and 3 both point to significant effects on attitudes, though the need for Walton to write to counter criticism allows you to infer that his views were not universally shared. Source 2 emphasises the importance of children as the 'supreme care of womanhood'. In spite of this, Source 2 recognises the role of women outside the home, while arguing for the need to take special steps to 'guard children', which you can infer would include the purchase of the company's products.

In coming to an overall conclusion, remember to take into account the nature of the sources. What priorities would one expect Glaxo to emphasise for the purpose of the advertisement?

# Glossary

**14 Points**   These were Wilson's peace aims, first outlined in January 1918. Wilson supported the principles of self-determination, reduction in armaments, and the establishment of a 'general association of nations' to preserve peace in future.

**1905 Moroccan crisis**   An international crisis resulting from Germany's challenge to France's growing influence in Morocco.

**1s. (one shilling)**   Twelve old pence (12d.) – or 5 pence in modern money.

**Admiralty**   The organisation that administers the Royal Navy.

**Armistice**   An agreement to suspend fighting.

**Autocracy**   A form of government where one (unelected) ruler has total power.

**Balance of payments**   The difference between a nation's total receipts (in all forms) from foreign countries and its total payment to foreign countries.

**Balkan crises**   There were crises in 1908–9 (over Bosnia) and two Balkan wars in 1912–13.

**Battalion**   Another name for a regiment, comprising in theory but rarely in practice 1000 men.

**Bioscope**   The first moving film apparatus.

**'Bite and hold'**   A term used to describe the tactic of capturing part of the enemy trench line and then defending it when the Germans counterattacked.

**Black and Tans**   Armed, auxiliary policemen, most of whom were ex-servicemen.

**Boer**   The Dutch word for farmer.

**Bosnian terrorists**   Serbs who wanted Bosnia (part of Austria-Hungary) to become part of Serbia and were prepared to use violence to achieve their aim.

**Boys' Brigade**   A movement, set up in the late nineteenth century, for the promotion of habits of obedience, reverence, discipline and self-respect.

**Breech-loading**   A firearm loaded at the side instead of the muzzle (the mouth of a gun).

**Capital ships**   Large warships.

**Chanak crisis**   An international crisis which almost resulted in a war between Britain and Turkey in 1922.

**Chartism**   A working-class movement for political reform, strong in Britain at various times in the 1830s and 1840s.

**Cholera**   An infection of the intestine caused by bacteria transmitted in contaminated water. The disease causes severe vomiting and diarrhoea which leads to dehydration that can be fatal.

**Christadelphians**   Members of a small religious sect.

**Collectivist schemes**   The idea that industry should be run by workers and the government rather than by big business.

**Combined arms tactics**   Fighting the enemy by blending together the different branches of the army (for example, artillery, infantry and tanks).

**Commando**   An armed group of Boers, varying in size from a few dozen men to several hundreds.

**Concert of Europe**   The various efforts by the great powers to co-operate in settling possible causes of conflict between themselves in order to maintain peace between 1815 and 1854.

**Creeping barrage**   An artillery bombardment where the shells are meant to keep falling just ahead of the attacking troops.

**Dáil**   The Irish parliament.

**Demographic**   To do with population size and distribution.

**Diamond rush**   A surge of miners, hoping to discover diamonds.

**Diphtheria**   A bacterial infection which produces a membrane across the throat that can choke a child.

**Division(al)**   A division was a formation of two or more brigades. It usually comprised some 4000–5000 men.

**D-Notice system**   Instructions sent by the government to newspapers, asking them not to publish certain information. (D is short for defence.)

**Drill** Basic training including marching and learning to handle weapons.

**Dumping** Exporting commodities for sale at below the cost of production to ruin overseas competition.

**Dysentery** An infection of the bowel causing painful diarrhoea. This results in dehydration which can be fatal. Dysentery occurs wherever there is poor sanitation.

**East India Company** A commercial company which established considerable political power in India in the eighteenth and early nineteenth centuries.

**Enfield rifle** An improved version of the minié rifle-musket.

*Esprit de corps* Morale.

**Establishment** The group or class in a community that holds power. Members of this group or class are usually linked socially and usually hold conservative opinions and conventional values.

**Executive** The body with the power and authority to devise policy and put laws into effect.

**Fabian Society** A society formed in London in 1884 for the purpose of peacefully promoting socialist ideas.

**Filibustering** Trying to obstruct new legislation by making lengthy speeches, hoping that there will not be enough time for the legislation to pass.

**Free trade** Unrestricted exchange of goods without protective duties.

**Frostbite** Damage to part of the body, usually a hand or foot, resulting from exposure to extreme cold. This may lead to gangrene.

**Gangrene** This usually results from infected wounds or frostbite. Body tissue decays as a result of failure in the blood supply, usually to an arm or a leg. Amputation of the affected limb was the only cure in the 1850s.

**Ghost-written** A book written by someone on behalf of another who is credited as the author.

**GHQ** General Head Quarters, comprising military staff officers who advised the Commander-in-Chief on policy and administration and helped him to carry out his plans.

**Going over the top** Attacking the enemy across no man's land.

**Government bonds** Securities issued by the government, allowing it to borrow money. Those who bought the bonds were guaranteed a return of their money in the future.

**Gross national product** The total value of all goods and services produced within a country plus the income from investments abroad.

**Guerrilla tactics** A method of warfare often used by non-regular soldiers who, instead of fighting pitched battles, operate in small bands, attacking the enemy's supply lines and striking against isolated enemy units.

**Heliograph** An apparatus for signalling by reflecting the sun's rays.

**Hindenburg line** A fortified German defence system, prepared over the winter of 1916–17.

**Horse Guards** The army's main administrative headquarters in Whitehall, London.

**Hun** The derogatory name for Germans in the First World War. Historically, the Huns were a barbarian tribe who had overrun much of Europe in the fifth century.

**Jewel in the crown** The most prized possession.

**Jingoism** Extremely patriotic. (The word came from a popular song of the 1870s when Disraeli threatened war with Russia. According to the lyrics, 'We don't want to fight but by jingo if we do; we've got the ships, we've got the men; we've got the money too.')

**Khaki** A dull-brownish cloth used for military uniforms. It provided better camouflage than red tunics.

*Laissez-faire* The principle that governments should not interfere in people's lives or in economic matters.

**Leader of the Commons** Prime Minister Salisbury, a peer, sat in the Lords. Therefore, Balfour led the Conservatives in the Commons.

**Liberal** In the mid-nineteenth century, liberals supported democracy and greater freedom generally (e.g. freedom of speech and religion).

**Little Englanders** Opponents of British imperialism.

**Magazine rifles** Rifles from which a succession of shots can be fired without reloading.

**Marriage bar** Married women were not allowed to work in many professions.

**Militia**   A home defence force raised from volunteers or by ballot in an emergency.

**Mills bomb**   A type of hand grenade.

**Minié rifle**   This fired the minié ball, an inch-long lead ball that expanded into the groove of the rifle-musket's barrel. It was far more accurate than the smoothbore musket. The latter had an effective range of less than 100 yards; the minié rifle was accurate at over 400 yards.

**Mortar**   A short-barrelled gun which lobs shells at the enemy.

**Munitionettes**   The name given to women who worked in the munitions industries.

**Muscular Christianity**   A vigorous combination of Christian living with devotion to athletic enjoyments.

**National bargaining**   The situation when wages and conditions of workers in a particular occupation are settled at national rather than at local level, ensuring all receive the same wages and work to the same conditions.

**National debt**   The money borrowed by a government and not yet paid back.

**National government**   A government made up of the most able men from all the political parties.

**Nationalised**   Taken over and run by the government.

**Navalists**   Those who believed that Britain's first and best line of defence was the Royal Navy.

**Navy estimates**   The money spent on the British fleet.

**Navy League**   A patriotic organisation set up in the mid-1890s to promote the interests of the Royal Navy. By 1914, it had 100,000 members.

**Near East**   The area which today comprises Turkey and many of the countries of the Middle East.

**Nonconformists**   Protestants who rejected the authority (and some of the practices) of the Church of England.

**Northern Rhodesia**   Modern Zambia.

**Peninsula War**   The war in Portugal and Spain between British and French forces (1808–14). The Duke of Wellington commanded British troops for most of the war.

**Poet Laureate**   A title bestowed by the monarch on a poet whose duties include the writing of commemorative odes on important occasions.

**Policy of confederation**   Britain hoped to unite its southern African colonies, plus the Orange Free State and Transvaal, into one country, under British supremacy.

**Poor Laws**   The measures passed to help those in severe poverty. Those who were desperate for help found refuge in the workhouse.

**Portuguese East Africa**   Modern Mozambique.

**Primrose League**   A patriotic organisation which campaigned on behalf of Britain's imperial interests.

**Principalities**   The two provinces of Moldavia and Wallachia.

**Privy council**   A committee of advisers to the monarch, comprising past and present members of the cabinet and other eminent people.

**Protectionist**   Someone who favours import duties to protect industry and agriculture.

**Radical Liberal**   Radical Liberals sympathised with the underdog, whether in Britain or abroad, and supported social reform.

**Radicals**   MPs who supported widespread economic and social change in Britain.

**RAF**   Royal Air Force.

***Reichstag* peace resolution**   The German parliament (*Reichstag*) passed a resolution in 1917 in favour of peace without annexations or indemnities.

**Requisitioning**   Government action forcing firms to supply materials for the war effort.

**Residential qualifications for voting**   Men had to live in a constituency for a year before an election to be entitled to vote.

**Retrenchment**   The cutting of government spending.

**Reuters**   An agency which supplied newspapers with international news.

**Rushed to the colours**   Volunteered to enlist in the army.

**Russophobia**   Fear and hatred of Russia and Russians.

**Salient**   A narrow area pushing into enemy lines which can therefore be attacked from several sides.

**Scurvy**   A disease caused by deficiency of vitamin C. The symptoms are weakness and aching joints and muscles, progressing to bleeding of the gums and other organs.

**Scuttled**   Deliberately sunk.

**Securities**   Bonds or certificates which provide evidence of holdings of property or money owed (by, for example, a government).

**Self-help**   The belief that people are best doing things for themselves without government assistance.

**Sepoys**   Indian soldiers who fought for Britain.

**Shop stewards**   Men who represent groups of workers.

**Social Darwinism**   Social Darwinists believed that only the fittest nations and social systems could thrive and prosper.

**Social Democratic Federation**   Created by an old Etonian, H.M. Hyndman, it advocated violent revolution to overthrow the capitalist system.

**Socialist**   It meant different things to different people, but most socialists wanted to improve life for the working class.

**Southern Rhodesia**   Modern Zimbabwe.

**Spanish–American War**   A short conflict, fought between Spain and the USA in 1898, which the USA easily won.

**Staff work**   Preparatory planning and administrative work undertaken by the commanding officer's personal team.

**Sterling**   The British currency.

**The Straits**   The Bosphorus and the Dardanelles, which link the Black Sea to the Mediterranean.

**Suzerainty**   Overlordship: ultimate power.

**Taxes on knowledge**   Taxes on items (like paper) that put up the cost of books, journals and newspapers.

**TNT**   A high explosive.

**Tommies**   The nickname for British soldiers in the First World War.

**Total war**   A conflict in which a nation utilises all its resources in an effort to secure victory.

**Trench foot**   As a result of prolonged exposure to water, soldiers' feet swelled, blistered and rotted. This could result in amputation.

**Tuberculosis**   A disease which affects the lungs. It is characterised by fever, lack of energy, weight loss and breathlessness

**TUC**   The Trades Union Congress.

**Typhoid**   An infectious disease, usually contracted by drinking infected water. The symptoms include fever, headache, loss of appetite and constipation.

**Typhus**   A dangerous fever transmitted by lice, fleas, mites or ticks. There are many different forms but they share the symptoms of fever, headache, pains in muscles and joints, and delirium.

**U-boats**   German submarines.

*Uitlanders*   White foreigners living in the Transvaal and the Orange Free State.

**Unionists**   Conservatives and Liberals who were united in their opposition to Irish Home Rule.

**Veldt**   Open, unforested grass-country.

**Venereal diseases**   Diseases transmitted predominantly by sexual intercourse.

**Volunteers**   Men (who had some basic military training) who could be called on to fight if Britain was invaded.

**War socialism**   The government's wartime control of many aspects of economic and social life.

**Waterloo**   The Battle of Waterloo was fought in 1815. British forces (led by Wellington) and Prussian forces (led by Blucher) defeated Napoleon Bonaparte.

*Weltpolitik*   A German word meaning 'world policy'; that is, Germany's imperialist ambitions.

**Whigs**   Aristocratic politicians who vied with the Conservatives for most of the eighteenth and early nineteenth centuries.

**Yeomanry**   Volunteer cavalry who served in Britain.

**Zeppelin**   A type of large airship, designed by Ferdinand von Zeppelin.

# Index